Delightfully Southern

A collection of recipes

By
Lucy Middleton Clark

Cover design, "Tea Party Time" in Grandmama's Backyard

Our grandchildren: Amy and Suzanna Willis
Elizabeth and Caroline Clark

Photography and Cover Design
Adkins Photography, Inc.
Cordele, Georgia

Delightfully Southern

Copyright © 2000 by Lucy Middleton Clark
Library of Congress Card Number 00-191772

ALL RIGHTS RESERVED

ISBN 0-9703793-0-7

First Printing, January 2001, 3000
Second Printing, August 2001, 5000

Printed in the USA by

WIMMER

The Wimmer Companies
Memphis

1-800-548-2537

 Dedication

This book is lovingly dedicated to our children, Lawana and Homer Willis; Dee and Charles Clark, and to our grandchildren; Amy and Suzanna Willis, and Elizabeth and Caroline Clark. They are all blessings from God and have brought joy to our lives, for which we are truly grateful.

Children, it is because of you that I did this book. You told me if I didn't write it down, you wouldn't know how to make these things! All your favorite recipes are included. Enjoy!

It is the desire of our hearts that you all honor God and your fellowman with your lives.

My Appreciation

To my husband, Lamar, without whom I would never have completed this book. He was my patient, kind, constant, supporter and encourager.

To my many friends and relatives who shared their wonderful recipes with me through the years. This would not have been possible without you. You were always there with not only recipes, but also support and encouragement.

In Loving Memory

Of my mother and father, Ella George Middleton, and Charlie William Middleton, RR, Blakely; Early County, Georgia.

We always lived in the same place on a farm ten miles south of Blakely. I have a treasure of wonderful childhood memories from our family and home. My parents reared six children to adulthood, and gave to us a rich Christian heritage, which to me, is the most valuable gift parents can give to their children.

I cannot remember when my mother did not allow me to help her cook! She always had the time and patience to share with me the joy of cooking. Both of my parents have had a tremendous influence in my life, and to them I am eternally grateful.

Of Lamar's mother and father, Susie Gray Clark and James Wade Clark, Dothan; Houston County, Alabama.

Mrs. Clark always inspired me with her relaxed manner in turning out "tons" of delicious food for their family of nine children, and, it seemed, whomever decided to drop in! I have never appreciated "mother-in-law" jokes because of my love and respect for her. Lamar and I both are grateful for having had wonderful Christian parents.

Gleanings from Life - Age 76

These "page fillers" are from my personal collection of what I consider to be profound statements that have been meaningful to me in my life.

I make no claim for originality. They are from pastor's sermons, things I have read, memories from "somewhere" . . . Probably, some I have slightly paraphrased.

Table of Contents

Appetizers & Beverages

Cheese Ball with Dried Beef

2 (8-ounce) packages cream cheese,
    softened
2 tablespoons prepared horseradish
2 tablespoons Worcestershire Sauce

1 package smoked or dried beef,
    chipped
Garnish: Parsley flakes or chopped
    nuts

Mix all ingredients. Roll in finely chopped parsley flakes and/or chopped nuts.
Wrap in plastic wrap and refrigerate.

Cheese Ball with Ranch Dressing

2 (8-ounce) packages lite cream cheese
    or non-fat cream cheese
1 (0.7-ounce) package dry original
    Ranch Dressing mix

1/2 cup finely chopped green onion
Bacon bits for garnish

Combine cream cheese, dressing mix and onion. Form into ball and roll in bacon
bits. Yield: 10 to 12 servings.

Cheese Crisps

2 cups sharp New York cheese, grated
1 stick margarine
1 cup plain flour
1/2 teaspoon salt

1/8-1/4 teaspoon cayenne pepper
    (optional)
2 cups Rice Krispies

Blend cheese and margarine; add flour, salt and cayenne, mixing well. Add Rice
Crispies and work into other ingredients. Form into very small balls. Place on
cookie sheet; flatten balls with hand to make wafer size. Cook 7 to 9 minutes at
400 degrees until they are lightly browned. Remove from cookie sheet immediately.

Judy's Cheese Straws

1 pound mild cheddar cheese
1/2 pound butter

3 1/2 cups self-rising flour
1 teaspoon red pepper

Blend cheese and butter; add flour and pepper. Press dough through cookie press,
using star-shape tip. Bake at 325 degrees until straws are firm. Do not brown or
you will kill the cheese flavor. They will not break as easily if you make them round
rather than long.

Cheese Ring

1 (16-ounce) package extra sharp
   cheddar cheese
1 (16-ounce) package medium
   cheddar cheese
1 cup mayonnaise

1 small onion, grated
1 teaspoon red pepper
1 cup chopped nuts
Parsley sprigs
Strawberry preserves, optional

Grate both cheeses. Combine cheeses, mayonnaise, onion and red pepper. Sprinkle pecans in an oiled 7-cup ring mold; press cheese mixture into mold. Chill overnight. Unmold on serving platter. Fill center with strawberry preserves: garnish with parsley sprigs and serve on crackers.

Hot Olive-Cheese Puffs

1 cup cheese, grated
3 tablespoons butter, softened
1/2 cup all-purpose flour, sifted

1/4 teaspoon salt
1/2 teaspoon paprika
48 stuffed olives, drained until dry

Blend cheese with butter; stir in flour, salt and paprika. Mix well. Wrap small amount of cheese dough around each olive. Place on ungreased cookie sheet and bake in 400 degree oven 10 to 15 minutes or until golden brown. Serve hot or warm.

Mexican Roll-Ups

1 (8-ounce) package cream cheese,
   softened
1 (4-ounce) can chopped black olives
1 (4-ounce) can chopped green chiles

1 (14-ounce) jar picante sauce
Garlic powder to taste
Flour tortillas

Combine cream cheese, olives, chiles, and 1 teaspoon of picante sauce. Spread on flour tortillas and roll up. Refrigerate at least 1 hour. Slice in 3/4-inch slices. Insert a toothpick. Serve with a bowl of picante sauce for dipping.

Picante Dip

1 (8-ounce) package cream cheese

1 (8-ounce) medium picante sauce

Blend and serve with favorite chips or crackers.

Rotel-Cheese Dip

1 pound pasteurized process cheese
  spread, cubed

1 (10-ounce) can Ro-tel tomatoes
  and green chiles

Place ingredients in covered casserole in microwave. Microwave on high until cheese spread is melted, about 5 minutes, stirring once. Serve with tortilla chips, crackers or vegetables. Makes 8 servings.

Tex-Mex Dip

3 medium-size avocados
2 tablespoons lemon juice
1/2 teaspoon salt
1/4 teaspoon pepper
1 (8-ounce) carton sour cream
1/2 cup mayonnaise
1 package taco seasoning mix
2 (10 1/2-ounce) cans bean dip,
  plain or jalapeño

1 large bunch green onions with green
  tops to make 1 cup
3 medium tomatoes, chopped to make
  2 cups
2 (3 1/2-ounce) cans pitted ripe olives,
  sliced
1 (8-ounce) package shredded cheddar
  cheese
Large round tortilla chips

Peel and mash avocados in medium size bowl with lemon juice, salt and pepper. Set aside. Combine sour cream, mayonnaise and taco seasoning in another bowl. To assemble: Spread bean dip in large shallow serving platter or plate. Top with seasoned avocado mixture. Layer with sour cream taco mixture. Sprinkle with chopped onions, tomatoes and olives. Cover with shredded cheese. Serve with tortilla chips.

Velveeta Cheese Dip

1 pound Velveeta cheese
1 (12-ounce) can evaporated milk
1 cup chopped olives

1 cup chopped nuts
1 small chopped onion
1 cup mayonnaise (not salad dressing)

In microwave bowl, combine the cheese and milk; cook and stir until cheese is melted, checking at 2-minute intervals. Cool to room temperature; add olives, nuts, onions and mayonnaise. Stir and chill. This dip can be frozen.

Frozen Fruit Slush

(My most shared recipe!)

3 cups sugar
3 cups water
1 (16-ounce) can orange juice
　concentrate
2 (20-ounce) cans crushed pineapple

8-10 bananas quartered lengthwise and
　chopped
1 orange juice can water
1 (10-ounce) jar maraschino cherries,
　drained and chopped

Combine sugar and water and bring to a boil. Cool. In 5-quart container with cover, combine orange juice, pineapple and chopped bananas. Stir well, as this prevents bananas from turning dark. Add orange juice can of water, chopped cherries and simple syrup, (made from sugar and water.) Freeze, stirring several times during freezing process as cherries will settle to the bottom. If this is not convenient, just freeze and remove from freezer later; allow to thaw until you can stir to a slushy consistency.

Note: Serve frozen as an appetizer, dessert (delicious on angel food cake with whipped topping, or over ice cream), snack, in punch bowl for parties or wedding receptions, for gifts for friends, and especially good for sick people.

Coconut Dip for Fruit

1 (8-ounce) package cream cheese,
　softened

1 (8.5-ounce) can cream of coconut
　(Coco Lopez)
Fruit for dipping

Beat cream cheese with electric mixer until fluffy. Gradually add the cream of coconut, continuing to beat on low speed. Refrigerate until ready to serve.

Suggestion: Serve in compote-style dish and top with just a little flaked coconut. Serve with fresh fruit such as strawberries, sliced apples, pineapple, or your choice. Place compote in middle of tray and surround with assorted fresh fruit.

Stuffed Dates

Stuff each date with one pecan half or quarter. Make sugar cookie dough. Form balls of dough just big enough to cover stuffed date. In hand, press each ball of dough around pecan-stuffed date. Bake in 350 degree oven until very lightly browned. Serve as is, or dip in your choice of icing. (To dip 1/2 would be nice). An **Orange Glaze** is very good, as is used on **Orange Blossoms**!

Pine-Apples

5 or 6 apples, depending on size   1 (20-ounce) can pineapple chunks

Wash apples and cut, unpeeled, into wedges. Slice away core. Marinate in pineapple, with juice, in sealed container in refrigerator, turning occasionally to keep apples from darkening. So simple, but a favorite of "children of all ages". They will keep for up to one week in fridge. Crisp, very firm apples should be used.
Favorite variation: Serve wedges around dip bowl filled with **Yogurt Fruit Dressing** topped with almonds for parties. At Christmas alternate groups of red and green apple slices. Also delicious with coconut dip for fruit. Both dip recipes are listed in appetizers.

Strawberries-With-Cream Dip

1 (8-ounce) cream cheese, softened   1 (8-ounce) carton Lite Cool Whip
1 cup strawberry low-fat yogurt   1 quart fresh strawberries, divided
2-3 tablespoons honey (to taste)   (May need more - Get with stems,
1/2 cup chopped strawberries   if possible)

Combine cream cheese, yogurt and honey in small bowl. (Combine a small amount first, and then the remainder, to prevent lumps of cream cheese.) Beat at medium speed with hand mixer just to blend; fold in Lite Cool Whip and chopped strawberries just enough to mix. Serve as dip with fresh strawberries. This can be used as a dip with other fresh fruits such as apples, peaches or banana chunks that have been marinated in pineapple juice.
Note: You may omit cream cheese for a lighter dip.

Taffy Apple Dip

1 (8-ounce) package cream cheese,   1 tablespoon vanilla extract
   softened   1/2 cup roasted peanuts, chopped
3/4 cup brown sugar, packed   6 apples, cut into wedges

In small bowl, beat cream cheese, brown sugar and vanilla until smooth and sugar is dissolved. Mound mixture on a compote-type dish in the middle of a small, round, serving tray. Top with roasted, chopped peanuts. Fan apple wedges around compote.
Favorite tip: Group red and green apple wedges for Christmas!

Yogurt Fruit Dressing or Dip

1 pint vanilla-flavored low-fat yogurt
2-3 tablespoons honey

1 (8-ounce) carton Lite Cool Whip
(more if desired)
Lightly toasted almonds for topping

Blend all ingredients. When serving, top with toasted almonds. This is a family favorite!

Favorite tip: Use generous dollop to top fresh fruit on lettuce leaf for salad; to top fruit cup as appetizer or as a light dessert, using toasted almonds on top. This is a very versatile dressing or dip for any fruit. Add desired flavor with fruit extracts or liqueur.

Thank you Lord for the obstacles in life. It is most often because of these that we turn to you.

Chicken Log

2 (8-ounce) packages cream cheese
1 tablespoon bottled steak sauce
1/2 teaspoon curry powder
1 1/2 cups minced, cooked chicken

1/3 cup minced celery
1/4 cup chopped parsley
1/4 cup chopped toasted almonds

Beat together first three ingredients. Blend in chicken, celery and 2 tablespoons of the parsley; refrigerate remaining parsley. Shape mixture into 9-inch log. Wrap in plastic wrap and chill 4 hours or overnight. Toss together remaining parsley and almonds; use to coat log. Makes about 3 cups of spread. Serve with favorite crackers.

Ham Rolls

2 sticks butter-softened (or margarine)
1-2 tablespoons horseradish mustard
2 tablespoons poppy seeds
1 teaspoon Worcestershire sauce

1 medium onion, minced
3 dozen Pepperidge Farm Dinner Rolls
16 ounces cooked ham, thinly sliced
2 cups Swiss cheese, grated

Mix butter, mustard, poppy seeds, Worcestershire and onion. Split package of rolls horizontally through center. Spread butter mixture on both sides of rolls. Layer bottom half with ham. Sprinkle Swiss cheese on top of ham. Replace tops. Bake at 400 degrees for 10-15 minutes. These freeze well. Cut into individual rolls before freezing so a few may be used at a time. Great for families or parties.

Hot Smoked Beef Dip

2 (8-ounce) packages cream cheese,
    softened
1 cup sour cream,
    plus 4 tablespoons milk
1 tablespoon horseradish, optional

1/4 teaspoon Worcestershire sauce
Tabasco sauce to taste
1 tablespoon minced onion
1 (6-ounce) package smoked beef, chipped
1 cup chopped pecans, toasted

Beat cream cheese with milk, sour cream, horseradish, Worcestershire, Tabasco and onion. Beat in beef and place in ovenproof serving bowl. Top with pecans and bake at 350 degrees for 20 minutes. Makes about 4 cups.

Little Links in Oriental Sauce

1 cup firmly packed brown sugar
3 tablespoons all-purpose flour
2 teaspoons dry mustard
1 cup pineapple juice
1/2 cup apple cider vinegar

1 1/2 teaspoons soy sauce
1 (1-pound) package cocktail weiners
1 (1-pound) package smoked cocktail
   sausages

Combine all ingredients, except weiners and sausages. Heat to boiling, stirring constantly. Boil for 1 minute. Stir in weiners and sausages. Cook slowly for 5 minutes. Transfer to chafing dish and keep warm for serving.
Note: This sauce is great for spareribs.

Cocktail Meatballs

3 pounds lean ground beef
3 eggs
2 1/2 cups bread crumbs

2 onions, chopped fine
3 garlic cloves, chopped fine
Salt and pepper

Sauce:
1 (12-ounce) jar chili sauce
1 (7-ounce) jar grape jelly

1 (7-ounce) jar water

Mix together first 6 ingredients. Roll into small balls. Place on rack in baking pan and bake in 350 degree oven for 15 to 18 minutes or until done. Drain. Heat chili sauce, jelly and water. Add meatballs; simmer for 30 minutes. Transfer to chafing dish and serve warm.

Sausage Balls

3 cups Bisquick or Betty Crocker
   Buttermilk Biscuit Mix
1 pound pork sausage, ground

1 (10-ounce) package Cracker Barrel
   cheese, sharp

Combine all ingredients. Roll into small balls and bake 13 to 15 minutes in 375 degree oven.

Sweet Potato - Sausage Balls

3 cups Bisquick or Betty Crocker
　Buttermilk Biscuit Mix
1 cup sharp cheddar cheese, shredded

2 cups cooked, mashed sweet potatoes
1 pound sausage

Combine all ingredients well. Roll into balls and place on sheet pan. Bake at 350 degrees for 20 minutes, until brown.

Sausage-Cheese Bites

1 pound breakfast sausage, browned
　and drained
1 pound processed cheese spread,
　melted
1 tablespoon catsup

1 tablespoon Worcestershire sauce
Garlic salt
Oregano
English muffins

Mix all ingredients and spread on English muffins. This amount will cover 6 to 8 muffins, split into halves. Cut the halves into 8 wedges, like a pie. Bake on cookie sheet at 400 degrees for 8 to 10 minutes until bubbly. (Can be frozen before baking.)
Note: For breakfast, leave out last 3 ingredients.

To discern what is right, seek in the proper manner. The wrong map for the right treasure does not work.

Clam Bake

1 (8-ounce) package cream cheese
1 (8-ounce) carton sour cream
1/2 cup mayonnaise
1 small can minced clams

1 small onion, minced
1 green onion, minced
1 teaspoon parsley

Blend cream cheese, sour cream and mayonnaise. Add remaining ingredients. Mix all together and bake in small casserole until well heated and bubbly. Serve hot with your favorite crackers or corn chips.

Crab Dip

1 (8-ounce) package cream cheese
1 (6-ounce) can white crabmeat
1/4 cup mayonnaise
3 teaspoons onion, chopped fine

1 teaspoon fresh garlic, grated, optional
1 teaspoon prepared mustard
2 drops Tabasco sauce
Slivered, toasted almonds for top

Combine all ingredients. Place in oiled baking dish; top with slivered almonds and bake at 325 degrees for 15 minutes. Serve hot with crackers or corn chips. (You will probably want to make about 3 times this amount for a party.)

Crabmeat Mold

3 (8-ounce) packages cream cheese
2 (7-ounce) cans crabmeat
6 tablespoons mayonnaise
1/4 teaspoon salt

1/4 teaspoon curry powder
2 tablespoons fresh onion, grated
1 tablespoon lemon juice
1 tablespoon Worcestershire sauce

Combine cream cheese and all other ingredients except crabmeat. Blend well; add crabmeat and mix. Place in lightly oiled mold. Refrigerate overnight. Invert on serving dish and garnish with parsley, other greens and pimiento. Serve with favorite crackers.

Crab Spread

1 (8-ounce) package cream cheese,
  softened
2 tablespoons Worcestershire sauce

1/2 cup onion, chopped
Cocktail sauce (purchased)
1 (7-ounce) can shredded crabmeat

Combine first 3 ingredients. Spread on bottom of small, flat serving dish. Cover with cocktail sauce and top with shredded crabmeat. Serve with your favorite crackers. Delicious and quick!

Salmon Ball

1 (1-pound) can red salmon
1 (8-ounce) package cream cheese
1 tablespoon lemon juice
2 teaspoons grated onion
1/4 teaspoon liquid smoke, to taste

1-2 teaspoons horseradish
1/2 teaspoon salt
1/2 cup pecans, chopped
2 tablespoons chopped parsley

Combine cream cheese and next 5 ingredients. Blend well; add salmon and mix. Form into 6-inch ball or logs. Mix pecans and parsley; roll ball or logs in these, coating well. Serve with favorite crackers.

Shrimp Dip

1 (8-ounce) package cream cheese,
  softened
1/4 cup fresh lemon juice
1 pound shrimp meat, boiled, peeled
  and coarsely chopped
1 cup finely chopped green onions

1 cup mayonnaise
1 tablespoon Worcestershire sauce
Hot sauce or ground cayenne pepper,
  to taste
Salt, to taste

Blend together cream cheese and lemon juice. Stir shrimp and onions into cream cheese. Add enough mayonnaise to give mixture the consistency of a dip. Stir in the hot sauce, Worcestershire sauce, and salt. Put into serving dish and chill. Dish is better made a day ahead. Serve with crackers, melba toast or chips.

Shrimp Mousse

1 (10 3/4-ounce) can tomato soup or
   cream of shrimp soup
1 (8-ounce) package cream cheese
2 envelopes unflavored gelatin
1/2 cup cold water
1/4 cup chopped bell pepper, optional

1/2 cup chopped onion
1/2 cup chopped celery
1/4 teaspoon dry mustard
1 cup mayonnaise
2 (4 1/2-ounce) cans small shrimp,
   save a few for garnish

Lightly oil 4-cup mold (shell or fish mold is great!). In a saucepan heat soup and beat in cheese until smooth. Sprinkle gelatin in cold water. Add to hot soup mixture and cool. Add remaining ingredients and blend well. Pour into mold and chill overnight. Serve with your favorite crackers.

Shrimp Puffs

1/2 cup water
1/4 cup butter
1/2 cup plain flour

2 eggs
Shrimp Filling (recipe follows)

Bring water and butter to a boil. Add flour and mix; then remove from heat. Beat in eggs one at a time, mixing well. Drop by the spoonful on a greased baking sheet. Bake at 400 degrees for 25 to 30 minutes. Remove from oven and cool. Break off top of puff when cool and fill each with shrimp filling. The puffs may also be stuffed with chicken salad or ham.

Shrimp Filling:
1 minced celery rib
1/4 cup green pepper, minced
1 can of small shrimp, rinsed
   and drained

1 teaspoon minced onion
1/2 cup mayonnaise
Pinch of tarragon

Combine all ingredients and fill puffs.

Tuna or Salmon Mousse: Please go to Seafood in Meats for this recipe as it is ideal for a meal or parties!

Almond Bark Pecans

6 squares vanilla-flavored   4 cups pecans, toasted
   Almond Bark

Toast pecans in 300 degree oven for about 30 minutes, being careful not to over cook. Taste them for doneness. Melt almond bark in microwave; stir in pecans to coat. Pour out on wax paper. Separate nuts with a fork. A talented friend does these for many of our social gatherings at the church, and he does a perfect job! Everyone loves them. Try roasted peanuts, also!

Frosted Peanuts

2 cups peanuts (raw)   1/2 teaspoon vanilla extract
1 cup sugar   3-4 drops red food coloring (if desired)
1/2 cup water   1/2 teaspoon salt

Combine all ingredients except salt in saucepan over medium heat and cook for about 10 minutes. Spread on buttered pan, salt and bake in 275 degree oven for about 30 minutes, stirring once or twice.

Praline Crunch

1/2 cup brown sugar   1/2 teaspoon soda
1/2 cup Karo syrup   1 (16-ounce) box Toasted Oatmeal Squares
1/2 stick margarine   Cereal (Quaker)
1 teaspoon vanilla extract   2 cups pecans

Preheat oven to 250 degrees. Place sugar, syrup and margarine in microwave and cook for 1 1/2 minutes. Stir. Cook 2 more minutes or until it comes to a boil. Remove from microwave; add soda and vanilla and stir. In large bowl place Oatmeal Squares and nuts; drizzle sugar/Karo syrup mixture over cereal and nuts. Stir until coated. Pour into jelly-roll pan and place in oven for 1 hour, stirring about every 20 minutes. Remove, cool and break up. Store in airtight container until ready to serve. (Be sure not to over cook, or it will be too hard.)
Note: A very popular recipe from a friend.

Pecan Dainties

1 egg white
Dash of salt

1 cup light brown sugar
2 cups pecan halves

Beat egg white and salt until soft peaks form. Add brown sugar in 2 additions, beating after each. (Mixture will be much thinner than for meringue.) Stir in nuts and drop about 1 1/2 inches apart onto a greased cookie sheet. (If you want these to be just perfect, remove each half with your fingers and make sure it is covered in meringue before placing on cookie sheet.) Bake in very slow oven (250 degrees), for about 30 minutes. Remove from cookie sheet immediately; allow to cool. Store in airtight container. Delicious!

Sugared Pecans

2 1/2 cups pecan halves
1/2 cup water
1 cup sugar

1 teaspoon cinnamon
1/2 teaspoon salt
1 teaspoon vanilla extract

Toast the nuts in 300 degree oven for 20 minutes. Remove and cool. Boil the water, sugar, cinnamon and salt until it forms a soft ball in cold water. Remove from heat and add vanilla and nuts. Stir until nuts are coated. Pour out on waxed paper and separate, using two forks.

Pecan Tarts

1 (3-ounce) package cream cheese
1 stick butter or margarine
1 cup flour

Pinch of salt
Filling (recipe follows)

Combine above ingredients and form into 1-inch balls; press into small muffin tins.

Filling:
3/4 cup light brown sugar
1 large egg, beaten
2 tablespoons butter

Dash of salt
1 teaspoon vanilla extract
Pecans, broken coarsely

Combine all filling ingredients except pecans. Put a few pecans in each pastry shell. Fill shells 2/3 full of filling. Top with a few more nuts. Bake at 350 degrees until lightly browned.

(All sandwich recipes here, since many sandwiches can be made party-size or family-size.)

Barbecued Beef Sandwiches
(A teenage favorite!)

2 pounds ground beef (ground
    round or chuck, if you prefer)
1 onion, chopped
1 cup celery, chopped
1 (12-ounce) bottle chili sauce
1 cup catsup (or more)
2-3 tablespoons vinegar

3 tablespoons Worcestershire sauce
1 tablespoon dry mustard
1 tablespoon brown sugar
1 teaspoon Morton's Natures
    Seasoning, optional
Few drops Tabasco sauce, optional
Salt, pepper, paprika to taste

Brown beef, drain well. Combine with remaining ingredients. Bake covered at 250 degrees for 2 hours. Stir occasionally. Adjust seasonings. If dry, add more catsup. Serve on hamburger buns with cole slaw. Flavor improves if made a day ahead. Freezes well. Makes about 12 sandwiches.

Carnation Sloppy Joes

1 1/2 pounds ground beef
1 cup chopped onions
1 teaspoon salt
1 teaspoon garlic salt

1 tablespoon chili powder
2 tablespoons all-purpose flour
1 cup evaporated milk
1 cup catsup

There usually is enough fat in beef to brown it. If necessary, add a little oil. Combine beef and onions and cook until beef is brown and onions are tender. Drain well. Sprinkle in seasonings and flour. Stir well. Gradually add evaporated milk. Cook over low heat, stirring constantly until thickened; add catsup and blend. Heat to serving temperature. Serve on toasted buns.

Chicken Mushroom Sandwiches

2 cups chicken, finely chopped
2/3 cup almonds, lightly toasted
  and chopped
2 tablespoons instant minced
  onion, optional
2 (3-ounce) cans mushrooms,
  drained and chopped

1 cup celery, diced
1/2-1 teaspoon salt
1/4 teaspoon pepper
1 teaspoon curry powder
1 cup mayonnaise
Bread rounds, whole wheat or white

Combine all ingredients. Mix well. Spread on bread rounds. May be served open-face with parsley garnish, or closed.

Chicken or Turkey Sandwiches

10 slices white or whole wheat bread
2 (5-ounce) cans chicken
  (or same amount of turkey)

1/4 cup walnuts, chopped
2 tablespoons mayonnaise
2 tablespoons sweet pickle relish

Trim crusts from bread with electric knife. Combine all other ingredients and spread on bread. Cut each sandwich in fourths.

Chili Dogs

1 pound ground beef
1 cup chopped onion
1 can tomato sauce
1 teaspoon chili powder

1/2 teaspoon salt
1 pound weiners
Buns

Sauté beef and 1/2 cup of the onions. Add tomato sauce, chili powder and salt. Cover and simmer 15 minutes. Cook weiners 5 minutes; put in buns and top with chili mix and uncooked onions. Always a favorite!

Cream Cheese and Olive Sandwiches

1 large jar olives
2 (8-ounce) packages cream cheese,
    softened (low-fat Neufchâtel)

Milk

Place olives in blender. Add about 2 cups of water to blender. Chop and drain. Cut cream cheese into fourths and place in blender. Add just a little milk and begin to pulse blender; keep adding milk, but just as little as possible to get cheese to a softer consistency. Add olives to cream cheese and pulse, adding more milk if necessary for desired spreading consistency for sandwiches. Use as a filling for your favorite bread. These are so good and without the mayonnaise that we do not need.

Cream Puffs

These are listed with Seafood Appetizers filled with a shrimp filling, but they are good with so many different fillings. Not only are they good with meat fillings, but also with custards for cream puffs. I believe people think they are difficult to make, but they really are very easy!

1/2 cup water
1/4 cup butter
1/2 cup plain flour

2 eggs
1/2 teaspoon salt

Bring water and butter to a boil. Add the flour and mix; then remove from heat. Beat in eggs, 1 at a time, mixing well. Drop by spoonfuls on a greased baking sheet. Bake at 400 degrees 25 to 30 minutes. Remove from oven and cool. Break off top of puff when cool and fill each with desired filling. (Put out in very small amounts, because they really do rise.)

Egg Salad Sandwiches
(with bacon, mustard & green onions)

6 hard-boiled eggs, peeled and
    coarsely chopped
1/2 cup mayonnaise (or more, if desired)
1/2 teaspoon grainy Creole mustard or
    other coarse mustard
1/2 teaspoon celery seed

1 stalk celery, minced (more, if desired)
3 green onions with some green tops,
    minced
1/4 cup minced parsley
1/2 cup crisp-cooked, crumbled bacon
    (or purchased Real Bacon Bits)

Mix together eggs, mayonnaise, mustard and celery seed. Blend. Add all other ingredients and mix well. Use as desired for sandwiches, closed or open-face.

Hot Ham Sandwiches

1/4 cup butter, softened
2 tablespoons poppy seed
2 tablespoons horseradish mustard
  (or 1 tablespoon horseradish and
  1 tablespoon mustard)

2 tablespoons finely chopped onion
Slivered ham
Sliced Swiss cheese

Mix butter, poppy seed, mustard and onion; spread on both sides of bun. Top with ham and slice of Swiss cheese. Wrap in foil. Bake for 20 minutes at 350 degrees. Serves four. You may freeze for later. Thaw and warm in microwave.

Pimiento Cheese

1 (16-ounce) package sharp cheddar
  cheese
2 tablespoons lemon juice

1 medium onion, chopped (or to taste)
1 (4-ounce) jar diced pimientos, drained
1 cup mayonnaise, or to taste

Mix all ingredients. Use for sandwiches or with crackers.

Pimiento Cheese - (Cheddar and Cream Cheese)

1 (16-ounce) package sharp cheddar
  cheese, finely grated
1 (8-ounce) package cream cheese,
  softened to room temperature

1 1/2 cups Hellmann's mayonnaise
1/2 cup sour cream
1 (4-ounce) jar chopped pimientos,
  undrained

In a medium bowl, mix cheeses with mayonnaise, sour cream and pimientos, stirring until combined. Store in refrigerator. This will keep 3 to 4 weeks. For an extra twist, chopped jalapeño peppers or olives may be added.

Baked Cheese Sandwiches

12 slices bread
Natural cheddar cheese for 6 sandwiches,
  sliced
4 eggs, beaten

2 2/3 cups milk
1/2 teaspoon salt
Paprika, optional

Butter a 9x13-inch baking dish and put 6 slices of bread in bottom. Put cheese slices on top of bread and cover with remaining bread slices. Beat milk, eggs and salt well. Pour over sandwiches and let stand 45 to 60 minutes, or overnight. Sprinkle with paprika, if desired. Bake in a 325 degree oven for about 45 minutes or until sandwiches are browned. Serve immediately. Yield: 6 sandwiches that are nice reminders of cheese soufflé or strata.

Tuna Toasties

2 cans white tuna
2/3 cup mayonnaise
1/2 cup chopped ripe olives

4 hard-boiled eggs, finely chopped
1 giant loaf sandwich bread
Frosting (recipe follows)

Mix first 4 ingredients together.

Frosting:
2 jars Old English Cheese, (sharp)
2 eggs, beaten

1 stick margarine

Heat and mix well in double boiler.

Two decker sandwiches: Cut 3 slices bread with tuna can. Put tuna mixture between slices. Cover with frosting and refrigerate. (May be wrapped individually and frozen. Best to thaw completely before cooking.) Bake at 450 degrees for 10 minutes. Place ripe olive in center slice before serving. Great for a luncheon!
Suggestion: Serve fresh fruit salad with this, and a good dessert.

Vegetable Sandwiches

1 bell pepper
1 carrot
1 onion (medium size)
1 cucumber

1 (8-ounce) package cream cheese
1/2 cup mayonnaise (try 1/4 and test
    consistency)
Salt to taste, if needed

Finely chop all vegetables in blender, chopping softer vegetables first (so there will be juice). Place vegetables in large tea strainer or fine sieve, pressing to remove all juice. Return vegetables to blender; add cream cheese, mayonnaise, and salt, if desired. Blend. Refrigerate before spreading on sandwiches. Nice for open-face sandwiches, garnished with tiny wedge of cucumber slice.

Sweet Appetizers

Of course, many family desserts may be used as appetizers if made in miniature size. Please refer to **Desserts - Candy, Desserts - Cookies, Desserts - Frozen** - especially see **Lemon Cheesecake - Light**. Refer to **Pecan Tarts** in **Appetizers - Nuts** for pastry recipe - as these delicious morsels are " party-pretty." Also see **Desserts -Pies**, which also may be used to fill miniature pastries.

Artichoke Dip

1 (14-ounce) jar artichoke hearts,
  drained and chopped
1 cup Hellman's mayonnaise
1 cup grated parmesan cheese

1 tablespoon lemon juice
1/8 teaspoon Tabasco sauce
Garlic powder

Combine all ingredients and mix well. Bake at 350 degrees for 30 minutes or until brown. Serve hot with crackers.

Broccoli Dip

1 envelope Lipton vegetable soup mix
1 cup grated cheddar cheese
1 cup sour cream

1 (10-ounce) package frozen chopped
  broccoli, thawed

Combine all ingredients and bake until hot and cheese is melted. Serve with your favorite crackers or toasted sesame seed bread sticks.

Cheesy Cherry Tomatoes

2 dozen cherry tomatoes
1 (8-ounce) package cream cheese,
  softened
6 slices bacon, cooked crisp and
  crumbled (or Bacon-Bits or Bacos to
  equal this amount)

1/4 teaspoon celery salt or celery seed
1/4 teaspoon Worcestershire sauce
Dash onion powder or just a little
  fresh onion and tops
Small fresh parsley for garnish

Cut off top of each tomato; scoop out pulp. Invert tomato shells on paper towels. Combine cream cheese and next 4 ingredients in small bowl; beat at medium speed. Spoon or pipe (use large round tip if piping) into tomato shells. Garnish serving dish with parsley.

Cucumber Dill Spread

2 (8-ounce) packages cream cheese,
   softened
2 teaspoons lemon juice
2 teaspoons minced onion

1/2 teaspoon dill weed
1/4 teaspoon prepared horseradish
Dash hot pepper sauce
3/4 cup finely diced, seeded cucumber

In a mixing bowl beat cream cheese, adding next 5 ingredients. Fold in cucumbers. Cover and chill at least one hour. Serve with favorite crackers or raw vegetables.

Hot Vidalia Onion Dip

1 cup Vidalia finely chopped onion
1 cup grated Swiss cheese

1 cup mayonnaise

Mix together and put into a small casserole dish. Bake at 350 degrees until bubbly.

Radish Dip

1 (8-ounce) package cream cheese
1/4 cup margarine
1/2 teaspoon celery salt
Dash of paprika

1/2 teaspoon Worcestershire sauce
1 cup finely chopped radishes
1/2 cup finely chopped green onions

Soften cream cheese and margarine. Mix all ingredients together. Chill and serve with crackers or vegetables. Makes 2 cups.

Spinach Dip

1 (10-ounce) package frozen spinach
  (thaw and drain)
1 package Knorr vegetable soup mix
1 can sliced water chestnuts
  (chopped a little)

3 green onions (chopped)
1 (8-ounce) carton sour cream
1 cup mayonnaise
Raw vegetables

Mix all ingredients together thoroughly. Great with Vegetable Thins or other crackers or chips used for dips.

Note: Purchase one round loaf of bread. Cut a 1 1/2-inch slice off the top of the bread, and hollow out the inside part, leaving a thick shell. Tear all removed bread into bite-size pieces. Fill the shell with dip; set on a large platter. Arrange the bread pieces and raw vegetables around it and serve immediately. Yield: 10 to 15 servings.

We may gain a higher judgment, and an enlightened ability; a gift only from God, but we must use this unique ability and not be misled by opinions of others.

Eggnog - Chocolate

3 quarts eggnog, chilled
1 1/4 cups chocolate syrup
3/4 cup rum (optional)
1 1/2 cups heavy or whipping cream

3 tablespoons granulated sugar
1 tablespoon cocoa
Garnish: About 1/2 square (1-ounce)
  semi-sweet chocolate, grated

About 20 minutes before serving: In large punch bowl, combine eggnog, chocolate syrup and rum. In small bowl with electric mixer at high speed, whip cream, sugar and cocoa until stiff. Spoon cream onto eggnog. Sprinkle with grated chocolate. Makes 24 (1/2-cup) servings.

Hot Chocolate for 100 - (Dry Mix)

1 (1-pound) can Nestle's Quik
1 (16-ounce) box Carnation dry milk

2 cups Coffee-mate
1 (1-pound) box powdered sugar

Combine all ingredients and mix well. Add desired amount to each cup of hot water. Especially nice for families with children.

Hot Spicy Cider - So-o-o Easy

4 cups apple cider or apple juice
1/4 cup red hots (candy)

Orange slices, cinnamon sticks,
  or both for garnish

Combine cider or juice and candies in a saucepan. Stir over medium heat until candies melt and cider is hot. Pour into mugs and garnish each with 1/2 orange slice and/or cinnamon stick. For large amounts you may serve in tureen, topped with orange slices and cinnamon. You may also make this in electric percolator, putting candies in basket.

Hot Tomato Bouillon

1 (10-ounce) can condensed
  beef bouillon
2 cups tomato juice
1 teaspoon Worcestershire sauce

Salt, to taste
Garlic, optional
Tabasco sauce, optional
Garnish: Paper-thin lemon slices

Mix all ingredients except lemon slices. Heat and serve. Garnish with lemon slices, if desired.

Iced Coffee

1/2 gallon frozen coffee (sweetened)
1 gallon strong coffee (sweetened)
6 cartons whipping cream

1/2 gallon vanilla ice cream
1 gallon milk
1/2 cup rum

Freeze 1/2 gallon sweetened coffee. Whip cream and sweeten. Cut away ice cream box. Slice the block of ice cream into 3/4-inch slices. Cut each slice into six squares. Place frozen coffee into punch bowl; add strong coffee, milk and rum. Top with ice cream and whipped cream. Stir gently. Serve in punch cups. Delicious! You can make this a diet coffee by using artificial sweetener, whipped topping, and non-fat, no-sugar-added ice cream.

Iced - Coffee Rum Punch

5 quarts strong coffee
4 cups powdered milk
1 cup granulated sugar

2 cups dark rum or less, or optional
1/2 gallon vanilla ice cream
Ice cream to replenish as needed

Make the coffee. While it is still hot, stir in powdered milk and sugar. After it cools, stir in rum. Cut away ice cream box. Slice the block of ice cream into 3/4-inch slices. Cut each slice into six squares. To serve, pour cold coffee mixture into a punch bowl and float ice cream squares on top. Replenish ice cream as needed.

Citric Acid Punch for 50

1 ounce (2 tablespoons) citric acid   2 quarts boiling water

Pour boiling water over acid and let set overnight.

Day to be served: Dissolve 8 cups of sugar in warm water - about 1/2 gallon.
Add:

2 large (46 ounce) cans
  pineapple juice
1 (12- to 16-ounce) can frozen
  orange juice

1 small (6 ounce) can frozen lemonade
2 gallons cold water
Food coloring, if desired

Combine acid, water and remaining ingredients. Makes about 3 1/2 gallons.

Christmas Eve Punch (or Red Punch for Anytime)
(This is especially good)

1 (32-ounce) jar cranberry juice
  cocktail
1 (46-ounce) can unsweetened
  pineapple juice
2 cups orange juice

2/3 cup lemon juice
1/2 cup sugar
2 teaspoons almond extract
1 (1-liter) bottle ginger ale (chilled)

Combine first 6 ingredients; chill. To serve, add chilled ginger ale, stirring well.
Yield: 4 1/2 quarts. (Red food coloring may be added to enrich the color.)

Percolator Cranberry Punch

1 (1 1/2-quart) bottle cranberry juice
2 quarts apple juice
1/2 cup brown sugar

1/4 teaspoon salt
4 cinnamon sticks
1 1/2 teaspoons whole cloves

Pour juices into 30-cup coffee maker. Place remaining ingredients into basket and
place in coffee pot; perk ingredients. Remove basket and serve punch hot. These
ingredients also may be simmered for 2 hours in large saucepan.

Green Party Punch

1 small package lime Jell-O
1 large can pineapple juice

Juice of 3 lemons
Sugar to taste

Combine all ingredients, stirring to dissolve sugar. Serve chilled. Makes 1 gallon.

Slushy Banana Punch

1 cup sugar
2 3/4 cups water
2 ripe medium bananas, cut up
3 cups unsweetened pineapple juice

1 (6-ounce) can frozen orange
   juice concentrate
2 tablespoons lemon juice
1 (1-liter) bottle carbonated water or
   lemon-lime carbonated beverage, chilled

Stir together sugar and 2 3/4 cups water until sugar dissolves. In blender combine bananas, half of pineapple juice and the orange juice concentrate. Cover; blend until smooth. Add to sugar mixture. Stir in remaining pineapple juice and lemon juice. Transfer to 13x9x2-inch baking pan. Freeze for several hours or until firm.
When ready to serve, let mixture stand at room temperature for 20 to 30 minutes. To form a slush, scrape large spoon across the frozen mixture. Spoon into punch bowl. Slowly pour carbonated water down the side of the bowl. Stir gently to mix. Makes about 24 (4-ounce) servings. Delicious!

Instant Russian Tea (Sometimes called Spiced Tea)

2 cups Tang
1/2 cup instant tea with lemon
1 package dry lemonade
1 2/3 cups sugar

1 1/2 teaspoons ground cloves
   (add to taste)
1 1/2 teaspoons ground cinnamon
   (add to taste)

Combine all ingredients and store in air-tight container. To serve, add 1 1/2 tablespoons mix, or desired amount, to one cup of boiling water.

Tea Syrup

3 quarts boiling water   16 family-size tea bags
7 cups sugar

Boil water; add sugar and stir. Add tea bags and steep about 10 minutes or longer. Pour tea syrup into gallon container; cover and refrigerate. When ready to use, dilute tea syrup by using 1 cup syrup to 4 cups water or to taste. Tea syrup may be stored in refrigerator until ready to use.

"Keep your eyes open for spiritual danger; stand true to the Lord; act like men;
be strong; and whatever you do, do it with kindness and love." 1Cor.16:13-14 TLB

Breakfast, Brunch & Breads

(Please go to "Hot Fruit" in this book for other brunch ideas.)

Breakfast Sausage Casserole

8 slices bread
Butter or margarine
1 pound bulk pork sausage
1 1/2 cups cheddar cheese, shredded

8 eggs, beaten
2 cups milk
1 teaspoon salt
1/2 teaspoon pepper

Remove crusts from bread; spread bread slices with butter. Place in a 13x9x2-inch baking dish and set aside. Cook sausage until brown, stirring to crumble; drain well. Spoon over bread slices, sprinkle with cheese. Combine eggs, milk, salt and pepper; mix well and pour over cheese. Cover casserole and chill overnight. Remove from refrigerator 30 minutes before baking. Bake casserole, uncovered, at 350 degrees for 45 minutes or until set. Serves 10 to 12 people.

Breakfast Sausage Sandwiches

Softened butter or margarine
8 slices bread
1 pound bulk pork sausage, cooked,
    crumbled and drained

1 cup (4-ounces) shredded cheddar cheese
2 eggs, beaten
1 1/2 cups milk
1 1/2 teaspoons prepared mustard

Spread butter on one side of each bread slice. Place 4 slices, buttered side down, in a single layer in a lightly greased 8-inch square baking dish. Top each bread slice with sausage and remaining bread slices, buttered side up. Sprinkle with cheese. Combine remaining ingredients; pour over sandwiches. Cover and refrigerate at least 8 hours. Remove from refrigerator; let stand 30 minutes. Bake uncovered at 350 degrees for 45 minutes. Yield: 4 servings.

Delicious Sausage Muffins

1 cup Bisquick or Betty Crocker
  Buttermilk Biscuit Mix
1/2 cup shredded cheddar cheese
1 (3-ounce) package cream cheese,
  cut into small cubes

1/4 cup chopped green onions
1/4 pound sausage, browned and drained
2 large eggs, lightly beaten
2/3 cup milk

Mix biscuit mix, shredded cheese, cream cheese, onions and sausage together. Combine eggs and milk; add to first mixture and blend. Fill greased miniature muffin tins 2/3 full. Bake in a 350 degree oven 35 to 40 minutes, until lightly browned and firm. Yield: 2 dozen miniature muffins. Nice for breakfast, brunches, lunches and morning meetings. (They freeze well.)

Egg Brunch

Sauce:

2 (8-ounce) jars chipped beef
8 slices bacon, fried and crumbled
1/4 cup butter
1 (4-ounce) can sliced mushrooms

1/2 cup flour
1 quart milk
Pepper to taste

Put butter in pan to melt. Add crumbled bacon, chopped chipped beef and 1 can of the mushrooms. Sprinkle flour over top; add milk and cook, stirring and beating until thick. Season with pepper.

Eggs:

16 eggs
1/4 teaspoon salt
1 cup evaporated milk

1/4 cup melted butter
1 (4-ounce) can sliced mushrooms

Combine above ingredients and scramble eggs. Cook until well done, somewhat on the dry side to most people. Alternate layers of eggs and sauce in casserole dish. (2 of each). Cover with mushrooms; refrigerate 8 hours or overnight. Bake at 270 degrees for about 1 hour. It can bake even longer if you need to keep it warm to serve to others later.

French Omelet

2 eggs
1 tablespoon water
1/8 teaspoon salt

Dash of pepper
1 tablespoon margarine

In a bowl combine eggs, water, salt, and dash pepper. Using a fork, beat until combined, but not frothy. In an 8 or 10-inch skillet with flared sides, heat margarine until a drop of water sizzles. Lift and tilt the pan to coat the sides. Add egg mixture to skillet; cook over medium heat. As eggs set, run a spatula around the edge of the skillet, lifting eggs and letting uncooked portion flow underneath. When eggs are set but still shiny, remove from the heat. Fill your omelet as desired with one of the suggestions below (or your choice), by placing filling across center. Fold omelet in half. Transfer onto a warm plate. Serves 1.

Filling Suggestions:

Cheese: 1/4 cup cheddar, Monterey Jack, or Swiss, or a mixture. Sprinkle across center of omelet. Fold; top with shredded cheese.

Mushroom: Cook mushrooms in margarine; sprinkle 1/3 cup across omelet and fold.

Fruited: Spread 2 tablespoons sour cream (fat free is good), add about 1/4 cup fruit (strawberries, peaches, blueberries). Sprinkle with 1 tablespoon brown sugar (or just a little Sweet 'N Low Brown Sugar.) Fold.

Vegetable: Cook 1/3 cup your choice vegetable for each omelet. Spread vegetable and a sprinkle of grated Parmesan, shredded cheddar and fold. (Zucchini is very good and pretty.) Season to please your taste. (Morton's Nature's Seasons Seasoning Blend is good on any vegetable.)

Quiche: Flavor of Your Choice

Pastry for single-crust pie
3 beaten eggs
1 1/2 cups milk
1/4 cup sliced green onion
1/4 teaspoon salt
1/8 teaspoon pepper

3/4 cup chopped cooked chicken,
　crabmeat, ham, sausage, or bacon
1 1/2 cups shredded Swiss, cheddar,
　or Monterey Jack cheese,
　or a mixture of cheeses
1 tablespoon all-purpose flour

Bake pie crust. Stir together eggs, milk, onion, salt, and pepper. Stir in your choice of meat. Toss together shredded cheese and flour. Add to egg mixture, mix well. Pour egg mixture into hot pastry shell. Bake in 325 degree oven for 35 to 40 minutes or until a knife inserted near the center comes out clean. Let stand 10 minutes. Serves 6.

(These breads are great breakfast, brunch or dinner breads.)

Banana Nut Loaf

2/3 cup margarine
1 1/2 cups sugar
2 eggs, slightly beaten
1 teaspoon vanilla extract
4 tablespoons milk

1 cup mashed bananas
1 1/2 cups flour
2 teaspoons baking powder
1/4 teaspoon salt
1/2 cup pecans

Blend margarine and sugar; add eggs, vanilla, milk and bananas. Sift dry ingredients and add to mixture along with pecans. Stir in just until moistened. Bake in oiled loaf pan in 350 degree oven about 1 hour or until done to touch.

Brown Bread

(To make this bread, you need to save 4 [16-ounce] empty cans.)

1 cup raisins
2 cups water
1 cup sugar
2 eggs
2 tablespoons Crisco

3 cups flour
2 teaspoons soda
1/2 teaspoon salt
1 cup nuts, chopped

Preheat oven to 325 degrees. Grease and flour 4 (16-ounce) cans. Boil raisins in water for 5 minutes. Mix sugar, eggs and shortening in mixing bowl until well blended. Add raisin mixture. Beat well. Add combined mixture of flour, soda, salt and nuts, mixing well. Pour into cans. Bake 40 to 45 minutes. Cool in cans about 10 minutes. Turn out; slice and serve. Especially good with cream cheese.
Great for Christmas gifts!

Orange-Date-Cranberry Bread

2 cups all-purpose flour
1 cup sugar
1 teaspoon baking soda
1/2 teaspoon salt
1 cup dates, chopped
1 cup pecans, chopped (or almonds)

2 eggs
1 (8 1/4-ounce) can crushed pineapple,
    including juice
1 cup whole berry cranberry sauce
3/4 cup vegetable oil
Zest from 1 orange

Combine flour, sugar, soda and salt. Stir in dates and nuts. Combine eggs, pineapple, cranberry sauce, oil and 1 tablespoon orange zest; stir into dry mixture. Pour batter into 2 well greased and floured loaf pans. Bake in 350 degree oven 1 hour or until pick inserted in center comes out clean. Cool in pan on rack 15 minutes. Remove from pan to complete cooling. Makes 20 servings.

Poppy Seed Bread

3 cups flour
1 1/2 teaspoons salt
1 1/2 teaspoons baking powder
3 eggs, lightly beaten
1 1/2 cups milk
2 1/4 cups sugar

1 cup plus 2 tablespoons oil
1 1/2 teaspoons vanilla extract
1 1/2 teaspoons butter extract
1 1/2 teaspoons almond extract
1-2 tablespoons poppy seed
Glaze (recipe follows)

Mix flour, salt and baking powder. Add to dry ingredients eggs, milk, sugar, oil and extracts. Mix well; fold in poppy seed. Bake in 2 well-greased loaf pans in 350 degree oven for 50 to 60 minutes or until done to touch and lightly browned. Brush glaze over loaves while hot. Cool and turn out.

Glaze:

1/2 teaspoon vanilla extract
1/2 teaspoon butter extract
1/2 teaspoon almond extract

1/2 cup orange juice
1 1/2 cups powdered sugar

Mix and beat until smooth. Brush over loaves while hot.
Favorite Variation: Omit glaze. Make miniature sandwiches filled with cream cheese softened with a little milk or orange juice. With orange juice, add a little grated rind.

Providential circumstances can be proof that God is going before you.

Strawberry Bread

2 cups sugar
3 eggs, slightly beaten
1 1/4 cups salad oil
3 cups flour
1 teaspoon salt

1 teaspoon soda
1 tablespoon cinnamon
2 (10-ounce) packages strawberries
1 1/2 cups nuts

Blend sugar, eggs and oil; add flour, salt, soda and cinnamon, mixing well. Stir in strawberries and nuts. Bake at 350 degrees for 55 minutes in well oiled and floured loaf pans. This is wonderful for miniature or regular size muffins. Delicious with cream cheese for party sandwiches, or serve hot strawberry muffins and cream cheese for breakfast!

Brunch Bubble Ring

1 1/2 cups Post Granola cereal
3/4 cup firmly packed brown sugar
2 teaspoons cinnamon
1/2 cup chopped pecans

2 (8-ounce) packages refrigerated
  biscuit dough
1/2 cup (1 stick) butter or margarine,
  melted

Preheat oven to 350 degrees. Grease 12-cup Bundt pan. Combine granola, brown sugar, cinnamon and nuts in a small bowl and mix well. Separate dough; cut each biscuit in half. Dip in melted butter; roll in the cereal mixture, coating generously and pressing into dough. Layer biscuits into the Bundt pan. Sprinkle with remaining butter. Bake 30 minutes. Turn out immediately onto plate. Serve warm.

Cinnamon Rolls - Mini (Easy)

2 (8-ounce) cans Pillsbury refrigerated
  crescent rolls
1/2 cup margarine, softened
1/4 cup sugar
1 teaspoon cinnamon

1/4 cup nuts or raisins (or both),
  optional
1/4 cup maraschino cherries,
  chopped, optional

Glaze:
1 cup powdered sugar

2 tablespoons apple juice, sweet milk
  or buttermilk

Preheat oven to 350 degrees. Separate rolls into rectangles; press perforations and spread with margarine. Combine sugar, cinnamon, raisins, cherries and nuts. Sprinkle mixture over rectangles. Roll up each rectangle from short end. Cut each roll into 5 slices. Place cut side down on ungreased baking sheet. Bake for 20 to 25 minutes or until golden brown. Mix glaze and drizzle on top of warm rolls. This recipe may be halved. Makes 40 mini rolls. Great for brunch!

Glazed Raisin Biscuits

2 1/2 cups biscuit mix (I prefer
    Betty Crocker Buttermilk Biscuit Mix)
2 tablespoons sugar
1 teaspoon ground cinnamon
1/2 cup raisins
1 egg, beaten
2/3 cup milk
Vanilla Glaze (recipe follows)

Combine first 4 ingredients in a medium bowl; add egg and milk, stirring just until dry ingredients are moistened. Turn dough out onto a lightly floured surface; knead 4 or 5 times.

Roll dough to 1/2-inch thickness; cut with a 2-inch biscuit cutter. Place on lightly greased baking sheets. Bake at 350 degrees for 15 minutes or until golden brown. Brush biscuits with Vanilla Glaze. Yield: 1 1/2 dozen.

Vanilla Glaze:
2/3 cup sifted powdered sugar
1 tablespoon water
1/2 teaspoon vanilla extract

Combine all ingredients. Yield: About 1/4 cup.

Sour Cream Coffee Cake

4 tablespoons brown sugar
2 teaspoons cinnamon
1 cup pecans, chopped
1 cup real butter
1 1/2 cups sugar
2 eggs, beaten
2 cups flour
1 1/2 teaspoons baking powder
1/2 teaspoon soda
1/2 teaspoon salt
1 cup sour cream
1 teaspoon vanilla extract

Make topping first by mixing brown sugar, cinnamon and pecans. Set aside. Cream butter and sugar; add eggs, mix well. Add dry ingredients alternately with sour cream. Stir in vanilla. Pour 1/2 of batter into well greased and floured tube or Bundt pan. Sprinkle with 1/2 topping. Add remaining batter; top with remainder of topping. Bake until wooden toothpick inserted in center comes out almost clean, about 1 hour. Cool on rack for 15 minutes. Remove from pan.

Favorite Variation: Use almonds instead of pecans, and substitute almond flavoring for vanilla.

Blueberry-Pecan Muffins

1/2 cup milk
1/4 cup salad oil
1 egg, slightly beaten
2 teaspoons lemon extract
1 1/2 cups flour

1/2 cup sugar
2 teaspoons baking powder
1/2 teaspoon salt
1 cup blueberries
1 cup pecans, chopped

Stir milk and salad oil into egg. Add lemon extract. Sift together all dry ingredients. Add egg mixture, stirring just until flour is moistened. Fold in blueberries and pecans. Batter should be lumpy. Fill greased muffin tins two-thirds full. Bake 20 to 25 minutes at 400 degrees. Remove when lightly browned.

Date-Citrus Muffins

1/3 cup honey
1/4 cup margarine, softened
1 egg
1 (8-ounce) can crushed pineapple
Zest from 1 orange
1 cup all-purpose flour

1 cup whole wheat flour
1 1/2 teaspoons baking powder
1/4 teaspoon salt
1/4 teaspoon nutmeg
1 cup dates, chopped
1/2 cup almonds or pecans, toasted

Beat honey and margarine together 1 minute. Beat in egg, then undrained pineapple and 1 tablespoon orange zest. Combine remaining ingredients. Stir into pineapple mixture until just blended. Spoon batter into greased muffin tins. Bake in 375 degree oven for 25 minutes. Turn out onto rack to cool. Makes 12 muffins.

Ever-Ready Bran Muffins

1 (15-ounce) package wheat-bran
  flakes cereal with raisins
5 cups all-purpose flour
3 cups sugar
1 tablespoon plus 2 teaspoons soda

2 teaspoons salt
4 eggs, slightly beaten
1 quart buttermilk
1 cup vegetable oil

Combine cereal, flour, sugar, soda and salt in a very large bowl. Make a well in center of mixture. Add eggs, buttermilk and oil; stir just enough to moisten dry ingredients. Cover and store in fridge until ready to bake. (Batter can be kept in refrigerator up to 6 weeks, tightly covered.) To bake, spoon batter into greased muffin tins, filling 2/3 full. Bake at 400 degrees for 12 to 15 minutes. Yield: About 5 1/2 dozen.

Sweet Potato Muffins

2 cups cooked and mashed
    sweet potatoes
2 cups self-rising flour
1 1/2 cups sugar

4 eggs
1 1/4 cups Puritan oil
1 cup pecans, chopped
2 tablespoons cinnamon

Combine and stir until mixed. Bake at 350 degrees for 25 to 30 minutes in well greased muffin tins. Yield: 30 to 34 muffins.

Upside-Down Pineapple-Bran Muffins

2 tablespoons margarine, melted
2 tablespoons honey
1 (8-ounce) can crushed pineapple
    in juice
1 egg, slightly beaten
1/4 cup vegetable oil

3/4 cup skim milk
2 cups sifted all-purpose flour
3 teaspoons baking powder
1/2 teaspoon salt
1 teaspoon cinnamon
2 cups raisin bran flake cereal

Preheat oven to 350 degrees. Drizzle melted margarine and honey in each of 12 muffin cups. Drain pineapple, reserving juice. Place 1 teaspoon pineapple in each cup. In small bowl combine egg, oil, milk and reserved pineapple juice (about 1/3 cup). Set aside. In medium bowl stir together flour, baking powder, salt and cinnamon. Stir in cereal. Beat egg mixture; add all at once to flour mixture. Stir until just moistened. Spoon batter into prepared muffin cups, filling 2/3 full. Batter will be sticky. Bake 20 to 25 minutes. Serve warm. Completely cool remaining muffins. Store in sealed plastic bags in freezer. Thaw and warm for serving.

Baked French Toast

10 whole wheat slices
1 1/2 cups (12-ounce can)
    evaporated skim milk
2 whole eggs, plus 4 egg whites,
    or 1 cup liquid egg substitute

1/3 cup dark brown sugar
1 teaspoon vanilla extract
1/2 teaspoon cinnamon

Lightly coat 9x13-inch baking pan with non-stick vegetable spray. Arrange bread slices in bottom of pan. Combine all remaining ingredients and mix well with whisk or egg beater. Pour mixture evenly over bread. Cover tightly and refrigerate several hours or overnight. To bake, preheat oven to 350 degrees. Remove bread from refrigerator and spray lightly with non-stick vegetable spray. Bake 30 to 35 minutes until lightly browned.

Baked Tomato French Toast
(Easy brunch or breakfast dish)

3 large (1 1/2 pounds) fresh tomatoes
16 slices firm white bread, crusts
   removed
2 tablespoons butter, melted
12 slices Canadian bacon
   (or thin sliced ham)

2 cups sharp cheddar cheese, grated
8 eggs
3 cups half-and-half
1 teaspoon salt
1/4 teaspoon black pepper

Core tomatoes. Cut off a thin slice from top and bottom. Cut each tomato in 4 slices; set aside. In 15x10x1-inch baking pan, place bread in a single layer, cutting to fit, if necessary. Butter bread on one side, turning buttered side down in pan. Arrange bacon over bread; sprinkle with 1 3/4 cups of grated cheese; set aside. In a bowl, beat eggs, half-and-half, salt and pepper; pour over bread and cheese. Bake, uncovered, in 350-degree oven until nearly firm, about 15 minutes. Arrange reserved tomato slices over the top; bake until set, about 8 minutes. Sprinkle with 1/4 cup cheese; cut into squares and serve.

Biscuits and Rolls

Angel Biscuits

5 cups self-rising flour
1/3 cup sugar
1 teaspoon soda
2 packages dry yeast

1/4 cup warm water
1 cup Crisco
2 cups buttermilk

Sift flour, sugar and soda. Dissolve yeast in warm water. Cut Crisco into sifted ingredients with pastry cutter. Add buttermilk and yeast mixture. Mix lightly and toss onto floured board or wax paper. Cut or roll biscuits into desired size. Bake 10 to 12 minutes in 450 degree oven, or until browned. Dough may be made up and stored in refrigerator until needed.

Best-Ever Biscuits

2 cups all-purpose flour
1 tablespoon baking powder
2 teaspoons sugar
1/2 teaspoon cream of tartar

1/4 teaspoon salt
1/2 cup shortening
2/3 cup milk

In a medium mixing bowl stir together flour, baking powder, sugar, cream of tartar, and salt. Mix well. Using a pastry blender, cut shortening into flour mixture until it resembles coarse crumbs. Gently push the mixture against the sides of the bowl, making well in center. Pour milk into the well all at once. Using a fork, stir just until the mixture follows the fork around the bowl and forms a soft dough. Turn dough onto a lightly floured surface. Knead gently 10 to 12 strokes. Cut or roll biscuit into desired size, handling just as little as possible. Bake in 450 degree oven 10 to 12 minutes or until biscuits are golden on top and bottom. Makes 10 to 12 biscuits.

Biscuits - Easy

1 3/4 cups self-rising flour
1/2 pint heavy whipping cream

Flour to roll out

Mix ingredients. Add enough flour to knead and roll out thick. Cut with biscuit cutter and bake in 450 degree oven 10 to 12 minutes. Yield: 12 to 14 biscuits.

Sour Cream Biscuits (Rich, but good!)

1 cup margarine, melted
1 (8-ounce) carton sour cream

2 cups self-rising flour

Preheat oven to 450 degrees. Combine margarine and sour cream; mix well. Add flour and mix well. Drop by teaspoonfuls into ungreased miniature muffin tins. Bake 15 minutes. Makes about 28 biscuits.

Biscuit from Mix

(I highly recommend Betty Crocker Buttermilk Biscuit Mix.)

(I buy 5-pound boxes of this mix at Sam's. You may find smaller boxes or bags of this in grocery; I am not sure.)

If you like to keep a mix on hand for quick use, Betty Crocker Buttermilk Biscuit Mix is wonderful! Bake as directed on box. You will find listed other recipes shown on box for Betty Crocker Biscuit Mix, as they sometimes change packaging and leave off recipes we may have liked.

A good idea from a friend for delicious waffle biscuits! Great to serve Curried Chicken over for a luncheon, or for breakfast with butter and your favorite sweet.

Waffles: Just add ice water to mix until you achieve the consistency of waffle mix. Cook in waffle iron. Delicious!

From box - Drop Biscuits: Prepare dough for 2-inch biscuits. Drop by 1/4 cupfuls onto lightly greased cookie sheet. Bake 9 to 11 minutes or until golden brown. 7 biscuits.

Cheese Biscuits: Prepare dough for 2-inch biscuits as directed — except add 3/4 cup shredded cheddar or Swiss cheese with the biscuit mix. Bake on lightly greased cookie sheet. Brush hot biscuits with mixture of 2 tablespoons melted margarine or butter and 1/8 teaspoon garlic powder, if desired.

Herb Biscuits: Prepare dough for 2-inch biscuits as directed — except add 2 teaspoons dried dill weed or 1 1/2 teaspoons dried basil leaves and 1/2 teaspoon dried oregano leaves with the biscuit mix. 12 or 13 biscuits.

Bunker Hill Biscuits: Mix 1/2 cup sugar and 1 tablespoon ground cinnamon; reserve. Prepare dough for 2-inch biscuits as directed. Drop by 9 rounded table-spoonfuls into 1/4 cup melted margarine or butter; roll to coat. Roll in sugar mixture, randomly twisting and pinching dough to incorporate mixture throughout. (Dough will have irregular appearance.) Place in rows in greased square pan, 8x8x2 inches. Bake 13 to 15 minutes or until deep golden brown. Loosen edges and immediately invert onto heat-proof plate. Serve warm. 9 biscuits.

Bisquick Rolls

(Betty Crocker Buttermilk Biscuit Mix Rolls)

6 cups Bisquick or Betty Crocker
   Buttermilk Biscuit Mix
1/4 cup sugar

2 packages dry yeast
1/3 cup shortening
2 cups warm water

Combine Bisquick mix, sugar and yeast. Cut in shortening with pastry blender. Add 1 3/4 cups warm water to make soft dough. Add rest of water, if needed. Roll out, cut and place on ungreased sheet. Brush with melted butter (optional). Bake in 425 degree oven 10 to 12 minutes. Makes about 4 dozen. You may remove them from oven before they brown, cool and freeze. Take out of freezer as needed and brown.

Janie's Rolls

2 cups milk, scalded
1 stick margarine
1/2 cup sugar
1 package yeast
1/4 cup lukewarm water

3 cups flour
2 cups flour
1 teaspoon baking powder
1/4 teaspoon soda
2 teaspoons salt

Combine margarine and sugar with hot milk. Stir until margarine is melted and sugar is dissolved. Allow to get lukewarm (115 degrees). Dissolve yeast in lukewarm water. Add this mixture to first mixture, adding 3 cups sifted flour, stirring to make soft dough. Let set for 2 to 3 hours or until about doubled in size. Combine the other two cups of flour, baking powder, soda and salt. Sift into soft dough mixture and mix well. Knead about 10 to 15 times. Put in refrigerator overnight, or until chilled. Toss onto floured board; knead a few times and shape into desired size. Let rise 2 hours or until about double in size. Bake in 375 degree oven for about 8 to 10 minutes for pre-cooked rolls. Cool completely and freeze in plastic bags.

Mama's Refrigerator Rolls

2 cups boiling water
1/2 cup sugar
1 tablespoon salt
6 tablespoons shortening
2 packages yeast

1/4 cup lukewarm water
1 teaspoon sugar
2 beaten eggs
8 cups flour (sifted)

Mix boiling water, sugar, salt and shortening together; cool until lukewarm. Soften yeast in 1/4 cup lukewarm water; add 1 teaspoon sugar and stir into first mixture. Add beaten eggs and stir in 4 cups flour; beat thoroughly. Stir in 4 more cups flour and mix well. Do not knead. Brush top of dough with melted butter; cover tightly and store in refrigerator until ready to use. Shape into rolls, put in a warm place to rise. When about doubled in size, bake in 425 degree oven for 10 to 15 minutes or until browned. Two cups of graham or wheat flour may be substituted for same amount of white flour. (This is my mother's recipe. She made them many, many times and they were so good!)

Cornbreads - A Favorite of the South

Cornbread tips: Buy fine ground meal. Do not buy cornbread mix unless the recipe calls for that. **Dixie Lily Cornmeal - Fine Ground** is my favorite. If I cannot get Dixie Lily, I use Alabama. It is very important to have good corn meal. Order it from somewhere, if need be!

When using mixes, do not beat batter until smooth, and your bread will peak on top with a very nice texture.

For a crisp outer crust, preheat griddle and then oil before filling with batter.

After baking, if not serving bread immediately, remove bread from baker onto serving dish and prop up on something so that air can get under it to prevent sweating.

When using iron bakers, be sure they are well "seasoned". Instructions come on most of these for "seasoning".

Do not boil anything in your iron bakers, or your bread will stick the next time. Do not cover bread with anything after cooking; this will cause it to sweat and not be crisp.

Cornmeal Lace Cakes or Hoe Cakes

1 cup cornmeal
1/4 teaspoon salt

Water to make very soft consistency
Corn oil

Heat small amount of oil in small, 5- to 6-inch, preferably iron, fry pan. Add oil as needed to make bread brown pretty. Combine meal, salt and water to very soft consistency. Spoon about 3 tablespoons of thin batter into hot fry pan, tapping bottom of pan when adding batter to make it spread to size of fry pan. Experience will help you get the perfect consistency. Turn with spatula as needed to get a perfect brown on both sides. Sprinkle lightly with salt as it drains on paper towel. **A Southern delicacy!**

Charles' Corn Bread

1 cup all-purpose flour	1 cup cornmeal
1/4 cup sugar	2 eggs
4 teaspoons baking powder	1 cup milk
3/4 teaspoon salt	1/4 cup liquid shortening

Mix first five ingredients; add eggs, milk and shortening. Beat just until mixed. (Do not over-beat.) Use your favorite baking pans that have been well oiled. Pie-shaped iron pans, corn cornstick pans or small muffin tins are my favorites. If you use large muffin tins, put a small amount of batter so that they will not be too thick. I use Baker's Joy on muffin tins instead of oil.
Remember to preheat iron pans and then oil! Bake in 425 degree oven 20 to 25 minutes or until brown. For corn sticks and muffins, about 12 to 15 minutes or until brown. Delicious warmed over in regular oven. (When Charles came home from college for break, he very often would want me to make these for him to take back.)

Corn Sticks with Cream Corn

1 cup sifted all-purpose flour	1 egg, beaten
2 tablespoons sugar	1 cup canned cream corn or
2 teaspoons baking powder	1 (8.5-ounce) can is fine
3/4 teaspoon salt	3/4 cup milk
1 cup cornmeal	2 tablespoons vegetable oil

Preheat iron cornstick baking pan; then grease generously. Combine first five ingredients; add egg, corn, milk and oil. Stir just until moistened. Fill hot pans 2/3 full; bake at 425 degrees until brown.

Corn Pone or Cracklin' Bread

3 cups Dixie Lily plain cornmeal	1 1/2-2 cups liquid —
1 1/2 teaspoons salt	(half milk and half water)
1 1/2 teaspoons baking powder	1 cup cracklings, optional
3 tablespoons oil	

Combine all ingredients, using enough liquid for a stiff consistency. Form pones with hands or drop by rounded tablespoons onto a hot oiled jelly-roll pan or griddle. Bake in 425 degree oven about 20 minutes or until brown. Remove from pan and sprinkle lightly with salt.

Egg Bread
(This is great used to make Chicken Dressing.)

2 1/2 cups cornmeal
3 teaspoons baking powder
1 teaspoon salt
1 teaspoon soda

2 eggs (beat until light)
3 tablespoons shortening
2 cups buttermilk

Preheat oven to 400 degrees. Combine above ingredients in order listed. Pour into well greased pan or skillet and cook for about 30 minutes. Cut into squares or use to make dressing.

Fried Cornbread

1 cup Dixie Lily cornmeal
1/4 cup all-purpose flour
1/4 teaspoon salt
2 teaspoons baking powder

Half water and half milk to make
soft batter
Oil for frying (Wesson Vegetable Oil)

Mix all ingredients. Spoon into medium hot oil in small amounts, forming patties (not too thick), or deep fry in very small amounts, like hushpuppies. Keep turning; browning on both sides. Have dough as soft as possible; but if it disintegrates in the oil, it is too soft. Add oil as needed. Drain thoroughly on paper towel, sprinkling lightly with salt. Delicious, but not on anyone's diet!
Favorite tip: Add onions and serve with fish or vegetables!

Fried Cornbread
or Hushpuppies (made with Buttermilk)

1 cup cornmeal (Dixie Lily)
1/4 cup all-purpose flour
1 teaspoon baking powder
1/4 teaspoon baking soda
1/2 teaspoon salt

1-1 1/2 cups buttermilk (as soft as
you can make it without it
disintegrating in oil)
1 large onion, chopped, optional

Combine ingredients and drop by teaspoonfuls into hot oil and cook until brown, turning as they cook. Drain well on paper towel. Sprinkle lightly with salt. **Do not cover with anything. These are our favorites!** (Do not cook so fast that they do not cook in the middle.)

Hushpuppies - with White Lily Cornmeal Mix

1 cup White Lily cornmeal mix
1/4 cup self-rising flour
1 egg

1 large onion, chopped
Enough buttermilk to make a stiff batter

Combine ingredients. Drop by teaspoonfuls into deep, medium hot oil until perfectly browned; drain. Sprinkle lightly with salt, if desired. A small ice cream dipper with spring release works great for these.

Broccoli Corn Bread

1 (10-ounce) package frozen,
    chopped broccoli, steamed
1 small onion, chopped
1 (8-ounce) carton cottage cheese

1 stick margarine, melted
3/4 teaspoon salt
4 eggs, beaten
1 box Jiffy Cornbread Mix

Mix all ingredients, adding corn bread mix last. Bake in 9x13-inch pan, (or in your choice of pan), at 400 degrees for 25 minutes.

Jalapeño Corn Bread

1 cup cornmeal
1/2 teaspoon salt
1/2 teaspoon baking soda
1 cup canned cream-style corn
2 eggs, beaten

2/3 cup buttermilk
1/3 cup melted shortening
1 cup longhorn cheese, grated
1/4-1/2 cup seeded, canned, jalapeño
    peppers, chopped fine

Preheat oven to 350 degrees. Mix cornmeal, salt and baking soda. Combine corn, eggs, buttermilk and shortening and mix with dry ingredients. Pour half of the mixture into a greased 9x9x2-inch pan, or your choice of pan. Sprinkle with cheese and peppers and remaining mixture. Bake 30 to 40 minutes or until brown.

Mexican Corn Bread

2 jalapeño peppers
1/2 cup sweet milk
3 eggs, beaten
1 cup onion, chopped
1 cup grated cheddar cheese

Dash garlic salt
1/2 cup vegetable oil
1 cup cream-style corn
1 1/2 cups self-rising cornmeal

Blend peppers in blender with milk. Combine all ingredients and pour into greased 8x10-inch baking dish. Bake for 40 to 50 minutes at 400 degrees or until golden brown.

Don't ignore inward impressions that continue to "bug" you. You may need to act and be obedient if you feel these are from God.

Be sure you recognize and know the Voice before you follow.
Christ chose us to have His salvation. We choose whether or not to receive it.

Have an intent to discern God's plans.

Choose God's choices.

The Spirit of God will honor your desiring of His will.

"Be humble and gentle. Be patient with each other, making allowance for each others faults because of your love." (Ephes.4:2 TLB)

Self is conscious of the impression it makes upon people. Christ in us makes us unconscious of ourselves.

Angels will hover over you as you do your best and share your best with your loved ones and friends.

Desserts

1-2-3-4 Cake Layers

1 cup shortening (butter or margarine)   1/2 teaspoon salt
2 cups sugar   3 teaspoons baking powder
4 eggs   1 cup milk
3 cups flour   1 teaspoon vanilla extract

Blend shortening and sugar until light and fluffy; add eggs one at a time, beating after each just until egg-color disappears. Sift flour once; add salt and baking powder and sift twice. Add dry ingredients alternately with milk. Stir in vanilla and pour into 3 layer cake pans and bake at 350 degrees until light brown — about 25 minutes. Cool in pans for about 10 minutes and turn out on racks to finish cooling. Frost with your favorite frosting.

Hot Milk Layer

These layers are spongier and finer texture than 1-2-3-4 layers.
They are delicious!

4 large eggs   5 large eggs
2 cups sugar   2 1/2 cups sugar
1 cup milk   1 1/4 cups milk
1 stick margarine   1 1/4 sticks margarine
2 cups all-purpose flour   2 1/2 cups all-purpose flour
1/2 teaspoon salt   3/4 teaspoon salt
1 teaspoon baking powder   1 1/4 teaspoons baking powder
2 teaspoons vanilla   2 1/2 teaspoons vanilla extract

First column of ingredients will make a small 3-layer cake. 2nd column of ingredients will make 3 layers about the size of 1-2-3-4 recipe. Beat eggs at high speed until foamy. Gradually add sugar, continuing to beat until very stiff and lemon-colored. Reduce speed; place milk and margarine in small saucepan and heat to just below boiling. Sift flour, salt and baking powder together 3 times. Remove egg mixture from mixer stand and with large spoon fold in dry ingredients. When combined, add heated milk/butter mixture; add vanilla and fold together. Divide, dipping from bottom of bowl, into 3 greased layer cake pans. Beat out air bubbles in each pan by bumping firmly on cabinet top several times. Bake immediately in 300 degree oven until layers spring back when touched, and are lightly browned. Expect batter to be very thin.

Hot Milk Layer (1)

2 eggs
1 cup sugar
1/2 cup milk
1 tablespoon butter

1 teaspoon vanilla extract
1 cup flour
1 teaspoon baking powder
1/4 teaspoon salt

Follow above directions for combining ingredients and baking.

Yellow Cake Layers (from mix - hard to beat)

1 box Duncan Hines Butter Recipe
  Golden Cake Mix
3 eggs

2/3 cup buttermilk
1 stick Blue Bonnet margarine

A friend shared her cake with me, and I thought the layers were outstanding! I have shared her idea with many people and everyone seems to like it. Such information can mean so much to one who cooks!
I always use the buttermilk and the Blue Bonnet Margarine. I slice the margarine into a saucer and put it in the microwave just 10 seconds. I think it needs to be just a little soft, but not too soft.

Combine all ingredients in mixer bowl: mix just enough to moisten.
Turn mixer to medium speed and beat for 4 full minutes. Divide into layers or bake in 9x13-inch, 2 (8x8-inch), or 10x15-inch pan, as directed on box. It is great to use the 8x8-inch and make two, icing both; freeze one for later use, or use as a gift! This recipe is great for Strawberry Shortcake or many other uses.
Note: For chocolate layers, I use the **Duncan Hines Butter Recipe Fudge Cake Mix** with same changes, except 3/4 cup buttermilk. This is good for layers, cup cakes and many other chocolate desserts. Save your foil pie pans with covers from purchased pie crusts; divide this cake batter between 3 pie pans, ice each and serve as is, or serve in pie-shaped wedges covered with strawberries or cherry pie filling and Lite Cool Whip or ice cream. Delicious and a very light dessert!

The requirement to receive God's Word is to be open to it.

Yellow Cake Layers

3 cups flour, sifted twice
3 teaspoons baking powder
1/2 cup margarine
2 cups sugar

1 1/2 cups cold water
1 teaspoon vanilla extract
4 egg whites, stiffly beaten

Sift flour and baking powder together. Cream butter or margarine and sugar. Add dry ingredients and water alternately to sugar mixture; add vanilla and blend well. Fold in stiffly beaten egg whites. Bake in 3 (9-inch) pans at 350 degrees for 25 to 30 minutes or until light brown and cake begins to leave sides of pans. This is especially good for coconut cake with white icing and lots of coconut.

Carrot Cake

4 eggs
1 1/2 cups Wesson oil
2 cups plain flour
2 cups sugar
2 teaspoons cinnamon

3 cups carrots, grated
1 cup pecans, chopped
2 teaspoons soda
Cream Cheese Icing (recipe follows)

Preheat oven to 325 degrees. Grease and flour 3 (9-inch) layer cake pans. In large mixer bowl, combine eggs and oil. Beat until foamy on medium speed. Sift flour, sugar and cinnamon; add to first mixture, beating well. Add carrots and chopped pecans and stir in by hand until thoroughly mixed. Add baking soda last; stir quickly to mix. Immediately pour batter into prepared pans. Bake about 25 minutes or until wooden pick inserted in center comes out clean. Cool 10 minutes in pans. Turn out and cool completely on wire rack.

Cream Cheese Icing:

1/2 stick margarine
1 (8-ounce) package cream cheese
1 box powdered sugar

2 teaspoons vanilla extract
1/2 cup pecans, lightly toasted

Cream margarine and cream cheese; beat until smooth. Add powdered sugar and vanilla and beat until well blended. Spread on layers, top and sides. Sprinkle nuts on top.

Heavenly Chocolate-Cherry Cake

Easy and Special
(One for a family of 8, and one to give to a special friend!)

1 box Duncan Hines Moist Deluxe
   Butter Recipe Fudge Cake Mix
1 stick Blue Bonnet margarine (1/2 cup)
3/4 cup buttermilk
1 can cherry pie filling

1 (8-ounce) carton whipped topping
Garnish: Toasted sliced almonds
   or pecans, optional
Glossy Chocolate Sour Cream
   Frosting (recipe follows)

This is one of my most favorite cakes - and so simple!
Prepare cake mix as directed on box, except using the Blue Bonnet margarine and the 3/4 cup buttermilk as listed above. Beat ingredients just until moistened and then set mixer on medium speed and beat for 4 full minutes. Bake in two (9-inch) round layer cake pans that have been greased, or heart-shaped pans for Valentines, or for someone on a special occasion! Cool 5 minutes in pans and turn out on wire rack to completely cool. Frost the two layers as individual cakes on sides and tops. You will have a heavy icing on top, but this is so good. The cake tastes like chocolate covered cherries but even better, not as "sweet, sweet" as the chocolate covered cherries.

Glossy Chocolate Sour Cream Frosting:
1 1/2 cups semi-sweet real chocolate
   chips (not the whole bag!)
3/4 cup sour cream (Not 8 ounces, just
   3/4 cup – I have made that mistake!)

2 cups confectioners' sugar
1 teaspoon vanilla extract

Melt mini-chips in top of double boiler over hot water, stirring constantly. Remove from heat and beat in remaining ingredients. Frost cakes, sides and tops.

Cherry Pie Filling and Whipped Topping:
Dip whipped topping onto cakes around outer edge in connecting dollops, following shape of pan. (This will take up about 2 inches.) Dip equal amounts of cherry pie filling onto middle of the top of each cake, filling in to the whipped topping.
Yield: 8 nice pie-shaped servings.
Garnish: Sprinkle a few lightly toasted, sliced almonds or chopped pecans on whipped topping, if desired.
Note: If you want a lighter dessert, leave off the frosting and use the cherry pie filling or fresh strawberries and the whipped topping. You may like to sweeten strawberries a little.

Chocolate Mound Cake

Layers: 1, 2, 3, 4 Cake Layers (recipe on page 54)
Filling (recipe below)
Frosting (recipe below)

Filling:

1 cup sugar
1 cup milk
3 (6-ounce) bags frozen, grated coconut

12 large marshmallows
1 teaspoon vanilla extract

Prepare filling while cake is baking. Place sugar and milk in saucepan and bring to a boil; add coconut and marshmallows. Stir and boil 5 minutes. Add vanilla; spread on layers, stacking cake while warm.

Frosting:

3/4 cup cocoa
4 cups powdered sugar
1/2 cup butter

1 teaspoon vanilla
1/2 cup evaporated milk

Mix cocoa and sugar. Cream 1/2 of cocoa/sugar mixture with butter; blend in vanilla and 1/2 of milk. Add remaining milk and cocoa/sugar mixture and blend. Frost cake top and sides. (If you prefer, use Glossy Chocolate Sour Cream Frosting – listed in icings, also in Chocolate-Cherry Cake previously listed.)

To believe in the basic worth of each individual makes it easier to deal with their differences.

Coconut Cake

(This glaze is an old idea given to me by a wonderful lady who made many delicious cakes for various functions at our church.)

1,2,3,4 Cake Layers (recipe listed with Cake Layers) baked into 3 layers

Coconut Glaze to soak into layers (recipe follows)
Seven-Minute Icing (recipe follows)

Coconut Glaze:
1 (12-ounce) bag frozen grated coconut (or flaked), divided

1/3 cup water
1/4 cup sugar

In small saucepan, cook about 1/2 cup coconut with water and sugar just long enough to dissolve sugar. Spoon over each of the 3 layers, allowing to soak into layer. Do this as you stack the cake.

Seven-Minute Icing:
3 egg whites
2 1/4 cups sugar
6 tablespoons water

1/3 cup Karo syrup
1/2 teaspoon cream of tartar
1 teaspoon vanilla extract

Beat all ingredients in top of double boiler for 1 minute before placing above boiling water. Cook approximately 7 minutes, or until it is a good spreading consistency. Stack the cake by glazing each layer, spreading with icing, and topping icing with coconut; using remainder of icing and coconut for top and sides. Delicious!

Devil's Food Cake (Easy)

Use Duncan Hines Chocolate Butter Recipe Fudge Cake mix, using Blue Bonnet margarine and 3/4 cup of buttermilk. You may make 3 layers instead of 2. Be careful not to overbake the thinner layers. Use **Seven Minute Frosting** listed in Icings, or in above recipe.

Fresh Coconut Cake

1-2-3-4 cake layers (recipe listed on page 54) baked into 3 layers, or your choice

Filling:

1 (12-ounce) package frozen, grated, coconut
2 1/2 cups water
2 teaspoons coconut extract, divided
2 cups sugar

1 teaspoon vanilla extract
1 teaspoon lemon juice
1/4 teaspoon salt
2 heaping tablespoons cornstarch
1/4 cup water

Bring coconut, water, coconut extract and sugar to a rapid boil. Boil for 5 to 8 minutes. Add vanilla, remaining coconut extract, lemon juice and salt. Mix cornstarch in 1/4 cup water; pour into filling, stirring constantly. Let boil for 2 minutes. Cool in fridge until completely cold and stiff. Spread between layers and on top of cake. This is an "old-fashioned coconut cake." This recipe is seldom seen any more, but very good and popular in the South.

Coconut Cake
(Bagged or Canned Coconut)

Make your our choice of layers: **1,2,3,4, Hot Milk** or **Duncan Hines Butter Cake Mix.** If you use mix, I suggest making 3 layers.

Icing: (I have not had this fail!)

5 egg whites
1 1/4 cups light corn syrup
1 1/4 cups sugar

1 teaspoon vanilla extract
1 (12-ounce) bag coconut

Put egg whites, corn syrup and sugar in a large double boiler, (or a metal mixing bowl sitting in, but not touching bottom, of a boiler) and beat until mixed; place over boiling water and cook and beat until beaters make deep tracks in icing and icing peaks and turns glossy. This takes about 8 to 10 minutes, depending on the heat used. Be sure to cook long enough. Add vanilla and mix. Spread icing thick on cake layers and sides of cake when you have finished stacking; cover each layer and sides of cake generously with coconut. This makes a lot of icing. This icing does not form a crust, but stays where you put it, and is great with lots of coconut.

Coconut-Pineapple Cake

1,2,3,4 layer (recipe on page 54) or your choice of 3-layer recipe
Pineapple Filling
Seven-Minute Frosting

Pineapple Filling:

1 cup sugar
3 tablespoons all-purpose flour
2 eggs, beaten
1 (8-ounce) can crushed pineapple, undrained

1 lemon, juice and rind (grated)
1 tablespoon butter or margarine
1 (12-ounce) bag coconut, divided (for layers and topping)

(If you like a lot of filling, double these ingredients except the coconut, and frost tops of all 3 layers with this filling. Then spread top and sides with **Seven Minute Frosting**.)

Combine sugar and flour in a small saucepan; add remaining ingredients, except coconut. Cook over medium heat, stirring constantly, until thickened (about 2 minutes).) Cool. Yield: 1 1/3 cups.

Seven-Minute Frosting:

1 1/2 cups sugar
1/4 cup plus 1 tablespoon cold water
2 egg whites

1 tablespoon light corn syrup
Dash of salt
1 teaspoon vanilla extract

Combine all ingredients except vanilla in top of a large double boiler. Beat at low speed of an electric mixer 30 seconds or just until blended. Place over boiling water; beat constantly on high speed 7 minutes or until stiff peaks form. Remove from heat. Add vanilla; beat 2 minutes or until beaters make deep tracks and frosting is thick enough to spread. Yield: 4 1/4 cups.

Spread 1 layer with half of Pineapple Filling; sprinkle 1/3 cup coconut over filling. Repeat with next layer. Spread Seven-Minute Frosting on top and sides of cake, and sprinkle with remaining coconut. Yield: One 3-layer cake.

Variation: Make cake the same but use **Lemon Cheese Icing** (listed in Icings) instead of pineapple. You will have more filling, so frost tops all three layers and then the sides. Spread **Seven-Minute Frosting** on top and sides, but leave a circle of lemon filling showing in center of top. Pretty and delicious!

Hummingbird Cake

3 cups all-purpose flour
1 teaspoon baking soda
1/2 teaspoon salt
2 cups sugar
1 teaspoon ground cinnamon
3 eggs, beaten
3/4 cup vegetable oil

1 1/2 teaspoons vanilla extract
1 (8-ounce) can crushed pineapple, undrained
1 cup chopped pecans
1 3/4 cups mashed bananas
1/2 cup chopped pecans (for frosting)
Cream Cheese Frosting (recipe follows)

Combine first 5 ingredients in a large bowl; add eggs and oil, stirring until dry ingredients are moistened. Do not beat. Stir in vanilla, pineapple, pecans, and bananas. Pour batter into 3 greased and floured 9-inch round cake pans. Bake at 350 degrees for 23 to 28 minutes or until a wooden pick inserted in center comes out clean. Cool in pans 10 minutes; remove from pans, and let cool completely on wire racks. Stir 1/2 cup pecans into Cream Cheese Frosting, if desired, or reserve them to sprinkle over top of frosted cake. Spread frosting between layers and on top and sides of cake.

Cream Cheese Frosting:

1/2 cup butter or margarine, softened
1 (8-ounce) package cream cheese, softened

1 (16-ounce) package powdered sugar, sifted
1 teaspoon vanilla extract

Cream butter and softened cream cheese. Gradually add powdered sugar; beat until light and fluffy. Stir in vanilla. Yield: Enough for one 3-layer cake.

Self is the principle which governs us in our natural life, and, if we allow it, takes in our being the place God claims is His.

Italian Cream Cake

1 stick butter or margarine	1 cup buttermilk
1/2 cup Crisco	1 teaspoon vanilla extract
2 cups sugar	1 small can coconut
5 egg yolks	1 cup chopped nuts, lightly toasted
2 cups flour	5 egg whites, beaten
1 teaspoon soda	**Cream Cheese Frosting** (recipe follows)

Preheat oven to 350 degrees. Cream butter or margarine, Crisco and sugar, beating well. Beat in egg yolks just until yellow is blended in. Sift flour and soda together; combine buttermilk and vanilla and add these two mixtures alternately. Fold in coconut and nuts. Lastly, fold in stiffly beaten egg whites. Bake in 3 greased and floured 9-inch layer cake pans at 350 degrees for 25 to 30 minutes, or until tests done when wooden pick comes out clean when inserted in center.

Cream Cheese Frosting:

1 (8-ounce) package cream cheese	1 box powdered sugar
1/2 stick margarine	1 teaspoon vanilla extract
1 cup chopped pecans, lightly toasted	

Beat cream cheese and margarine. Add sugar and vanilla. Mix well. Spread icing on cake. Sprinkle nuts between layers and on top.

When there is a fault in someone; there is a need. As Christians we are only to dwell on the need, and, if possible, help meet it.

Lemon Cheese Cake

1 cup butter
2 cups sugar
3 cups flour
1 teaspoon baking soda
1 cup buttermilk
1 teaspoon vanilla extract

8 egg whites, stiffly beaten
    (with cream of tartar added)
1 teaspoon cream of tartar
Lemon Cheese Filling (recipe follows)
Seven-minute Frosting, optional
    (recipe follows)

Cream butter well, adding sugar a small amount at the time, beating until light and fluffy. Sift flour 3 times; add baking soda to buttermilk and add flour and buttermilk alternately to butter/sugar mixture. Add vanilla, mixing well; fold in stiffly beaten egg whites to which cream of tartar has been added. Pour into greased and floured pans and bake in 350 degree oven until lightly browned, and cake leaves sides of pans. Cool in pans 10 minutes. Turn out on rack and cool completely. (Good white layer for any cake.)

Lemon Cheese Filling:

2 cups sugar
3 tablespoons flour
1 cup butter
1 cup milk

8 egg yolks, beaten
3 lemons, rind and juice
    (rind finely grated)

Combine sugar and flour in top of double boiler, mixing well. Add all other ingredients and cook until thick and of spreading consistency. Spread on layers, top and sides of cake. Top this filling with **Seven-Minute Frosting,** if desired. This is enough for 3 layers.

Seven-Minute Frosting:

2 egg whites, unbeaten
1 1/2 cups sugar
1/8 teaspoon salt

1/4 cup, plus 1 tablespoon water
1 tablespoon light corn syrup
1 teaspoon vanilla extract

Combine all ingredients in top of double boiler; beat with hand mixer 1 minute. Place over boiling water and beat about 7 minutes. Remove from boiling water when frosting stands in glossy peaks. Continue beating until frosting is cool and thick enough to hold firm swirls. Makes enough frosting for two 8- or 9-inch layers or 1 tube cake.

Red Velvet Cake - (Old-Fashioned)

1 1/2 cups Wesson Oil
1 1/2 cups sugar
2 eggs
1 teaspoon vinegar
2 ounces red food coloring
1 teaspoon vanilla extract
2 1/2 cups plain flour

3 teaspoons baking powder
1 teaspoon salt
2 tablespoons cocoa
1 cup buttermilk
1 teaspoon soda
Cream Cheese Icing (recipe follows)

Combine oil, sugar and eggs, beat well; add vinegar, food coloring and vanilla, mixing thoroughly. Sift together flour, baking powder, salt and cocoa. Combine buttermilk and soda; mix dry ingredients and buttermilk mixture alternately into first mixture, stirring just enough to blend. Pour into 3 greased and floured layer-cake pans. Bake about 25 minutes or until done to touch in center. (No indentation from touch of finger.)

Cream Cheese Icing:
1 (8-ounce) package cream cheese
1/2 stick butter or margarine, softened
1 box powdered sugar

1 teaspoon vanilla extract
1 cup chopped pecans, slightly toasted

Combine all ingredients, except pecans; blend well. Ice layers, top and sides of cake. Pecans may be put into icing or sprinkled on layers and top.

Red Velvet Cake (Easy)

1 Duncan Hines Yellow Cake Mix
1 (3-ounce) box Jell-O Instant
   Chocolate Pudding Mix
2 ounces red food coloring

Cream Cheese Icing (recipe follows)
   or 2 cans Betty Crocker Cream
   Cheese Icing

Prepare batter according to directions on box, adding the chocolate pudding mix and the red food coloring. Bake three layers; allow layers to cool completely. Ice with cream cheese icing.

Cream Cheese Icing:
1 (8-ounce) package cream cheese
1/2 stick butter or margarine, softened
1 box 4x powdered sugar

1 teaspoon vanilla extract
1 cup chopped pecans, optional

Cream together butter or margarine and cream cheese; slowly adding sugar and then vanilla. When well mixed, add pecans and frost cake. If you prefer, you may add your pecans on top of the icing instead of in it.

Toasted Pecan Cake

2 cups pecans
1 1/4 cups butter, divided
2 teaspoons baking powder
3 cups flour
1/2 teaspoon salt

2 cups sugar
4 eggs
1 cup milk
2 teaspoons vanilla extract
Icing (recipe follows)

Toast pecans in 1/4 cup butter in 300-degree oven about 20 minutes, stirring frequently and being careful to not over-cook. Oven temperatures vary, be careful as an over-cooked pecan loses it's flavor. Sift baking powder, flour and salt; cream the 1 remaining cup of softened butter, gradually adding sugar. Blend eggs in one at a time. Add dry ingredients alternately with milk, beginning and ending with dry ingredients and mixing well. Stir in vanilla and 1 1/3 cups toasted pecans. Bake in 3 (9-inch) greased and floured layer-cake pans at 350 degrees 25 to 30 minutes, or until light brown.

Icing:
1 stick butter, softened
1 box powdered sugar
1 teaspoon vanilla extract

4-6 tablespoons milk
Remaining nuts

Combine softened butter, approximately 1/2 sugar and vanilla, mixing well. Add the other half of sugar, adding a little milk as necessary to reach a nice spreading consistency. Ice layers, top and sides; sprinkle with remaining nuts.
Note: You may use **Cream Cheese Icing,** if you prefer. See **Red Velvet Cake** recipe, page 65.

Genuine moral integrity means holding firm even when costly.

Caramel Icing

3/4 cup sugar + 3 cups sugar

Brown 3/4 cup sugar in small fry pan on top of stove. Let it get to a golden brown, but be careful not to over cook. If you use an iron fry pan, it will continue to cook a little after you remove it from heat.

1 1/2 sticks margarine   1 teaspoon vanilla extract
1 1/2 cups milk

At the same time, bring to boil the 3 cups of sugar, milk and margarine in saucepan. Add browned sugar and cook, stirring constantly, until it reaches soft ball stage, (240 degrees). Add vanilla and beat with hand mixer until of spreading consistency. (Allow it to cool from time to time during the beating process as it has to be almost completely cool before it is ready to spread.) This is not difficult. Just be patient and you will be richly rewarded!

*"The law of the Lord is perfect, reviving the soul.
The statutes of the Lord are trustworthy, making wise the simple.
The precepts of the Lord are right, giving joy to the heart.
The commands of the Lord are radiant, giving light to the eyes."   (Psalm 19)*

Caramel Frosting - Easy
(I hope many young cooks will conquer this simple task, and you will enjoy it many times!)

1 1/2 sticks butter (do not substitute)   1 box light brown sugar
1 (5-ounce) can evaporated milk   1 cup chopped, toasted pecans (optional)

Melt butter on low heat with milk; add sugar. Heat to a boil; reduce heat to a gentle rolling boil and cook for about 11 minutes, stirring occasionally. Remove from heat. Test by putting a tablespoonful in saucer; cool and beat with fork to see if it reaches spreading consistency. Let this sample cool completely. You don't have to beat constantly, just at intervals. When it is cool and ready, it turns a much lighter color and you will know it has cooked enough. You will be able to cut through the sample and where you cut it will not run back together. If this test is not positive, return boiler of filling to burner and cook a little more until when tested, as above, you know it is of spreading consistency. (If you let it cook too much, you can beat in just a **little** milk.) When right, add nuts (optional), and frost cake.
Note: This is a wonderful, simple recipe given to me by a friend. She does many of these for friends and family, and everyone loves them. For the cakes, we use the Duncan Hines Butter Cake Mix, using Blue Bonnet margarine instead of butter, and buttermilk instead of water. Follow directions on box for mixing, being sure to beat the full 4 minutes at medium speed. This batter will make 2 (8x8-inch) cakes which can be iced individually and served in squares. Bake 25 to 30 minutes at 300 degrees, or until lightly browned and firm to touch. The 8x8's fit perfectly in 1-gallon Zip-Lock bags for storage in freezer or for gifts.
(Or use jelly-roll pan for thinner squares.)

Chocolate Cream Icing
(start day before needed) So easy!

1 1/2 cups whipping cream   1 (6-ounce) package chocolate chips

Melt chips in heated cream. Place in refrigerator. The next day whip cream until stiff for icing cake. This can be used in many ways – on your favorite cake, as a delicious topping for parfaits or many other desserts.

Chocolate Cream Cheese Frosting

1 (8-ounce) package cream cheese,
   softened
1/2 cup margarine or butter, softened
2 teaspoons vanilla extract

6 1/2 cups sifted powdered sugar
1/3 cup unsweetened cocoa powder
1-2 tablespoons milk

Beat together the cream cheese, butter and vanilla until light and fluffy. Gradually add 2 cups sifted powdered sugar and cocoa powder, beating well. Gradually beat in remaining powdered sugar until smooth. Beat in milk if needed, to reach spreading consistency. Makes about 3 1/2 cups frosting.

Chocolate Fudge Icing - Easy and delicious!
(A favorite!)

2 cups sugar
1 (5-ounce) can evaporated milk
1 stick margarine
10 large marshmallows
   (or 1 cup of small)

1 (11.5-ounce) package chocolate
   chips (Milk chocolate or semi-sweet;
   we prefer milk chocolate.)
1 teaspoon vanilla extract

Bring sugar, milk and margarine to a boil. Boil 2 minutes, stirring occasionally as it boils. Turn burner off and leave boiler on the burner. Immediately add remaining ingredients. Beat with hand mixer until marshmallows and chocolate chips are melted. Continue beating until of spreading consistency. Spread on layers. It usually does not take long.

Glossy Chocolate Sour Cream Frosting
This is a wonderful dark-chocolate frosting especially good combined with fruits, such as cherries or strawberries.

1 1/2 cups semi-sweet chocolate
   mini-chips
3/4 cup sour cream

2 cups confectioners' sugar
1 teaspoon vanilla extract

Melt mini-chips in top of double boiler over hot water, stirring until melted. Remove from heat and beat in remaining ingredients. Makes enough for 3-layer cake or 2 individual 1-layer cakes such as the **Heavenly Chocolate-Cherry Cake.**

White Chocolate Frosting
(This frosting really sets off a dark chocolate cake.)

1 cup heavy cream or canned milk
1 1/4 cups granulated sugar
4 ounces white chocolate, chopped

1/2 cup butter
1 teaspoon vanilla extract

In a medium saucepan, bring the cream and sugar to boil over medium to medium-high heat, stirring constantly. Reduce the heat to medium low and simmer 5 minutes. Remove from heat and add the white chocolate, butter and vanilla. Stir until melted and combined. Refrigerate until thick, 1 to 1 1/2 hours. Beat at high speed with a mixer until thick and creamy, 1 to 2 minutes. Spread on cake.

White Chocolate Glaze
(For Petit Fours etc.)

3/4 cup whipping cream

24 ounces white chocolate

Heat whipping cream in large heavy saucepan over medium heat until hot. Add white chocolate and cook over very low heat, stirring constantly until chocolate melts. Dip (1 1/2-inch) pound cake squares, 1/2 of cookies, fruit, etc.

Chocolate Glaze

1 cup chocolate chips

6 tablespoons butter or margarine

Melt chocolate chips and butter together. Let cool until desired consistency to drizzle or spread as needed.

Lemon Cheese Filling

2 cups sugar
1 cup butter
8 egg yolks, slightly beaten

3 lemons, grated rind and juice
(more if desired)

Combine in top of double boiler and cook until of spreading consistency; ice cake. (You may cook over low heat in saucepan, stirring constantly, until thickened.)

Lemon Cream-Cheese Frosting

1 (3-ounce) package cream cheese
2 tablespoons margarine
1 teaspoon finely grated lemon peel

1 tablespoon lemon juice
1 1/2-2 cups, sifted, powdered sugar

Combine cream cheese, margarine, lemon peel and lemon juice. Add powdered sugar to achieve desired spreading consistency. (Try 3 tablespoons margarine and enough sugar-free dry lemonade mix to get desired lemon flavor – such as Crystal Light.)

Orange Glaze

2 cups sifted powdered sugar
3 tablespoons butter, softened
1 teaspoon finely shredded orange peel

2-3 tablespoons orange juice,
(or orange juice concentrate), just enough to achieve desired spreading consistency

Combine and beat to smooth texture. Delicious to dip 1/2 of ginger, chocolate or vanilla cookies, or to use over gingerbread etc.

Pineapple Icing

1 stick oleo
2 cups sugar
4 tablespoons flour

1 (20-ounce) can crushed pineapple
2 tablespoons lemon juice
Lemon rind to taste

Combine and cook ingredients until thickened over medium heat, stirring constantly, or use double boiler. Test small amount in saucer to be sure if thick enough.

Praline Cake Icing - Broiled

1/2 cup margarine
2 tablespoons milk
1 cup brown sugar

1 cup flaked coconut
1 cup chopped pecans

This icing is to go on cake while it is still hot. This would be good on the 1 layer hot milk cake, or your choice. Combine margarine, milk and brown sugar in small saucepan. Bring to a boil and boil 1 minute; remove from heat. Add coconut and pecans. Spread icing on cake while it is hot. Place under broiler until icing bubbles, watching carefully.

Rum Butter-Cream Frosting
(Delicious, especially with glaze.)

1 stick butter, softened
1 (1-pound) box powdered sugar
3-4 tablespoons rum

Chocolate Glaze, optional
    (Recipe listed with icings)

Blend butter with half of sugar. Beat in remaining sugar alternately with 3 to 4 tablespoons rum until spreading consistency. Ice cake and let stand until firm. (Enough for a cake, brownies or cookies.)

Seven-Minute Icing *(Never Fails)*

NOTE: If you want more icing, use amounts in right column.

Regular Amount:
3 egg whites
3/4 cup sugar
3/4 cup light corn syrup
1/2 teaspoon vanilla extract
1/2 teaspoon coconut extract, if desired

Additional Amount:
5 egg whites
1 1/4 cups sugar
1 1/4 cups light corn syrup
1 teaspoon vanilla extract
1 teaspoon coconut extract, if desired

Place all ingredients except extracts in top of double boiler; place water in bottom of double boiler and let it come to a boil. Meanwhile, blend all ingredients; place on boiling water and continue beating. Beat as it cooks until it stands in peaks, 7 to 10 minutes. Remove from heat; add extracts and beat until just right to spread on cake. Spread layers, top and sides with icing and with plenty of Angel Flake or frozen, grated coconut, if desired. This is a wonderful icing, especially for a coconut cake. I have not had it fail. It does not form a crust or glaze over the top, but stays where you put it. With coconut on it, to me it is perfect!

Seven Minute Icing
This recipe forms a thin crust on top.
(Some people prefer this.)

3 egg whites
2 1/4 cups sugar
1/2 teaspoon cream of tartar

6 tablespoons water
1/3 cup Karo syrup (5 tablespoons)
1 teaspoon vanilla extract

Beat all ingredients 1 minute before putting over boiling water in double boiler. Cook approximately 7 to 10 minutes, beating constantly, or until right consistency to spread on cake. (It takes 7 to 10 minutes depending on how fast you are cooking it.)

Almond Dump Cake or Cherry Dump Cake

1 (21-ounce) can crushed pineapple, undrained
1 (20-ounce) can cherry pie filling
1 box yellow cake mix

2 sticks butter (They say use real butter, but I don't.)
1 (8-ounce) bag sliced almonds

Spray 9x13-inch pan with nonstick spray. Dump pineapple in and cover bottom. Dump pie filling to cover pineapple. Dump cake mix to cover fruit. Cut butter into pats. Place all over cake mix. Bake 40 minutes at 350 degrees. Remove from oven and add nuts to cover top. Return to oven. Bake 25 to 30 minutes more or until lightly browned.

Apple or Pear Cake

1 1/2 cups Wesson oil
2 cups sugar
3 cups flour
1 teaspoon salt
1 teaspoon soda
1 teaspoon cinnamon

3 eggs
2 teaspoons vanilla extract
3 cups apples, chopped
1 cup coconut
1 cup pecans, chopped
Filling or Sauce (recipe follows)

In large bowl mix oil and sugar. Add next 4 ingredients; add eggs one at a time, beating well. Add vanilla, coconut, chopped apples and chopped pecans, stirring to mix well. Pour into greased 9x13-inch pan; bake at 325 degrees for 45 minutes. Check and bake longer if not firm in middle. Lower temperature if it starts to brown.

Filling or Sauce:
1/2 cup margarine (1 stick)
1 cup light brown sugar
1 can sweetened condensed milk

1/3 can evaporated milk or plain milk
1 teaspoon vanilla extract

Bring first 4 ingredients to a rolling boil and boil slowly for 3 minutes, stirring constantly. Remove from heat. Add vanilla and pour over warm cake, or if you want it to be more like filling than sauce, let the cake cool before you put it on.

Chocolate Sheet Cake

2 cups all-purpose flour
2 cups sugar
1 teaspoon cinnamon
4 tablespoons cocoa
1 cup water
2 sticks margarine

1 teaspoon soda
1/2 cup buttermilk
2 eggs, slightly beaten
1 teaspoon vanilla extract
Icing (recipe follows)

Sift flour, sugar, and cinnamon into bowl. Put cocoa, water and margarine into saucepan and bring to a boil; pour hot mixture into flour and sugar and mix well. Combine soda and buttermilk; add this mixture, eggs, and vanilla to original mixture. Mix well and pour into greased jelly-roll pan (10x15-inch) and bake for 20 minutes at 400 degrees.

Icing:

1 stick margarine
6 tablespoons buttermilk
4 tablespoons cocoa
1 box 10X sugar

1 teaspoon vanilla extract
1 cup or more of small marshmallows
   (optional)
1 cup nuts, chopped, optional

Place margarine, buttermilk and cocoa into same saucepan as used for batter, and bring to a boil. (It is not necessary to wash pan.) Turn off heat; add powdered sugar and vanilla. Beat with hand mixer until smooth. Place marshmallows on hot cake (use as many as you like.) Gently pour hot icing over marshmallows onto warm cake and sprinkle with nuts. This is an old favorite!

German Chocolate Cake

(Easy does it.)

1 package German chocolate cake mix
   (Duncan Hines, if available)
1 1/2 cups chopped pecans
1 1/2 cups shredded coconut

1/2 cup margarine
1 (8-ounce) package cream cheese
4 cups powdered sugar

Prepare cake mix according to package directions. Preheat oven to 350 degrees. Grease and flour a 9x13-inch pan. Combine pecans and coconut. Sprinkle in bottom of pan. Pour prepared cake mix over pecans and coconut mixture. Melt margarine and cream cheese together in sauce pan. Add powdered sugar. Mix well. Pour mixture over cake batter. Bake 45 minutes or until cake tests done. Remove from oven. Cool. Cut into squares. Makes 16 squares. Flavor improves daily.

Hawaiian Cream Cake

1 package yellow cake mix
   (Duncan Hines)
1 (20-ounce) can crushed pineapple
   in juice

3/4 cup sugar
2 packages instant vanilla pudding mix
3 cups cold milk

Topping:
1 cup heavy whipping cream
1/4 cup 4X sugar

1 teaspoon vanilla extract
3/4 cup flaked coconut, toasted

Combine first five ingredients and mix well. Pour into 9x13-inch greased and floured pan and bake in 350 degree oven for 30 to 40 minutes.
Topping: Whip cream, adding sugar and vanilla. Spread over cooled cake and top with toasted coconut. Cut into squares and serve.

Pineapple Upside-Down Cake

First make this topping:
3 tablespoons butter or margarine
1/3 cup heavy cream or canned milk
1/2 cup brown sugar, firmly packed
1/2 cup coconut

1/2 teaspoon ground ginger
1 (20-ounce) can pineapple slices
8 maraschino cherries, drained
   (or 16 if you make smaller servings)

Heat butter, cream or milk and brown sugar in a heavy 9-inch skillet until it is a smooth paste. Remove from heat. Sprinkle coconut and ginger over it; arrange pineapple slices around edge with a cherry in the middle of each slice. If you would like smaller servings, cut each pineapple slice in half and arrange with each half turned the same way around edge with cherry in the middle of each.

Batter:
1 cup flour
1 teaspoon baking powder
1/2 teaspoon salt
2 eggs

1 cup sugar
1/2 cup milk
1 tablespoon butter or margarine

Start oven at 350 degrees. Sift flour, baking powder and salt several times. Beat eggs until thick; add sugar one tablespoon at the time, beating hard. Stir flour into egg/sugar mixture just enough to mix. Heat milk and butter to warm, and mix into batter. Pour over pineapple and bake 40 to 50 minutes. Cool 5 minutes and then turn upside down and serve with or without whipped cream or whipped topping.
Note: I have had this recipe over 40 years and we have enjoyed it many times!

Praline Cake

1 cup regular oats
1 cup cold water
1 cup sugar
1 cup brown sugar
1 cup vegetable oil

2 eggs
1 1/2 cups flour
1 teaspoon soda
1 teaspoon cinnamon
Icing (recipe follows)

Combine oats and water; let stand. Cream sugars, oil and eggs. Add oat mixture, flour, soda and cinnamon. Bake 35 minutes in 9x13-inch lightly oiled pan.

Icing:

1/2 cup margarine
2 tablespoons milk
1 cup brown sugar

1 cup flaked coconut
1 cup chopped pecans

After cake has baked, combine margarine, milk and brown sugar in saucepan. Boil 1 minute. Add coconut and pecans. Spread icing on cake while cake is hot. Place cake under broiler until icing bubbles, watching it carefully. Cut into squares.

Be sure that through your actions you create melody notes in your life.

It is more important in families to focus on relationships than on rules.

Refrigerator cakes are great "do ahead" desserts.

Blueberry Refrigerator Cake

3 layers of your favorite yellow cake mix
1 (8- to 9-ounce) carton frozen whipped
   topping, thawed
1 (8-ounce) package cream cheese

1 cup powdered sugar
1 teaspoon vanilla flavoring
1 (21-ounce) can blueberry pie filling

Mix whipped topping, cream cheese, sugar, and vanilla flavoring. Spread on each cake layer. Spoon blueberry pie filling between cake layers and on top layer. Place in a cake saver and refrigerate until all is served. A nice do-ahead dessert. **Suggestion:** Use Duncan Hines Yellow Butter Cake mix using Blue Bonnet margarine and buttermilk instead of water.

Coconut Refrigerator Cake

1 package Duncan Hines butter cake mix
   (Use buttermilk instead of water and
   Blue Bonnet margarine)
2 (6-ounce) packages frozen coconut
2 cups milk

1/2 stick margarine
1 teaspoon coconut flavoring
1 cup sugar
1 (12-ounce) carton Cool Whip, thawed

Mix cake mix by directions on box, except substitute buttermilk for water, and use Blue Bonnet margarine. Be sure to beat the full 4 minutes at medium speed of mixer. Bake in 9x13-inch baking dish. When almost done, mix milk, sugar, margarine, coconut flavoring and 1 package frozen coconut in boiler. Bring to a boil. When cake is done, place it on serving tray (or leave it in glass bake dish) and punch holes about an inch apart with fork. Slowly pour mixture on cake and let it absorb. Cool thoroughly. Mix other package of coconut with Cool Whip and ice cake. Keep refrigerated.

Coconut-Sour Cream Layer Cake

1 box Duncan Hines Butter Cake Mix   **Frosting** (recipe follows)

Bake by directions on box, substituting buttermilk for water and use Blue Bonnet margarine. Be sure to beat the full 4 minutes at medium speed of mixer. Make 2 layers. Split each layer, making 4 layers. (An easy way to split cake layers evenly is to push 6 wooden picks into sides of layer just below half the height of the cake. Use a sharp, long-bladed knife to cut just above the picks.) Place bottom layer on cake plate.

Frosting:

2 cups powdered sugar
1 (16-ounce) carton commercial
  sour cream

1 (12-ounce) package frozen coconut, thawed (divided) (Save 1/4 of the coconut to go on top of cake)
1 (12-ounce) carton frozen whipped topping, thawed

When cake layers are completely cool, split both layers, making four. Combine sugar, sour cream, and 3/4 of the coconut, blending well. Chill. When chilled, with a knife, mark the filling into 4 parts. Use 1/4 of the filling on each of 3 layers. Combine the other fourth of the filling with the whipped topping and frost the cake, top and sides. Use reserved coconut on top and sides of frosting.

Lemon Refrigerator Cake

1 box Duncan Hines Butter Cake Mix
3 eggs
2/3 cup buttermilk

1 stick Blue Bonnet margarine, just slightly softened
Lemon Filling (recipe follows)

Combine above ingredients until moistened; beat 4 full minutes with mixer on medium speed. Bake in two layer cake pans that have been sprayed with Baker's Joy. Allow to cool. Cut each layer horizontally, making 4 layers. (Easy way to cut layers given in Coconut Sour Cream Refrigerator cake just before this recipe.)

Lemon Filling:

1 (6-ounce) can frozen lemonade
  concentrate, thawed
1 small instant lemon pie filling mix

1 (14-ounce) can sweetened condensed
  milk
1 (12-ounce) carton Cool Whip

Combine ingredients and ice cake layers, top and sides. Keep refrigerated.

Mandarin Orange Refrigerator Cake

1 box Duncan Hines yellow butter
cake mix
4 eggs
1/2 cup Crisco oil

1 can Mandarin oranges, drained and
chopped
Icing (recipe follows)

Combine eggs, oil and cake mix until moistened. Beat about 4 minutes on medium speed. Fold in Mandarin oranges. Bake in 3 layers at 350 degrees until done.

Icing:

1 small box instant vanilla pudding mix
1 (12-ounce) carton Cool Whip, thawed

1 (20-ounce) can crushed pineapple,
well drained

Combine ingredients and ice cake layers, top and sides. Keep refrigerated.

Strawberry Refrigerator Cake

1 Duncan Hines Yellow Butter cake mix   **Filling** (recipe follows)

Bake cake as per directions except substituting buttermilk for water and using Blue Bonnet margarine. Bake in jelly-roll pan.

Filling:

1 (12-ounce) carton Cool Whip, thawed
2 cups sour cream

2 cups confectioners' sugar
2 pints strawberries, sliced

Mix filling ingredients and ice cake. Keep refrigerated.

Peace is not the absence of conflict, but the harvest of love.

Fresh Apple or Pear Cake

2 cups sugar
3 eggs, beaten
1 1/2 cups oil
3 cups all-purpose flour
   (You may use 3 cups self-rising
   and omit salt and soda.)
1 teaspoon salt

1 teaspoon soda
2 teaspoons vanilla extract
2 teaspoons ground cinnamon
1 cup pecans or walnuts, chopped
3-4 cups diced apples or pears (Use fresh
   fruit, not canned.)
Brown Sugar Glaze (recipe follows)

Combine sugar, eggs and oil; beat well. Add flour, soda and salt. Mix well with sugar mixture. Stir in vanilla, cinnamon, nuts and diced fruit (apples or pears). Pour batter into greased and floured 10-inch tube pan. Bake at 350 degrees for one hour or until done. Remove from pan and let cool. Top with glaze.

Brown Sugar Glaze:

1/2 cup (1 stick) butter or margarine
1/2 cup brown sugar

2 tablespoons brandy (or vanilla extract)

In a small saucepan, melt 1/2 cup (1 stick) butter or margarine. Stir in 1/2 cup brown sugar and 2 tablespoons brandy (or use vanilla). Bring to a boil and cook for 2 minutes. Pour over cake.

Lemon Jell-O Cake

(Easy and good!)

1 (18 1/2-ounce) box yellow cake mix
2/3 cup cooking oil
1 (3-ounce) package lemon gelatin

3/4 cup hot water
4 eggs
Glaze (recipe follows)

Put all ingredients except eggs in mixer bowl; add 1 egg at a time and beat until blended. Pour into a greased and floured tube pan. Bake for 1 hour in a 325 degree oven or until done when checked with cake tester.

1 (6-ounce) can frozen lemonade
   concentrate

3/4 cup sugar

Glaze:

Mix frozen lemonade concentrate and sugar. Heat to dissolve sugar. Punch holes in cake and pour over hot cake. Let stand over night.

Frosted Peach Pound Cake

1 cup (2 sticks) butter or margarine
1/2 cup shortening
3 cups granulated sugar
6 large eggs
3 3/4 cups all-purpose flour
1/2 teaspoon baking powder

3/4 cup milk combined with
   1/4 cup peach juice (see note)
1 teaspoon almond extract
2 cups sliced fresh peaches, divided
   (see note)
Peach Frosting (recipe follows)

Preheat oven to 325 degrees. Grease and flour 10-inch tube pan and set aside. In the large bowl of an electric mixer, beat together the butter and shortening, slowly adding the sugar. Beat until light and fluffy. Add the eggs one at a time, beating well after each addition. In a mixing bowl, sift together the flour and baking powder. Add to creamed mixture alternately with milk-juice mixture, beginning and ending with dry ingredients. Fold in the almond extract and half the cooked peaches. Pour batter into prepared pan. Bake 1 1/2 hours. Cool in pan 10 minutes, remove from pan and allow to cool completely on a wire rack. Frost when completely cool.

Note: Place 2 cups sliced fresh peaches in a saucepan. Add just enough water to cover, about 1/2 cup. Cook over medium heat about 20 minutes, until peaches have cooked down to a generous cup. Drain, reserving 1/4 cup juice for the cake. Divide the cooked peaches in half, using half in the cake and half in the frosting. If you want to use canned peaches, do not cook them. Chop them or process in food processor.

Peach Frosting:

2 (3-ounce) packages cream cheese,
   softened
1/4 cup (1/2 stick) butter
1 (1-pound) box confectioners' sugar
1/2 teaspoon almond extract

1/2 cup chopped pecans or walnuts
1 (6-ounce) package frozen grated
   coconut, thawed
Remainder of peaches (see note)

In large bowl of an electric mixer, beat together the cream cheese, butter and sugar. Fold in the almond extract, nuts, coconut and peaches. Frost top and sides of cake.

Plum Cake

3 eggs
2 cups sugar
1 cup Wesson oil
2 (4-ounce) baby food jars of plums

2 cups self-rising flour (sifted)
1 cup pecans, chopped
1/2 teaspoon ground cloves
1 teaspoon ground cinnamon

Mix in order given. Cook in greased and floured bundt pan in 325 degree oven for 1 hour and 15 minutes. This is good plain or with cream-cheese icing as you would use on carrot cake. It is so nice baked in loaf pans for gifts!

Pound Cake - Buttermilk

2 cups sugar
1 cup shortening, preferably butter
    flavored
4 eggs
3 cups flour

1 teaspoon salt
1/2 teaspoon baking powder
1/2 teaspoon soda
1 cup buttermilk
3 teaspoons vanilla extract

Cream sugar and shortening; add all 4 eggs and beat well. Sift flour, salt, baking powder and soda together and add to first mixture, alternating flour and buttermilk twice. Do not overbeat after adding flour. Stir in vanilla and bake in tube or Bundt pan 1 hour and 15 minutes in a 325 degree oven. Serve plain or topped with fruit, ice cream or your favorite sauce.

Christian concept of self: We should value ourself as God values us, no more, no less.

Pound Cake - Cherry (Very pretty and good!)

1 cup shortening
  (Crisco - Butter Flavor)
1/2 cup margarine
3 cups sugar
6 eggs
1 teaspoon vanilla extract

1 teaspoon almond flavoring
3 3/4 cups flour
3/4 cup milk
1 (10-ounce) jar maraschino cherries,
  drained and chopped
Frosting (recipe follows)

Cream shortening and margarine with sugar until fluffy. Add eggs one at a time, beating well. Add flavorings, then flour and milk alternately, just until blended. Fold in chopped cherries. Bake in greased bundt or tube pan in 300 degree oven for 1 hour and 45 minutes. Do not preheat oven. Start cake in cold oven. After baking, cool cake in pan for 15 minutes and then remove from pan.

Frosting:

1 (3-ounce) package cream cheese
1/2 stick margarine
2 cups powdered sugar
1 teaspoon almond flavoring

1/2 cup coconut
1/2 cup pecans, chopped
1 (10-ounce) jar maraschino cherries,
  drained and chopped

Combine softened cream cheese, margarine and powdered sugar and beat well. Stir in flavoring, nuts, coconut and cherries. Spread on top and sides of cake.

Achievement is what matters, not IQ. IQ makes the road easier, but achievement through perseverance, training and commitment, is what matters. History has proven this.

Pound Cake - Chocolate

1/2 cup shortening	3 cups flour
2 sticks butter or margarine	1/2 cup cocoa
3 cups sugar	1/2 teaspoon baking powder
6 eggs	1/2 teaspoon salt
2 teaspoons vanilla extract	1 1/4 cups milk

Cream shortening, butter and sugar thoroughly. Add eggs 1 at a time, beating just until yellow disappears. Add vanilla. Sift together flour, cocoa, baking powder and salt. Add dry ingredients, alternating with milk. Mix just until blended. Bake in greased and floured tube pan in 300 degree oven for 1 hour and 25 minutes.

Frosting: (if desired)

2 1/4 cups sugar	3/4 stick margarine
3 squares semi-sweet chocolate	1 cup pecans, chopped
3/4 cup milk	2 teaspoons vanilla extract
2 1/4 tablespoons white Karo corn syrup	

Cook sugar, chocolate, milk and Karo syrup to 230 degrees on candy thermometer. Add margarine and vanilla. Beat until spreading consistency and ice cake. **Suggestion: White Chocolate Frosting** or **Rum-Butter Frosting** are also very good on this cake and very pretty. Wonderful for a gift! These recipes may be found in cake icing section of this book.

Christ's lifestyle in you springs from the mental quality of discernment.

Pound Cake
Coconut Cream Cheese (and Plain Cream Cheese)

1/2 cup butter or margarine, softened
1/2 cup shortening
1 (8-ounce) package cream cheese, softened
3 cups sugar
6 eggs
3 cups all-purpose flour

1/2 teaspoon baking soda
1/2 teaspoon salt
1 (6-ounce) package frozen coconut, thawed
1 teaspoon vanilla extract
1 teaspoon coconut extract
(or almond extract, if preferred)

Cream butter, shortening and cream cheese; gradually add sugar, beating well at medium speed of mixer. Add eggs, one at a time, beating after each addition. Combine flour, soda, salt; add to creamed mixture, stirring just until blended. Stir in remaining ingredients. Pour batter into a greased and floured, (Baker's Joy is wonderful!), 10-inch tube pan. Bake at 325 degrees for 1 1/2 hours or until a wooden pick inserted in center of cake comes out clean. Cool in pan 10 to 15 minutes; remove from pan, and let cool on a wire rack.

For plain cream cheese pound cake:
Add 1 additional stick of margarine; leave out the coconut, the coconut flavoring, and use 1 teaspoon lemon extract, 1 teaspoon almond extract, and 1 teaspoon vanilla extract. (Or use your choice of extracts.)

Pound Cake - Sour Cream

1 cup butter
3 cups sugar
6 eggs
2 teaspoons vanilla extract
1 teaspoon almond extract

3 cups flour
1/4 teaspoon baking powder
1/4 teaspoon baking soda
1/4 teaspoon salt
1 cup sour cream

Blend butter and sugar thoroughly. Add eggs, one at a time, beating after each until yellow disappears. Add vanilla and almond extracts. Sift together flour, baking powder, baking soda and salt; add dry ingredients and sour cream alternately, beginning and ending with flour. Pour into a greased and floured tube pan and bake in 300-degree oven for approximately 1-1/2 hours or until tests done.

Pound Cake - Red Velvet

1 cup butter, softened
3 cups sugar
6 eggs
2 teaspoons vanilla
1 (1-ounce) bottle red food coloring
3 cups flour

1/4 teaspoon salt
1 tablespoon cocoa
1 tablespoon cider vinegar
1 teaspoon baking soda
1 cup buttermilk
Cream Cheese Frosting (recipe follows)

Lightly grease and flour a 10-inch tube pan; set aside. In a large mixing bowl or the bowl of an electric mixer, cream the butter and sugar until light and fluffy. Add eggs one at a time, beating well after each addition. Stir in the vanilla and food coloring. In another large bowl, combine the flour, salt and cocoa. Dissolve the baking soda in the vinegar and add to the buttermilk. Stir in the flour alternately with the buttermilk, beginning and ending with the flour. Pour batter into prepared pan. Bake at 325 degrees for about 1 hour and 20 minutes or until cake is done. Cool in pan about 10 minutes. Remove cake from pan to a wire rack to cool completely before frosting.

Cream Cheese Frosting:

1/2 cup butter, softened
1 (8-ounce) package cream cheese, softened

1 teaspoon vanilla
1 (1-pound) box powdered sugar, sifted
1 or 2 tablespoons milk, if needed

Combine butter and cream cheese and blend until smooth. Stir in vanilla. Mix well. Stir in powdered sugar; beat frosting until creamy. Add milk, if needed, to make frosting the spreading consistency you prefer.

Ambrosia Cake

3/4 cup Crisco
2 cups sugar
3 eggs
3 cups cake flour
2 teaspoons baking soda
1 1/2 tablespoons powdered cocoa

1 teaspoon cinnamon
1 teaspoon nutmeg
1/2 teaspoon cloves
1 cup buttermilk
1 apple, peeled and diced
Filling (recipe follows)

Combine Crisco and sugar and beat thoroughly; add eggs, beating after each. Sift together all dry ingredients and add alternately with buttermilk. Stir in diced apple. Pour into 2 oiled and floured 9x13-inch pans and bake in 350 degree oven until done to touch in middle (when it has risen up in middle) and pulls away from the sides of pans. Let sit 5 minutes and turn out on cake rack to cool.

Filling:
1 teaspoon baking powder
Pinch of soda
2 1/2 cups sugar

1 pint heavy cream or Carnation milk
1 stick butter

Mix baking powder, soda and sugar together; add milk and butter. Cook in heavy boiler (Presto is ideal) until thick. Punch holes in cake layers and add 1/3 of filling to layers to run in while hot, reserving remainder.

Icing:
1 cup raisins
1 whole orange (less seeds and
   membranes)

1 cup pecans, chopped
1 cup Angel Flake coconut

Grind ingredients and add to reserved 2/3 of filling; ice cake layers.

Merely providing resources to the underclass accomplishes very little. Motivation must be provided as well.

Fruitcake - Cherry

1 1/2 cups sifted flour
1 1/2 cups sugar
1 teaspoon baking powder
1/2 teaspoon salt
2 (16-ounce) jars maraschino cherries,
    drained

1 pound candied pineapple, diced
18 ounces pecans, chopped
    (about 5 1/2 cups)
6 eggs
1/3 cup dark rum
1/2 cup light corn syrup

Grease 2 9x3-inch loaf pans; line with foil, allowing a 2-inch overhand and grease again. Sift flour, sugar, baking powder and salt into a large mixing bowl; add fruits and pecans and toss until coated. Beat eggs and rum thoroughly; pour over fruit mixture. Toss until combined. Turn mixture into prepared loaf pans, pressing with metal spatula to pack tightly. Bake in a 300 degree oven for 1 3/4 hours or until toothpick inserted in center of loaves comes our clean. Allow cakes to cool in pans for 15 minutes, then remove from pans and tear off foil. Brush loaves with corn syrup while still warm. Cool thoroughly before serving or storing.

Fruitcake - Date Nut Loaf

1 1/2 pounds dates, chopped
1 pound chopped pecans,
    (about 4 cups)
1 cup sugar
1 1/2 cups flour

2 teaspoons baking powder
1/2 teaspoon salt
2 teaspoons vanilla extract
4 eggs, beaten

Combine dates and pecans; sift dry ingredients over them, mixing well. Mix vanilla extract into beaten eggs and combine with first mixture. Oil loaf pan and line with foil; oil again. Pour cake batter into pan and bake at 250 to 275 degrees for about 1 1/2 hours. Test for doneness. When done, sit pan on rack to cool for about 15 minutes. Turn out and peel off foil. Cool thoroughly before serving or storing.

Outward actions are a reflection of inner thoughts.

Fruit Cake - Icebox

1 pound candied pineapple
1 pound dates, chopped
1 pound candied cherries
1 pound graham cracker crumbs
1/2 pound marshmallows (small)

3 cups chopped pecans
2 tablespoons instant coffee dissolved
   in 1 tablespoon boiling water
1 cup cream, evaporated milk or
   half-and-half

Cut up fruit; combine with cracker crumbs, marshmallows and pecans. Combine dissolved instant coffee with cream and add to fruit mixture. Mix thoroughly and press into Saran lined loaf pan. You can make 1 or 2 loaves depending on how thick you prefer them. Place in refrigerator to chill; when thoroughly chilled, invert and wrap with several thicknesses of plastic wrap. Store in refrigerator until ready to serve. Small fingers of fruitcake rolled in powdered sugar are nice for parties or snacks. The coffee flavor is different and good. (Freezes well.)

Cranberry Cake
(A delicious coffee - cake type cake)

2 1/2 cups all-purpose flour
2 cups sugar, divided
1 teaspoon baking soda
1 teaspoon baking powder
1/2 teaspoon salt
Zest of 1 orange
2 oranges juiced

2 eggs, slightly beaten
1 cup buttermilk
1/2 cups vegetable oil
1 cup chopped dates
1 cup chopped nuts
1 cup fresh cranberries, cut in half

Preheat oven to 350 degrees. Grease and flour a 10-inch tube or Bundt pan. In a large bowl, sift together the flour, 1 cup sugar, baking soda, baking powder and salt. Stir in the orange zest. In a medium bowl combine the eggs, buttermilk and oil. Add to the dry ingredients along with the dates, nuts and cranberries; stir until thoroughly combined. Pour batter into prepared pan and bake for 1 hour or until cake tests done. Cool in pan for 15 minutes; turn out on rack and invert. Punch holes in cake for glaze to soak into. A cook forks works very well for this purpose. Put the remaining cup of sugar in a medium saucepan. Add enough water to the orange juice to make 1 cup and add to the sugar. Over medium heat, bring mixture to a boil. (Do not over cook.) Remove from heat and brush or spoon over warm cake and let soak in. (A basting brush works well for this.) Refrigerate the cake for 3 days before serving (or freezing). Can be served warm, if desired.

German Chocolate Cake

1 package German chocolate
1/2 cup boiling water
1 cup butter
2 cups sugar
4 egg yolks
1 teaspoon vanilla extract

2 1/2 cups sifted cake flour
1 teaspoon soda
1/2 teaspoon salt
1 cup buttermilk
4 egg whites, stiffly beaten
Coconut-Pecan Frosting (recipe follows)

Melt chocolate in boiling water; cool. Cream butter and sugar; add egg yolks and beat. Add vanilla; melted chocolate mixture, and mix until well blended. Sift flour with soda and salt. Add sifted dry ingredients alternately with buttermilk, beating after each addition until batter is smooth. Fold in stiffly beaten egg whites. Pour into 3 greased and floured layer cake pans and bake in 350 degree oven approximately 35 minutes or until firm to touch in the middle and leaving sides of pans. Cool.

Coconut-Pecan Frosting:

1 (12-ounce) can evaporated milk
1 1/2 cups sugar
3/4 cup (1 1/2 sticks) margarine or
    butter
4 egg yolks, slightly beaten

1 1/2 teaspoons vanilla extract
1 (7-ounce) package Angel Flake coconut
    (about 2 2/3 cups)
1 1/2 cups pecans, chopped

Mix milk, sugar, margarine, egg yolks and vanilla in large saucepan. Cook and stir on medium heat about 12 minutes or until thickened and golden brown. Remove from heat. Stir in coconut and pecans. Cool to room temperature and of spreading consistency. Frost each layer, top and sides of cake. A delicious, festive cake!

Most people who are wary of the future are the ones who fear change, even though change is one of the few certainties in this uncertain world.

Japanese Fruitcake

1 cup butter
2 cups sugar
4 eggs
3 cups flour, divided
1/2 pound raisins
1 cup chopped pecans
2 teaspoons baking powder

1 cup milk
1 teaspoon vanilla extract
1 teaspoon cinnamon
1 teaspoon cloves
1 teaspoon allspice
1/8 teaspoon nutmeg
Filling (recipe follows)

Cream butter and sugar until light and fluffy. Add eggs 1 at a time, beating after each addition just until yellow disappears. Add 2 tablespoons of flour and mix with raisins and nuts. Sift remaining flour and baking powder and add to batter alternately with milk. Stir in vanilla. Divide batter in half. To one half of batter add the spices, raisins and nuts. In well greased and floured layer-cake pans bake in 350 degree oven plain batter in 2 layers and the spiced batter in 2 layers. Turn out on cake racks to cool.

Filling:

2 1/2 cups sugar
3 tablespoons cornstarch
1 (6-ounce) package frozen coconut, thawed
1 orange, juice and grated rind
2 lemons, juice and grated rind

1 (8-ounce) can crushed pineapple, including juice
1 cup boiling water
1 (10-ounce) jar maraschino cherries, drained and halved

Blend sugar and cornstarch. Add all other ingredients except cherries and cook until thickened, stirring constantly. When of spreading consistency, remove from heat and spread between layers, top and sides of cake. Place a few cherry halves between layers, saving more of them to use as garnish on top. Delicious and beautiful!

Suggestion: For a quick cake with practically same flavor, use Duncan Hines Butter Cake Mix and add spices, raisins and nuts to all the batter, or you can remove 1/3 of the batter and have top and bottom layers with spices and nuts, and middle layer plain.

Each person has a great need for self reliance and a life of one's own.

Lane Cake

1 cup butter	1 cup milk
2 cups sugar	1 teaspoon vanilla extract
3 cups flour	8 egg whites, stiffly beaten
3 1/2 teaspoons baking powder	**Filling** (recipe follows)

Cream butter and sugar until very light. Sift flour and baking powder 3 times and add to first mixture, alternately, with combination of milk and vanilla. Fold in stiffly beaten egg whites and bake in three layers in preheated 350-degree oven about 25 minutes, or until lightly browned. Turn out on rack to cool.

Filling:

2 boxes raisins	1 cup butter or margarine
1 (12-ounce) bag coconut	2 teaspoons vanilla extract
1 quart pecans	1/2 cup brandy
8 egg yolks	1/2 cup grape juice
3/4 cup sugar	

Grind or chop finely raisins, coconut and pecans. Set aside. Combine in double boiler, egg yolks, sugar and butter; cook until thick. Let cool and add vanilla, brandy and grape juice; pour this mixture over ground raisins, coconut and pecans. Spread on cake layers, top and sides.

Cranberry Date Bars

12 ounces cranberries, fresh or frozen	2 cups oats, old-fashioned
8 ounces chopped dates	1 1/2 cups brown sugar
2 tablespoons water	1/2 teaspoon baking soda
1 teaspoon vanilla extract	1/2 teaspoon salt
2 cups all-purpose flour	1 cup butter or margarine, melted

Glaze:

2 cups confectioners' sugar	1/2 teaspoon vanilla extract
3 tablespoons orange juice	

Preheat oven to 350 degrees. In a medium saucepan over low heat, simmer cranberries, dates and water, covered, for 15 to 20 minutes, stirring occasionally, until the cranberries have popped. Remove from heat, stir in vanilla and set aside. In a large bowl combine flour, oats, brown sugar, baking soda and salt. Stir in melted butter until well-blended. Pat half of mixture into an ungreased 13x9x2-inch dish. Bake at 350 degrees for 8 minutes. Spoon cranberry mixture over crust and sprinkle with remaining oat mixture. Pat gently. Bake at 350 degrees for 25 to 30 minutes or until brown. Cool and cut into 36 bars. Stir together glaze ingredients and drizzle over bars.

Fruit Bars

1 stick margarine
1 1/2 cups light brown sugar
2 eggs
1 cup flour

1 teaspoon vanilla extract
1 pound crystallized cherries
1 pound crystallized pineapple
2 cups nuts

Cream margarine and sugar; add eggs and beat well. Add flour and then vanilla. Oil 9x13-inch dish or pan; pour mixed fruits and nuts in pan, and spread batter over them. Bake at 300 degrees for 1 hour or until test done.

Fruit Cake Cookies

1 cup brown sugar
1 cup butter or margarine, melted
3 eggs
1 teaspoon cinnamon
1 teaspoon vanilla extract
3 cups all-purpose flour, divided
1/2 pound red crystallized cherries,
   halved

1/2 pound green crystallized cherries,
   halved
1/2 pound white crystallized pineapple,
   chopped
1 box golden raisins
8 ounces chopped dates
3 cups chopped pecans

Cream sugar, margarine, eggs, cinnamon and vanilla; add 2 cups of the flour and mix well. Combine the remaining 1 cup of flour with fruit and nuts and toss; add to batter. Drop by teaspoons onto aluminum foil-lined cookie sheet that has been slightly oiled; bake in 300 degree oven until lightly browned. Cool and store in air-tight container.

Japanese Fruit Pie
(Begin the Season early with this festive pie!)

1 cup sugar
1 stick margarine
Pinch salt
2 eggs, beaten
1 tablespoon vinegar

1/2 cup flaked coconut
1/2 cup nuts
1/2 cup raisins
1 (9-inch) unbaked pie shell

Combine sugar, margarine, salt, eggs and vinegar; blend well. Add to this mixture coconut, nuts and raisins. Pour into 9-inch unbaked pie shell. Bake for 35 to 40 minutes in 325 degree oven. Serve with a dollop of whipped topping or ice cream. Begin the season early with a festive flavor!

Chocolate Drops

2 cups pecans, broken coarsely
and toasted
2 tablespoons peanut butter

1 (12-ounce) bag chocolate chips,
semi-sweet
1 (6-ounce) bag butterscotch chips

Toast pecans in 300 degree oven for 15 minutes. Set aside to cool. Combine peanut butter, chocolate and butterscotch chips in microwave-safe mixing bowl; heat until melted, stirring during process. Add toasted nuts and drop by spoonfuls on waxed paper.

Chocolate Fudge

4 1/2 cups granulated sugar

1 (12-ounce) can evaporated milk

Bring this to a boil in heavy boiler, stirring constantly. Boil for 10 minutes; pour this hot mixture over the following ingredients in large mixing bowl.

2 sticks margarine, partly melted
18 ounces chocolate chips, partly
melted

1 1/2 teaspoons vanilla extract
2 cups nuts, chopped

Combine all ingredients and mix well; press into pan. Cool and cut into squares. Makes 5 pounds.
Note: 1 cup peanut butter is delicious in this fudge.

Cinnamon Hard Candy

2 cups sugar
1 cup water
3/4 cup light corn syrup

1/2 teaspoon flavoring (oil of cinnamon,
peppermint or cloves)
Confectioners' sugar in which to roll candy

Cook first 3 ingredients to hard crack stage on candy thermometer. Add flavoring. (It will be very strong when you first pour it in.) Pour onto greased marble slab or large tray and let set. Cut into small pieces with scissors. You need 2 or more people to cut, because it will set quickly. Roll in confectioners' sugar to keep from sticking.

Coconut-Date Slices

2 cups sugar
1 tablespoon light corn syrup
3/4 cup evaporated milk
1 (8-ounce) package pitted dates
2 tablespoons butter

1 cup chopped nuts
1/2 teaspoon vanilla extract
1/8 teaspoon salt
1 1/2 cups flaked coconut, toasted

Mix first 3 ingredients in saucepan. Cook, stirring, until a small amount of mixture forms a soft ball when dropped in cold water (232 degrees). Add dates; cook, stirring, until mixture returns to 232 degrees. Remove from heat, and cool to lukewarm (110 degrees). Add remaining ingredients, except coconut, and beat until thick. Shape in 2 or 3 rolls 1 1/2-inch in diameter. Roll in coconut. When firm, cut in 1/2-inch slices. Makes about 7 dozen.

Coconut Macaroons

3 cups shredded coconut
1 teaspoon pure vanilla extract
1/8 teaspoon salt

2/3 cup sweetened condensed milk
2 egg whites, stiffly beaten

Preheat oven to 350 degrees. In medium bowl, combine coconut, vanilla, salt and condensed milk, making a thick paste. Beat egg whites until stiff and fold into batter. When combined, drop small amount from teaspoon, about 2 inches apart onto lightly oiled cookie sheet. Bake 8 to 10 minutes until edges are lightly browned. Cool slightly before removing from sheet.
Variation: Heat condensed milk and add 3 tablespoons unsweetened cocoa or 3/4 ounce of baker's chocolate, grated. Let mixture cool, then add coconut, vanilla and salt. Continue as for plain macaroons.

Cranberry Nut Bark

1 pound white vanilla coating,
    cut into pieces
1/2-1 cup nuts (macadamia, pecans or
    walnuts) chopped and lightly toasted

1/2-1 cup dried cranberries
    (sometimes packaged as Craisins)

Melt coating in microwave-safe bowl of sufficient size to accommodate nuts and cranberries. Melt at 2-minute intervals until soft. Add nuts and cranberries, mixing well. Spread thinly onto a foil-lined baking sheet. Cool. Break into pieces.
Yield: 1 1/4 pounds.

Divinity

2 1/2 cups sugar
1/2 cup water
1/2 cup light corn syrup

2 egg whites
1 teaspoon vanilla extract
1 cup chopped pecans, toasted

Combine first three ingredients in about a 7-inch saucepan; cook over low heat, stirring gently, until sugar dissolves. Bring to a boil over medium heat; cover and cook 2 to 3 minutes to wash down sugar crystals from sides of pan. Uncover and cook, without stirring, until mixture reaches hard ball stage or candy thermometer registers 260 degrees. Remove from heat. Beat egg whites in large mixing bowl at high speed until stiff peaks form. Pour hot syrup in thin stream over beaten egg whites while beating constantly at high speed. Add vanilla; beat until mixture holds shape (3 to 4 minutes). Stir in pecans. Drop by teaspoonfuls onto wax paper. Cool completely. **Note:** You may want to add red or green candied cherries at Christmas.

Brown Sugar Divinity

3 cups white sugar
1 box light brown sugar
1 1/2 cups water
3 egg whites, beaten

1 cup white Karo syrup
2 cups chopped nuts
1 tablespoon vanilla extract

Cook the sugars, water and syrup to 250 degrees on candy thermometer. Slowly pour half of mixture over beaten egg whites; beat well and continue cooking mixture. Cook to about 260 degrees, pour over first mixture and beat until consistency to drop. Add vanilla and nuts. Drop onto wax paper. About 75 pieces.

Haystacks

2 (6-ounce) packages butterscotch
  morsels
2 tablespoons creamy peanut butter

1 (6 ounce) can Chinese chow mein
  noodles
1 cup roasted peanuts, chopped

Melt morsels and peanut butter in double boiler (or in microwave bowl). Add other ingredients. Work quickly before it becomes hard. Drop by teaspoonfuls onto wax paper. (Spread wax paper on stove near double boiler and leave heat on low, if not using microwave. This makes it easier to work with.)

Chocolate-Oatmeal Fudge
(Quick)

3 cups oatmeal, regular
1 cup chopped nuts
2 cups sugar
1/2 cup cocoa

1/2 cup milk
1 stick margarine
1 teaspoon vanilla extract

Combine oatmeal and nuts. Bring sugar, cocoa, milk and margarine to a rolling boil, stirring constantly. Stir in vanilla and pour over oats and nuts. Drop by teaspoonfuls onto wax paper.

Peanut Brittle

3 cups sugar
1 cup white Karo syrup
1/2 cup water
3 cups raw peanuts

3 tablespoons margarine
1 teaspoon salt
2 heaping teaspoons baking soda

Combine first 5 ingredients; cook over medium heat, stirring until candy thermometer reaches 295 degrees and mixture is golden brown. Remove from heat; add mixture of soda and salt and mix rapidly until mixture is at maximum foam. Pour gently onto a marble slab or cookie sheets, greased with margarine. Do not spread. When candy hardens, break into pieces and store in airtight container.

Peanut Butter Fudge

1 cup granulated sugar
1 cup light brown sugar
1/4 teaspoon salt
1/2 cup milk

1 cup miniature marshmallows
1/2 cup peanut butter, plain or crunchy
1 teaspoon vanilla extract

Combine sugars, salt and milk in a saucepan and cook to 240 degrees (soft ball stage). Remove from heat and add marshmallows, peanut butter and vanilla. Beat with wooden spoon for several minutes until thick and creamy and gloss disappears. Spread in a buttered 8-inch square pan. Cut into squares.

Pralines

1 1/2 cups white sugar
1 1/2 cups brown sugar
Dash salt
1 cup buttermilk mixed with

1 teaspoon soda
4 tablespoons margarine
1 teaspoon vanilla extract
1 cup pecan halves

Use large 6-quart saucepan. Cook all ingredients, but the vanilla and pecans until soft ball stage or 240 degrees on a candy thermometer, stirring constantly with a wooden spoon. Remove from heat and add vanilla and pecans; beat until slightly thickened. Work quickly and drop by tablespoonfuls onto wax paper sprayed with vegetable cooking spray. Let cool and store in air-tight containers. Pralines may be wrapped in foil to use in gift boxes of candy.

Reese's Squares

2 sticks margarine
1 cup peanut butter
1 1/4 cups Graham cracker crumbs

1 box 10X sugar
1 (12-ounce) package chocolate chips

Melt margarine in a 2-cup measuring cup. Add peanut butter for easy measure. Mix with crumbs and sugar in 9x13-inch pan. Pat into even layer. Melt chocolate chips (can use same measuring cup) and pour over crust layer. Cool and slice at room temperature. Makes 100-plus small bites for parties or 60 family size. Quick, easy, and freezes well.

Rocky Road Fudge
(So-o-o easy and good!)

12 ounces (6 squares) Almond Bark,
  chocolate flavored
2 scant cups marshmallows

2 scant cups nuts (toasted pecans or
  roasted peanuts) (We prefer roasted,
  salted peanuts, but either is wonderful)

In microwave-safe bowl large enough to accommodate all ingredients, melt chocolate bark, stirring at 2-minute intervals. It takes about 4 minutes. Add marshmallows and nuts, stirring to coat. Drop by teaspoons onto wax paper or foil.

Syrup Candy

1 cup Blackburn Maid Syrup
1/2 teaspoon soda

1 tablespoon margarine
3 cups roasted nuts, chopped

Cook syrup 1 minute after it comes to a good boil. Add soda, butter and peanuts, stirring well. Pour into small buttered pyrex dish. As soon as it is cool enough to handle, butter hands; shape into desired serving pieces.

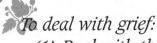*To deal with grief:*

(1) Deal with the reality of it.

(2) Write down memories.

(3) Look for a new investment.

(4) Rethink your faith.

Almond Angels

4 egg whites
1/4 teaspoon cream of tartar
1/4 teaspoon salt
1/2 teaspoon vanilla extract

1 teaspoon almond extract
1 1/2 cups sugar
1 cup blanched slivered almonds

Combine egg whites, cream of tartar and salt; beat until mixture holds soft peaks. Add flavorings and gradually beat in sugar until very stiff; fold in almonds. Very lightly spray cookie sheets with Baker's Joy. Spread spray with hand, removing excess, if any. Drop by teaspoons onto sheets. Bake at 275 degrees for 15 to 20 minutes, or until very lightly browned. Remove from cookie sheet immediately and cool on wire racks. Yield: 5 or 6 dozen, depending on size you make them. (When using cookie sheets for other bakings, it is not necessary to oil or wash.)

Almond-Butter Cookies

1 cup butter, softened
1/4 cup firmly packed light
   brown sugar
1 egg yolk
1/2 teaspoon vanilla extract

1 teaspoon almond extract
2 cups all-purpose flour
1/2 cup finely chopped almonds
1/2 cup finely chopped pecans
1/2-3/4 pound powdered sugar

Beat butter and brown sugar until fluffy with an electric mixer; add egg yolk and extracts, mixing well. Stir in flour, almonds, and pecans. Shape dough into 1-inch balls; place 1 inch apart on ungreased cookie sheets. Bake at 300 degrees for 30 to 40 minutes or until light brown. Roll warm cookies in powdered sugar. Cool on wire rack. Yield: about 6 dozen.

Almond Chips
(Homer's Favorite)

1 1/2 cups sugar
1 cup shortening (Crisco)
2 eggs
1 teaspoon vanilla extract

2 teaspoons almond extract
3-3 1/2 cups self-rising flour
1 cup flaked coconut
1/2 cup slivered almonds, optional

Cream sugar and shortening; add eggs and extracts, beating well. Continuing to beat, add flour, coconut and almonds. This batter will be very stiff. Form into four 1 1/2-inch rolls; place each roll on plastic wrap and roll up. Place in freezer until ready to bake. When ready to bake, remove one roll at the time; slice with sharp knife into very thin rounds and bake on ungreased cookie sheet, in 300 degree oven, for about 8 to 10 minutes or until very lightly browned. If you prefer, form 1-inch balls and place on cookie sheet and bake. Bake 1-inch balls at 325 degrees.

Amy's Cinnamon Twist

(Amy learned to make these in Home Economics in the 7th grade, and she shared this recipe with me.)

2 cups self-rising flour
1/4 cup shortening
3/4 cup milk

1/2 cup margarine, melted
1 cup sugar
2 teaspoons cinnamon

Heat oven to 400 degrees. Cut shortening into flour; add milk and stir with fork. Form a ball of dough. Turn out onto a floured cloth; knead until smooth. Roll out to 1/4 inch thick; cut into strips and then cut strips into approximately 4-inch lengths. Dip into margarine, then sugar/cinnamon mixture; twist. Place on lightly greased, foil-covered baking sheet. Bake 8 to 10 minutes.

Apricot-Date Balls

1/2 cup dried apricot halves
   (about 12)
1 1/2 cups pitted dates (about 18)
1 cup flaked coconut

1/2 cup sugar
1 tablespoon grated orange peel
1 tablespoon orange juice

Rinse apricots in cold water. Combine with 1/2 cup water in small saucepan; bring to boil. Reduce heat and simmer uncovered 30 minutes. Drain. Coarsely chop apricots and dates in chopper or food processor. In medium bowl combine apricots, dates, coconut, sugar, orange peel and orange juice. Mix well. Shape into 1 1/4-inch balls; refrigerate, covered, for 24 hours or longer. Just before ready to use, roll in powdered sugar.

Beehives

1/4 cup honey
1 egg, beaten
1 teaspoon vanilla extract
2 cups shredded coconut

1 cup coarsely chopped walnuts
1 cup chopped, pitted dates
2 tablespoons all-purpose flour

Combine honey, egg and vanilla in medium bowl. Beat until blended. Stir in coconut and nuts. Coat dates with flour; add to mixture and stir. Drop by tablespoonfuls onto greased baking sheets. Bake at 325 degrees for 12 minutes or until slightly brown. Cool on wire rack.

Brownies are such a favorite dessert,
I have included 7 delicious, different recipes here!

Brown Brownies

(Amy's and Suzanna's favorite)

1 (16-ounce) package light brown sugar
2/3 cup butter or shortening
3 eggs
1 teaspoon vanilla extract

2 1/2 teaspoons baking powder
2 3/4 cups flour
1 (6-ounce) bag chocolate morsels
1 1/2 cups pecans, chopped

Cream sugar and butter or shortening; add eggs and vanilla, mixing well. Add baking powder and flour; blend, and stir in chocolate morsels and nuts. Pour into oiled jelly-roll pan and bake in 350 degree oven for about 30 minutes or until done in middle, being careful not to over cook. Remove from oven and cool on cake rack. Cut into squares and serve or store.

Brownies - Crème De Menthe

1 cup sugar
1/2 cup butter
4 eggs, beaten
1 cup flour

1/2 teaspoon salt
1 (16-ounce) bottle chocolate syrup
1 teaspoon vanilla extract

Cream butter and sugar together. Add eggs and other ingredients in order given. Beat well. Pour into a greased 13x9-inch pan; bake 25 to 30 minutes at 350 degrees and cool.

Crème De Menthe Layer:

2 cups confectioners' sugar
1/2 cup butter or margarine, melted

2 tablespoons of Green Crème De Menthe

Mix together confectioners' sugar, melted butter and Green Crème De Menthe. Spread this mixture over the cooled brownies.

Glaze:

1 cup chocolate chips

6 tablespoons butter or margarine

Melt chocolate chips and butter together. Let cool until it will spread easily. Spread over the Crème De Menthe layer. Cool and cut into squares.

Brownies - Cup-Cake

1 cup plain flour
1 3/4 cups sugar
4 eggs
4 ounces semi-sweet chocolate

2 sticks margarine
2 teaspoons vanilla extract
2 cups pecans, chopped

Combine flour and sugar; add eggs. Stir as little as possible. Melt chocolate and margarine together; add to mixture along with vanilla and nuts. Fill paper-cup-lined large muffin tins half full. Bake at 325 degrees for 25 to 30 minutes. Cool in pans so paper will hug cup cakes. (Batter will be very thin.) Makes 24.
Variation: Cook in 9x13-inch pan. Frost with **Rum-Butter Frosting** and glaze with **Chocolate Glaze**. (Recipes in Icings, also listed with **Crème De Menthe Brownie** recipe.) The frosting is optional; they are delicious just as they are.

Brownies - German Sweet Chocolate (One Bowl)

1 (4-ounce) package German's
   Sweet Baking Chocolate
1/4 cup (1/2 stick) butter or margarine
3/4 cup firmly packed brown sugar,
   divided
2 eggs

1/2 cup flour
1 cup pecans or walnuts, chopped and
   divided, optional
1 1/3 cups (3 1/2-ounce) Angel Flake
   coconut
1/4 cup milk

Heat oven to 350 degrees (325 degrees for glass baking dish). Grease bottom and sides of 8-inch square pan. Microwave chocolate and butter in large microwavable bowl on High 1 1/2 minutes or until butter is melted. Stir until chocolate is completely melted. Stir 1/2 cup of the brown sugar into chocolate until well blended. Mix in eggs. Stir in flour and 1/2 cup of the nuts until well blended. Spread in prepared pan. Mix coconut, remaining 1/2 cup nuts and remaining 1/4 cup brown sugar in same bowl. Stir in milk until well blended. Spoon mixture evenly over brownie batter. Bake 35 minutes or until toothpick inserted in center comes out with fudgy crumbs. **Do Not Overbake.** Cool in pan. Cut into squares. Makes 16.
Tip: If omitting nuts, increase coconut to 2 2/3 cups (1 7-ounce package.)

Brownies - Heavenly Hash Brownies (or Plain Chocolate)

4 eggs, slightly beaten
2 cups sugar
1 1/2 cups self-rising flour
1 teaspoon vanilla extract
1 cup margarine, melted

1/3 cup cocoa
1 tablespoon dry instant coffee,
  (optional)
1 1/2 cups pecans, chopped
Marshmallows for top, if desired

Combine eggs, sugar, flour, and vanilla. Melt margarine; add cocoa and instant coffee (if desired), stir to dissolve and add to egg mixture and mix well. Fold in nuts; bake in 9x13-inch pan in 350 degree oven for 25 to 30 minutes. Do not over cook. As soon as brownies are done, put marshmallows on top and return to oven until marshmallows are slightly melted. Frost while still hot.
Note: For plain brownies leave off marshmallows and frosting.

Frosting: (Use recipe below or make two recipes of brownies and use **Chocolate Fudge Icing** listed in Cake Icings.)
2 cups powdered sugar
1/4 cup cocoa

1 stick butter or margarine, melted
1 teaspoon vanilla extract

Combine sugar, cocoa, melted butter and vanilla; beating well. If too stiff, add just a little warm milk until of the right consistency to pour on brownies and marshmallows. (A few chopped nuts may be added on top of icing, if desired.)

There probably is no factor more important in the life of a child than self-esteem. This should be a gift from parents.

Brownies - Marbled Peanut Butter

1 cup (2 sticks) butter or margarine
2 cups sugar
2 teaspoons vanilla extract
3 eggs
3/4 cup cocoa

1 1/4 cups all-purpose flour
1/2 teaspoon baking powder
1/4 teaspoon salt
1 cup milk chocolate chips

Peanut Butter Filling:
2 (3-ounce) packages softened
    cream cheese
1/2 cup creamy or crunchy
    peanut butter

1/4 cup sugar
1 egg
2 tablespoons milk

Heat oven to 350 degrees. Grease 13x9x2-inch baking pan. Prepare Peanut Butter Filling by beating cream cheese, peanut butter, sugar, egg and milk until creamy. For brownies, melt butter, stir in sugar and vanilla. Add eggs, 1 at a time; beat well with spoon after each addition. Beat in cocoa; add flour, baking powder and salt; beat well. Stir in chips. Remove 1 cup batter; pour remaining batter into pan. Spread Peanut Butter Filling over surface. Drop reserved chocolate batter by teaspoons over filling. With knife, gently swirl through top layers to marble. Bake 35 to 40 minutes or until wooden pick inserted in center comes out almost clean. Cool; cut into bars. About 36 brownies.

Young people: Be realistic about yourself as an independent person in this world. Set goals that will afford security, and be determined to reach those goals. You are very special. There is not anyone else like you.

Brownies - Texas

2 cups all-purpose flour
2 cups granulated sugar
1/2 cup (1 stick) butter or margarine
1/2 cup shortening
1 cup strong coffee or water
    (I use 3 heaping teaspoons
    instant coffee)

1/4 cup dark, unsweetened cocoa
1/2 cup buttermilk
2 eggs
1 teaspoon baking soda
2 teaspoons vanilla extract
1 cup nuts, chopped
Frosting (recipe follows)

In a large mixing bowl, combine flour and sugar. In heavy saucepan, combine butter, shortening, coffee or water and cocoa; stir and heat to boiling. Pour boiling mixture over the flour and sugar in mixing bowl. Add buttermilk, eggs, baking soda, and vanilla; mix well, using high speed on mixer. Add nuts; pour into well buttered 17 1/2x11-inch jelly-roll pan. Bake at 400 degrees for 20 minutes or until brownies test done in the center.

Frosting:
1/2 cup (1 stick) butter or margarine
2 tablespoons dark cocoa
1/4 cup milk

3 1/2 cups unsifted powdered sugar
1 teaspoon vanilla extract

While brownies bake, prepare frosting. In saucepan, combine the butter, cocoa and milk. Heat to boiling, stirring. Remove from heat. Mix in powdered sugar and vanilla until frosting is smooth. Pour warm frosting over brownies as soon as you take them out of the oven. Cool. Cut into 48 bars. **These are delicious!**
Note: If you do not have buttermilk on hand, substitute 2 teaspoons vinegar or lemon juice mixed into 1/2 cup milk.

Holiness is a distinctiveness in a life, and is evident to everyone who sees it.

Caramel Chocolate Squares

1 (14-ounce) bag caramels
2/3 cup evaporated milk, divided
1 (18 1/4-ounce) German Chocolate
  Cake Mix

3/4 cup margarine, melted
1 (6-ounce) package chocolate chips
1 cup chopped walnuts or pecans,
  divided

Combine caramels and 1/3 cup of evaporated milk in double boiler. Cover, place over boiling water. Stir until melted. Keep warm over hot water. Combine cake mix, margarine and remaining 1/3 cup of evaporated milk in bowl. Beat with mixer at medium speed for 2 minutes, scraping bowl occasionally. Spread one half of batter in a greased 9x13-inch baking pan. Bake in 350 degree oven for 6 minutes. Cool 2 minutes. Spread caramel mixture carefully over baked layer. Sprinkle with chocolate chips. Stir 1/2 cup nuts into the batter. Drop by spoonfuls over all. Sprinkle with remaining 1/2 cup nuts. Bake in 350 degree oven 18 minutes. Cut into 3x1-inch bars.

Chewy Peanut Butter Macaroons

1 (14-ounce) can sweetened
  condensed milk

1/2 cup creamy peanut butter
3 cups flaked coconut

Combine all ingredients. Drop by teaspoons onto lightly greased baking sheet. Bake at 325 degrees for 12 to 15 minutes. Cool. Store in airtight container up to 3 weeks or freeze up to 3 months. Yield: 5 dozen.

Greater is He that is in you than they that are in the world. (1 John 4:4)

Coconut Macaroons - Party Perfect

4 egg whites
1/4 teaspoon cream of tartar
1 teaspoon vanilla extract
1 1/3 cups sugar

1 cup chopped pecans
1 cup shredded coconut
3 cups corn flakes

In a large mixing bowl, beat egg whites until foamy. Add cream of tartar and vanilla. Gradually add sugar, beating until very stiff and glossy, about 15 minutes. Fold in pecans, coconut and corn flakes. Lightly spray baking sheet with Baker's Joy; spread with hand, removing any excess. Drop by teaspoons onto baking sheets. Bake at 275 degrees for 20 minutes or until very lightly browned. Let stay on sheet just a minute and then gently remove to racks to cool. (If using sheets for a second baking, it is not necessary to use Baker's Joy again or to wash sheets.) These are beautiful and so good!

Note: Make these very small for parties as they do crumble. They look like divinity candy!

Cornflake-Peanut Butter Cookies

6 cups corn flakes
1 cup sugar

1 cup corn syrup
1 cup peanut butter

Place corn flakes in large bowl. Heat sugar and syrup to boiling until sugar is melted. Remove from heat and stir in peanut butter. Pour over cornflakes, mix and spoon out or roll in balls and place on waxed paper to cool. Store in tightly covered container.

The important thing is not to win, but to be worthy of winning.

Crispy Oat Cookies
(Also called World's Best Cookies.)

1 cup butter or margarine
1 cup granulated sugar
1 cup firmly packed brown sugar
1 egg
1 cup vegetable oil
2 teaspoons vanilla extract
3 1/2 cups all-purpose flour

1 teaspoon baking soda
1/2 teaspoon salt
2 cups regular oats, uncooked
2 cups crushed cornflakes
1/2 cup flaked coconut
1 cup pecans, chopped
    (or slivered almonds)

Cream butter; gradually add sugars, beating well at medium speed of mixer. Add egg; beat well, and add oil and vanilla, mixing well. Combine flour, soda and salt; add to creamed mixture, mixing well. Stir in oats and remaining ingredients. Dough will be **very** stiff. Shape dough into 1-inch balls; place on ungreased cookie sheets and flatten each ball with tines of a fork. Bake at 325 degrees for 12 to 15 minutes. Cool slightly; remove from cookie sheets and cool. Yield: 10 dozen. If you drop by teaspoons, you need not flatten, and this recipe will make 250. These are very good.

Variation: Coconut Cookies: Use 1 teaspoon vanilla and 2 teaspoons coconut extract, 1 cup flaked coconut (instead of ½ cup), and 1 (6-ounce) bag of semi-sweet chocolate chips. Omit nuts. **Very good - with a real coconut flavor!**

Cup Cakes - Spicy with Caramel Icing

1/2 cup butter
1 cup brown sugar
1 egg
2 cups all-purpose flour
1/4 teaspoon salt

1 teaspoon cinnamon
1 teaspoon nutmeg
1 teaspoon cloves
1 teaspoon soda
1 cup buttermilk
Caramel Icing (recipe follows)

Blend butter and sugar; add egg, beating well. Sift all dry ingredients; add alternately with buttermilk, mixing well. Bake in paper-lined muffin tins, sprayed with Baker's Joy, in 325 degree oven until light brown and firm in the middle. Allow to cool and ice with caramel icing or serve plain.

Caramel Icing:

1/2 cup margarine (1 stick)
1 cup light brown sugar
1 can sweetened condensed milk

1/4 cup milk
1 teaspoon vanilla extract

Bring first 4 ingredients to a rolling boil and boil slowly for 3 minutes, **stirring constantly.** Remove from heat; add vanilla. Top cooled cup cakes with teaspoon (or more) of icing.

Date-Cheese Cookies

1/2 cup butter
1/4 pound sharp cheese, grated
1 cup plain flour

1/2 pound dates, chopped
1/2 cup light brown sugar
1/4 cup water

Cream butter and cheese; gradually add flour. Make a soft dough ball and put it in the refrigerator for at least 1 hour. Combine dates, brown sugar and water; cook over low heat, **stirring constantly,** until very thick. Take dough the size of a walnut and make a small ball. Flatten in the palm of hand and put a small amount of date mixture in middle. Fold over, forming a half moon. Crimp edges with fork tines. Bake at 325 degrees 15 to 18 minutes or until lightly browned.

Date Meringues

3 egg whites, stiffly beaten
1/2 teaspoon vinegar
1/2 teaspoon vanilla extract
1 cup sugar

1 cup dates, chopped
1 cup nuts
1/2 cup oatmeal

Beat egg whites; add vinegar and vanilla; add sugar gradually. Fold in dates, nuts and oats. Drop by teaspoons onto foil-lined, greased cookie sheet and bake at 275 degrees for about 25 minutes or until a **very** light brown. Remove from foil and cool on rack.

Date Nut Squares

1 1/2 sticks margarine
1 cup sugar
1/2 pound dates, chopped

2 1/2 cups Rice Krispies cereal
1/2 cup or more of pecans

In boiler, melt margarine and add sugar, blending well. Add dates; let come to bubbly boil and cook for 4 minutes, stirring constantly. Remove from heat; add Rice Crispies and nuts. Pour into pan and cut in squares.

Elegant Angel Bites

1 (10-inch) tube angel food cake, or loaf cakes – (You may like to bake your own. Duncan Hines mix is so easy. Loaf cakes trim up and cut into petit fours easier.)

Icing:

1 cup butter or margarine
1/2 cup light rum

1 (1-pound) box powdered sugar
2 (2 1/2-ounce) packages sliced almonds

Trim brown crumbs from cake. Cut cake into small petit four-size squares. Set cake squares on cooling rack over a sheet of aluminum foil or wax paper. Place butter in 4-cup glass measure. Microwave at high 2 to 3 minutes until melted. Add rum and powdered sugar, blending until smooth. Pour icing over angel food squares, coating all sides except bottom. Re-use icing which drips onto foil. Before icing sets, press or sprinkle almond slices onto top of cake squares. Once icing is set, cover angel bites with aluminum foil or place in airtight container. Makes 72 petit fours.

Fudgy Peanut Butter Bars

For cookie base:

1 1/2 cups all-purpose flour
3/4 cup finely chopped dry
    roasted peanuts

1/2 cup packed brown sugar
1/2 cup (1 stick) butter or
    margarine, melted

Combine the flour, peanuts, brown sugar and butter in a 9x13-inch baking pan. Press onto bottom of pan. Bake in a preheated 350 degree oven for 10 to 12 minutes, or until light brown around the edges.

For topping:

2 cups (12-ounce package) semisweet
    chocolate morsels

3/4 cup creamy or chunky peanut butter
1/3 cup sifted powdered sugar

Cook chocolate morsels and peanut butter in medium, microwave-safe bowl on high (100 percent power) for 1 minute; stir. Cook on high an additional 10 to 20 second intervals, stirring until smooth. Add powdered sugar. Stir vigorously until smooth. Spread over hot cookie base. Chill just until chocolate is no longer shiny. Serve at room temperature. Makes about 3 dozen cookies.

Gingerbread Boys or Girls (or Cookies)
(Children love to do these!)

3/4 cup Crisco
3/4 cup sugar
3/4 cup molasses
1 egg
3 1/4 cups sifted all-purpose flour
3/4 teaspoon salt

1 1/2 teaspoons baking powder
3/4 teaspoon soda
1 teaspoon ginger
1/4 teaspoon cloves
2 teaspoon cinnamon
1/2 teaspoon nutmeg

Cream Crisco and sugar in large mixer bowl; add molasses and egg. Beat well. Sift together all dry ingredients and add gradually to first mixture. Chill 1 hour and roll out to 1/4-inch thickness on floured surface. Cut into desired shapes. If you prefer, shape into 1-inch balls for cookies. Bake in 375 degree oven 8 to 10 minutes, or until lightly browned. **Children of all ages love these!**
Variation: For special occasions, shape cookies into small ovals and dip just 1/2 of cookie in vanilla or lemon icing. (See Cake Icings)

Ice Box Cookies

1 pound butter or margarine
1 pound dark brown sugar
1 large egg
2 teaspoons vanilla extract

1 1/2 cups pecans, toasted and chopped
5 cups all-purpose flour
1/2 teaspoon salt

Cream butter and sugar until well blended. Add egg, vanilla and nuts. Mix until well blended. Combine flour and salt and add to mixture 2 cups at a time. If dough gets too stiff, mix with spoon. Divide dough into 4 equal parts. Lightly flour area you will be working on. Flour hands; form 1/4 dough into roll. Wrap roll in plastic wrap, wrap again in foil and place in freezer. Repeat for other 3 pieces. When ready to bake, preheat oven to 375 degrees; slice in 1/4-inch slices. Bake for 12 minutes.

Understanding God's purpose for our life is the key that unlocks His plan for us.

Jam Cookies
(A favorite of Amy's, just plain)

3/4 cup butter or Crisco
3/4 cup sugar
1 egg

1 teaspoon butter flavoring
1 1/2 cups all-purpose flour

Cream butter and sugar; add egg and flavoring. Blend in flour. Shape into balls; press thumb print deeply into middle of ball. Fill with your favorite jam. Bake in 325 degree oven for 15 to 18 minutes or until lightly browned.
Suggestion: Place candied cherry on top: these make nice Christmas cookies.

Lemon-Cheese Bars
(Unusual, easy and good!)

1 Duncan Hines Lemon Supreme
   Cake Mix
1 egg

1 stick margarine
1 cup pecans, chopped
Topping (recipe follows)

Mix ingredients and pour into 9x13-inch pan.

Topping:
1 (8-ounce) package cream cheese
1 box powdered sugar (Reserve 3
   tablespoons to sift over top,
   as garnish)

2 large eggs
Juice of 2 to 3 lemons

Mix and spread on top of batter. Bake in 350 degree oven 30 to 40 minutes, until lightly browned. Remove from oven and while hot, with small tea strainer, sift reserved powdered sugar on top. Cut into small squares.

Lemon Drops
(Something new for parties, or anytime!)

2 cups plain flour
3/4 cup butter or margarine
4 tablespoons powdered sugar
1/2 teaspoon vanilla extract
1/2 teaspoon lemon extract
1/4 cup finely chopped pecans

1/4 cup shredded coconut, chopped
   (Put coconut into chopper and
   chop fine)
2 teaspoons cold water, if needed
Icing (recipe follows)

Combine flour, butter, powdered sugar, and extracts; blend well. With hands, work in coconut and nuts. Measure out by teaspoonfuls onto cookie sheet. (You can quickly do this by dipping teaspoon measure into batter and pressing the batter against side of mixer bowl while bringing to top of bowl.) Dip out as many as you can bake on your cookie sheet; then with hands roll into balls. Bake in 325 degree oven about 10 minutes, or until very lightly browned on bottom. (They stay just the size they are when placed in oven as they do not have leavening.) Immediately, while cookies are hot, with tongs dip into hot icing. Place on tin foil to harden. Yield: About 7 dozen.

Icing:

6 squares (12 ounces) Almond Bark,
   vanilla flavored

1 teaspoon dry lemonade mix
   (or to taste)

Melt almond bark in microwave at 2-minute intervals, stirring each time, until it is completely melted. Stir in dry lemonade mix. You may add 1 drop of yellow food coloring, if desired. (If you feel like splurging, use pure white chocolate instead of Almond Bark.)

Lemon Squares

2 1/4 cups flour, divided
1/2 cup confectioners' sugar
1 cup margarine, softened
4 eggs, beaten
1 3/4 cups sugar

1/2 cup lemon juice
5 tablespoons flour
1/2 teaspoon baking powder
Confectioners' sugar
Dry lemonade mix

Crust: Mix together flour, confectioners' sugar and margarine. Pat into 9x13-inch pan and bake at 350 degrees 25 minutes, or until very lightly browned.
Filling: Combine eggs, sugar, lemon juice, flour and baking powder and pour over baked crust. Bake at 350 degrees 25 to 30 minutes. Sprinkle with mixture of confectioners' sugar, and dry lemonade mix to please your taste.

Macaroon Kiss Cookies

1/3 cup butter or margarine
3 ounces cream cheese, softened
3/4 cup sugar
1 egg yolk
2 teaspoons almond extract
2 teaspoons orange juice
1 1/4 cups unsifted flour

2 teaspoons baking powder
1/4 teaspoon salt
5 cups flaked coconut (14-ounce package), divided
1 (9-ounce) package milk chocolate kisses, (about 54)

Cream first 3 ingredients; beat well, then add egg yolk, almond extract and orange juice, continuing to beat until blended. Combine flour, baking powder and salt; gradually blend into creamed mixture to form dough. Stir in 3 cups coconut. Cover; chill about 1 hour. Shape dough into 1-inch balls. Roll balls in remaining coconut; place on ungreased cookie sheet. Bake at 350 degrees 10 to 12 minutes or until bottom browns lightly. Remove from oven and press chocolate kiss into center of each cookie (optional). Cool 1 minute. Remove cookies from sheet and cool until kisses are firm.

Suggestion: For special occasions, tint coconut to roll cookies in with a drop or so of food coloring by shaking in covered jar.

Oatmeal Cookies
(Charles' favorite!)

1 cup shortening
1 cup brown sugar
1 cup granulated sugar
2 eggs
1 teaspoon vanilla extract
1 1/2 cups sifted all-purpose flour

1/2 teaspoon salt
1 teaspoon soda
3 1/2 cups oatmeal (If not using pecans, 4 cups oatmeal)
1 cup pecans, chopped, optional

Cream shortening and sugars; add eggs and vanilla. Beat until blended. Sift together flour, salt and soda; add to creamed mixture. Stir in oatmeal and nuts. Form into 1 1/2-inch rolls, wrap in plastic wrap, chill, slice and bake; or, dampen hands as needed, form into 1-inch balls and place on cookie sheet. Bake in 350 degree oven about 8 to 10 minutes or until very lightly browned.

Variation: For Choc-Oat cookies reduce oatmeal to 3 cups and add 1 (12-ounce) package semi-sweet chocolate morsels.

Old Rangers Cookies

1 cup granulated sugar
1 cup brown sugar
1 cup shortening
2 eggs
1 teaspoon vanilla extract
2 cups flour
1/2 teaspoon baking powder

1 teaspoon soda
Pinch of salt
2 cups oatmeal
2 cups Rice Krispies
1 cup flaked coconut
1 cup nuts, chopped (optional)

Cream sugars and shortening; add eggs and vanilla and blend. Sift dry ingredients and add to first mixture; add all other ingredients and form into 1-inch balls and place on cookie sheets. Dampen hands if necessary in handling dough. Bake 8 to 10 minutes in 350 degree oven.

Orange Blossoms

1 box Duncan Hines Yellow Cake Mix
1 small package lemon instant
    pudding mix

3/4 cup vegetable oil
3/4 cup cold water
Glaze (recipe follows)

Combine all ingredients and mix. Bake in small muffin tins at 350 degrees. Allow to cool on racks.

Glaze:

2 cups powdered sugar, sifted
3 tablespoons margarine, softened
1 teaspoon finely shredded orange peel

2-3 tablespoons orange juice or
    concentrate, as needed

Mix ingredients together. Place tinfoil or wax paper under rack; dip each muffin in glaze, and place muffins on rack to harden. You may use glaze that drops on foil again, if desired.

Orange Macadamia Nut Cookies
(Pecan or Walnut)

4 cups all-purpose flour
2 cups sifted powdered sugar
1 cup cornstarch
2 cups butter, or margarine
1 cup chopped macadamia nuts,
   toasted pecans or walnuts

2 egg yolks
1 tablespoon finely shredded orange peel
4-6 tablespoons orange juice
Granulated sugar
Orange Frosting (recipe follows)
Finely shredded orange peel, optional

In a large mixing bowl stir together flour, powdered sugar and cornstarch. Cut in butter until mixture resembles coarse crumbs. Stir in nuts. Combine egg yolks, 1 tablespoon orange peel and 4 tablespoons of the juice; add to flour mixture, stirring until moistened. If necessary, add remaining juice to moisten. On lightly floured surface, knead dough until it forms a ball. Shape dough into 1-inch balls. Arrange balls on an ungreased baking sheet; flatten with bottom of glass to 1/4-inch thickness, dipping glass into granulated sugar for each round. Bake in a 350 degree oven for 12 to 15 minutes or until edges begin to brown. Remove from baking sheet to a wire rack. Frost with Orange Frosting. Garnish, if desired, with finely shredded orange peel. Makes 6 dozen.

Orange Frosting:

2 cups sifted powdered sugar
3 tablespoons softened butter
   or margarine

1 teaspoon finely shredded orange
   peel, or to taste
2-3 tablespoons orange juice,
   or as needed

Stir together powdered sugar, softened butter, shredded orange peel and enough orange juice to make icing of spreading consistency.

Peanut Butter Cookies

1 cup shortening
1 cup brown sugar
2 eggs
1 cup peanut butter
3 cups flour

1 teaspoon baking powder
1 teaspoon soda
1/2 teaspoon salt
1 teaspoon vanilla extract
1 tablespoon cold water

Cream shortening, stir in sugar and eggs. Beat until light and creamy before adding peanut butter. Add peanut butter and blend thoroughly. Sift together, flour, baking powder, soda and salt. Add sifted dry ingredients to first mixture. Last, stir in vanilla and cold water. Shape dough into small teaspoon portions. Roll in hands into disk. Place on greased cookie sheet and press flat with fork that has been dipped in cold water. Bake 10 to 15 minutes at 350 degrees or until very light brown.

Peppermint Meringues
(Especially nice for Christmas!)

2 egg whites
Dash of salt
1/4 teaspoon cream of tarter
3/4 cup sugar

1 (6-ounce) package chocolate morsels
1 teaspoon peppermint extract
Few drops green or red food coloring

Preheat oven to 250 degrees for 30 minutes. Beat egg whites, salt, and cream of tarter until frothy. Gradually add sugar and beat until stiff and glossy; beating about 15 minutes on medium speed. Fold in chocolate morsels, peppermint extract and food coloring. (Elizabeth and I like 3 drops of food coloring.) Spray small amount of Baker's Joy on cookie sheets. Spread with hand, removing excess spray, if any. Drop mixture by teaspoonfuls (or very small, especially for parties), onto cookie sheet; bake 20 minutes. Remove from oven and allow to sit on sheet for just a minute. Remove to rack to cool. If you have made them teaspoonful-size you will have at least 4 dozen.
Note: If you bake them slow enough, they will retain their beautiful color. If you bake them too fast, of course, they will brown. **These are very pretty, and a tasteful surprise.** (Elizabeth liked them plain, without the chocolate chips.)

Praline Strips

Graham crackers to cover cookie sheet
1 cup chopped pecans

1 cup butter or margarine
1 cup brown sugar

Line cookie sheet which has sides with foil. Place on it a layer of graham crackers topped with pecans. Bring to boil butter or margarine and brown sugar. Cook just to dissolve sugar, about 2 minutes. Pour this mixture over Graham Crackers and nuts; bake in a 400 degree oven for 5 minutes. Just slightly cool and cut into strips, and then allow to finish cooling.

Raggedy Ann Cookies

1 1/2 cups raisins, divided
1/2 cup butter
1/2 cup sugar
2 eggs, well beaten
1 1/2 cups sifted all-purpose flour

1/2 teaspoon soda
1 teaspoon vanilla extract
4 cups uncrushed cornflakes
1 cup shredded coconut

Rinse raisins and drain well. Cream butter and sugar together thoroughly. Stir in well beaten eggs. Sift flour with soda and blend into mixture. Stir in vanilla, raisins, cornflakes and coconut. Drop by small spoonful about 2 inches apart on ungreased cookie sheet. Bake at 350 degrees for 12 to 15 minutes or until very lightly browned.

Sand Tarts, Crescents or Nut Fingers

2 cups plain flour
3/4 cup butter
4 tablespoons powdered sugar
2 teaspoons vanilla extract

1/2 cup pecans, chopped
2 teaspoons cold water, if needed
Powdered sugar

Combine flour, butter, powdered sugar and vanilla; add nuts. Add cold water if necessary to form a very stiff batter. Shape as desired, and bake at 325 degrees until very light brown. While still warm roll in powdered sugar. Shake off excess and store. (Shape as desired – fingers, crescents, balls, etc.)

Strawberry-Chocolate Cheesecake Squares

2/3 cup margarine, softened
1/2 cup sugar
2 egg yolks
2 cups all-purpose flour
2 (8-ounce) packages cream cheese, softened
1 cup mini chocolate chips

3/4 cup sugar
2 teaspoons vanilla extract
2 eggs
1/2 cup mini chocolate chips, finely chopped
1 cup strawberry jam

Preheat oven to 375 degrees. Grease 13x9x2-inch pan. Mix margarine, 1/2 cup sugar and egg yolks in medium bowl. Stir in flour. Press evenly in pan. Bake 18 to 20 minutes or until lightly browned; immediately sprinkle with 1 cup chocolate chips. Let stand until soft and spread over baked layer. Refrigerate 30 minutes. Beat cream cheese until smooth. Beat in 3/4 cup sugar, vanilla and eggs. Stir in chocolate chips. Pour over crust layer. Bake 30 minutes. Spread with jam. To make them look really great, melt 1/4 cup chocolate chips with 1 teaspoon shortening. Drizzle over top of jam layer. Refrigerate about 3 hours; cut into 1 1/2-inch squares.

Tea Cakes
(My Mother's Recipe)

2 cups sugar
1 cup butter-flavored Crisco
   (She did not have butter flavored,
   but it is better.)
2 eggs

1 teaspoon vanilla extract and
   1 teaspoon almond or 2 teaspoons
   vanilla extract and no almond extract
3-4 cups self-rising flour

Cream sugar and shortening. Add eggs and flavorings. Add some of the flour. Gradually beat in remaining flour. (About 3 1/2 cups of flour is usually enough, but the batter needs to be very stiff.) Form 1-inch balls and bake in 350 degree oven 9 to 12 minutes or until very lightly browned, or form batter into 4 rolls, freeze and slice very thin and bake. This makes many, depending on the size you make them. With 6 children, and always extra people around, my mother needed many! If you make 1-inch balls, you have about 120. This is a wonderful basic recipe.
Variations: Nuts, chocolate chips, chopped candied cherries all are good additions to these.

Toll House Cookies

2 1/4 cups all-purpose flour
1 teaspoon baking soda
1/2 teaspoon salt
1 cup (2 sticks) butter or margarine,
   softened
3/4 cup granulated sugar

3/4 cup brown sugar
1 teaspoon vanilla extract
2 eggs
1 (12-ounce) bag chocolate morsels
1 cup chopped nuts

Combine flour, baking soda and salt in small bowl. Beat butter, granulated sugar, brown sugar and vanilla in large mixer bowl. Add eggs one at a time, beating well after each addition; gradually beat into flour mixture. Stir in morsels and nuts. Drop by rounded tablespoons onto greased baking sheets. Bake at 375 degrees (or less depending on your oven) for 9 to 11 minutes or until lightly browned. Let stand a minute; then place on wire rack to cool. Makes about 5 dozen.

Turtle Cookies

2 cups flour
1 cup firmly packed brown sugar
1/2 cup butter, softened
1 cup pecans, chopped

Caramel Layer:
2/3 cup butter
1/2 cup brown sugar, firmly packed
Topping:
1 cup milk chocolate chips

Mix flour, 1 cup brown sugar and 1/2 cup butter; press into 9x13-inch pan. Sprinkle unbaked crust with pecans. Bring to boil over medium heat 2/3 cup butter and 1/2 cup brown sugar, stirring constantly, for 1 minute. Pour caramel over pecans and crust. Bake at 350 degrees for 18 to 20 minutes. Remove and immediately sprinkle with milk chocolate chips. Let sit 1 minute and slightly spread. Cool. Cut into squares to serve.

Yummy Squares

1 cup peanut butter, smooth or crunchy
1 stick butter or margarine
1 (16-ounce) box light brown sugar
3 eggs

2 teaspoons vanilla extract
2 cups self-rising flour
1 (12-ounce) package semi-sweet
    chocolate chips

Cream peanut butter, butter or margarine, and sugar until light and fluffy. Add eggs, one at a time, beating well after each addition. Blend in vanilla extract and flour. Fold in chocolate chips. Spread batter in a greased 9x13-inch pan. Bake in a 350 degree oven for 25 to 30 minutes or until lightly browned. Cake will sink slightly in the center. Cool for a while and cut into squares while warm. Yield: 35 squares.

Our ultimate purpose in life is to glorify God. The way you practice is the way you play the game.

Banana Split Dessert

1 1/4 cups graham cracker crumbs
1/4 cup margarine
1/4 cup sugar
1/2 cup nuts
1/2 gallon vanilla ice cream

3 large bananas, sliced
1 (20-ounce) can crushed pineapple,
　 well drained
Sauce (recipe follows)

Mix first 4 ingredients and put into 9x13-inch pan and bake at 350 degrees until lightly browned. Cool. Remove vanilla ice cream from carton, slice and spread onto crust. Slice 3 large bananas over ice cream; top bananas with pineapple, well drained. Freeze while you make sauce.

Sauce:

1 cup semi-sweet chocolate chips
1/2 cup margarine
1 (13-ounce) can evaporated milk
2 cups powdered sugar

1 teaspoon vanilla extract
1 (12-ounce) carton Cool Whip
1/2 cup chopped, toasted pecans
Maraschino cherries for garnish

Combine first 5 ingredients and cook 8 minutes from time you place on heat. When sauce is completely cool, pour over frozen mixture. Spread 1 large carton Cool Whip over sauce. Sprinkle with toasted chopped nuts. Freeze. Cut into squares and place a cherry on top of each serving.

Cherries à la Mode

3 tablespoons lemon juice
2 tablespoons brown sugar
1/8 teaspoon salt

1 (22-ounce) can cherry pie filling
Pound cake or Angel Food Cake
1 quart chocolate ice cream

Combine lemon juice, sugar, salt, and pie filling in a (1-quart) sauce pan; heat 5 minutes. Spoon sauce over pound cake slices, add scoop of ice cream, and top with additional cherry sauce. Serve immediately. Yield: 6 to 9 servings.

Coffee Crunch Pie or Parfaits

1 pie crust of your choice
  (if making pie)
1 quart coffee ice cream, softened
1 (2-ounce) package slivered almonds,
  lightly toasted

2 (1.4-ounce) English-flavored toffee
  candy bars, crushed
1/2 cup chocolate syrup
1 (8-ounce) whipped topping, divided
Chocolate curls

Bake pie crust, if necessary. Spoon ice cream into cooled pie crust; freeze for 15 minutes or until firm. Layer almonds, crushed candy bars and chocolate syrup evenly over pie. Cover and freeze. Top with whipped topping and chocolate curls.
Note: If making parfaits, spoon 1/4 cup ice cream into each of 8 (4-ounce) parfait glasses. Layer half of almonds, crushed candy bars and chocolate syrup evenly in glasses. Repeat layers. Finish as above.

Ice Cream Sandwich Dessert

Ice cream sandwiches (box of 12)
1 large carton whipped topping
Toasted pecans, chopped

Chocolate syrup or chocolate icing
Kahlúa (coffee liqueur)

Fill 9x13-inch dish with ice cream sandwiches. Spread whipped topping over sandwiches and top with toasted pecans. Drizzle with chocolate syrup or chocolate icing and Kahlúa. Freeze and cut into squares to serve.
Variation: You may layer sandwiches, cherry pie filling and whipped topping, making two layers. Freeze and slice as a cake or cut into squares. Garnish as desired. You will need approximately 19 sandwiches.

The most important aspect of life exists in relationships.

Ice Cream - Compotes, Pies or Parfaits (any flavor)

You will need 1 quart (approximately) ice cream per pie. Choose your crust and make your favorite ice cream pie! They always look and taste so special, and most hostesses like things that can be prepared ahead. Look under Pies and Crusts in this book for suggestions for crusts. For those watching sugar and fat, Eskimo Pie Ice Cream, and Breyers (no sugar added, and 1/3 to 50% less fat), are wonderful!. Purchase 1/2 gallon of your favorite vanilla ice cream and let your imagination go wild! There are so many different kinds of ice cream pie you can make. This amount will make 2 pies.

To prepare ice cream: Slice ice cream into medium slices and place in large mixer bowl. Beat until softened a little; proceed with your chosen flavor. For a lighter ice cream, fold in an (8 or 12-ounce) carton of frozen whipped topping. Cover tightly and freeze until a few minutes before you are ready to serve. It is best to garnish at this time.

Chocolate Ice Cream Pie: Use purchased chocolate, or chocolate-marshmallow Eskimo Pie Ice Cream (no sugar added), with a Pecan Crust, or crust of your choice. **Note:** A favorite of ours is a dish of chocolate-marshmallow ice cream (Eskimo Pie) topped with chopped roasted peanuts. Delicious!

Coffee Ice Cream Pie: Use purchased coffee ice cream; add rum, or rum flavoring to taste. Mix well. Garnish with a little whipped topping, shaved chocolate and a drizzle of Kahúa. Place in freezer until serving time. Chocolate-Rice Crispy or Coconut Crust.

Vanilla Ice Cream Pie with Glazed Bananas: on individual desserts, or as a topping on ice cream pie. **Recipe:** Melt 2 tablespoons brown sugar in a skillet over low heat; add 2 sliced bananas and cook, stirring often, until browned and glazed. Don't over cook or bananas will become mushy. Add 2 tablespoons rum, if desired. Arrange ice cream topped with bananas in compotes and sprinkle with toasted, flaked coconut, or top ice cream pie with bananas and coconut just before serving. This is only enough for about 4 compotes. Double as needed.

Hawaiian Ice Cream: Add coconut and cherries to the pineapple recipe below.

Lemon: Use frozen lemonade concentrate or 1 tub of dry lemonade mix. (You may like to use sugar-free lemonade mix.) You might like the Chocolate Crumb, the Gingersnap, or the plain Graham cracker crust.

Lemon: To 1/2 gallon vanilla ice cream (softened slightly), add juice of 1/2 lemon, rind of 2 lemons, finely grated, and 1 (6-ounce) can frozen lemonade, thawed. Refreeze immediately. Serve in individual dishes sprinkled with sautéed pecans and garnished with a thin lemon twist.

Peach: Use 1 tub dry lemonade mix and add 1 quart crushed peaches, fresh or from your freezer. Peaches are mild flavored, and you need to use more than most fruit. Also, the lemonade mix helps to bring out the flavor.

Pineapple: Add 1 tub of dry sugar free lemonade mix (optional), and 1 (20-ounce) can of crushed pineapple, in natural juice. Zesty and delicious! Small servings are satisfying. A palate cleaner!

Strawberry: Crush and use as many as you like, add a little artificial sweetener or sugar to the berries and let them sit a little before adding to vanilla ice cream.

Toasted Pecan: Use 1 1/2 cups toasted pecans and butter-nut flavoring to taste (not too much, it has a strong flavor). The Eskimo Pie purchased buttered-pecan ice cream is great, also.

Homemade Freezer Sherbet: Pineapple-Cherry

1 (20-ounce) can crushed pineapple
1 (10-ounce) jar chopped
   maraschino cherries
1 (14-ounce) can sweetened
   condensed milk

3 (12-ounce) cans milk
2 cans water
3/4 cup sugar
Juice of 1 lemon

Mix all ingredients well and freeze in electric freezer.

Lemon Cheesecake - (Light)

Crust: Make a double recipe of graham cracker crust as per recipe on box. Bake in 9x13-inch pan or two 9-inch pie plates.

1 (3-ounce) lemon-flavor gelatin
   (sugar-free, if desired)
1/2 cup boiling water
1 (8-ounce) package cream cheese
   (light-Neufchâtel)

1 cup sugar
1 or 2 lemons, juice and rind (zest)
1 large can evaporated milk, frozen and
   whipped (fat free, if desired)

Dissolve gelatin in boiling water. Set aside until room temperature. In small bowl, with hand mixer, blend cream cheese and sugar; add gelatin mixture. Whip frozen evaporated milk in large mixer bowl until it holds peaks. With mixer on low speed, mix in cream cheese-gelatin mixture, (a little at the time at first), and juice and rind of lemon. Pour into crust and freeze. Cut into serving pieces and garnish with a dollop of whipped topping and thinly sliced lemon twist. (Or save a few crumbs of crust for garnish.)

Suggestion:
Cheesecake Delights (Do ahead party food!)
Use above filling with the following pastry for finger food for parties. (You may substitute strawberry Jell-O with a few fresh strawberries instead of lemon, if desired.)

1 (3-ounce) package cream cheese
1 stick butter or margarine

1 cup all-purpose flour
Pinch of salt

Combine above ingredients and form into 1-inch balls; press into miniature muffin tins and bake in 350 degree oven until very lightly browned. Allow to cool a little and gently remove with blade of a paring knife. Fill with cheesecake; cover well and store in freezer until needed. These hold up well even if partly thawed.

Piña Colada Wedges

1 (8-ounce) package cream cheese
   (softened)
1/3 cup sugar
2 tablespoons rum or
   1/2 teaspoon rum extract

3 1/2 cups thawed whipped topping,
   divided
1 (20-ounce) can crushed pineapple in
   syrup
2 2/3 cups Angel Flake coconut, divided

Beat cream cheese with sugar and rum until smooth. Fold in 2 cups whipped topping, pineapple (with syrup) and 2 cups coconut. Spread into slightly buttered pie plate; add remaining whipped topping and sprinkle with remaining coconut. Freeze. Cut into wedges to serve. Delicious!

Easy Frozen Pumpkin Pie
(A delicious "do-ahead" for Thanksgiving!)

Crust of your choice

Filling:

1 quart butter pecan ice cream, softened
1 cup canned pumpkin
1/2 cup granulated sugar

1 teaspoon cinnamon
1/4 teaspoon ground ginger
1/4 teaspoon nutmeg

Prepare crust, if necessary. Chill. Prepare ice cream by slicing into slices and cutting slices into squares. Place in electric mixer bowl and beat just to slightly soften; add canned pumpkin, sugar, cinnamon, ginger and nutmeg. Blend thoroughly. Spread mixture over chilled crust, cover with plastic wrap or aluminum foil. Freeze for at least 2 hours. Remove from freezer 10 minutes before serving.

Make encouragement an element of your lifestyle.

Apple Dumplings - Easy

1 (5-ounce) can buttermilk biscuits
2 1/2 medium-size cooking apples,
   peeled, cored and quartered
3/4 cup sugar

1/4 cup margarine
1/2 teaspoon vanilla extract
1/4 teaspoon cinnamon

Roll each biscuit into a (5 1/2-inch) circle; cut each circle in half. Place one apple quarter on each piece of dough, placing straight edge of apple to straight edge of dough. Moisten edges with water; bring ends to center and pinch to seal. Place in 8-inch square casserole. Combine sugar and remaining ingredients; bring to a boil. Pour over dumplings. Bake in 350 degree oven for 30 minutes, basting with syrup at least twice. Serve warm. (Pears are also good used in this way.)

Banana Pudding

2 (1-ounce) packages instant vanilla
   pudding mix (sugar free, if desired)
1 (12-ounce) carton frozen Lite Cool Whip,
   divided

1 (12 ounce) box vanilla wafers
6-8 bananas

Mix pudding mix with milk according to directions on box. Fold in enough thawed, whipped topping to give a very light consistency. Layer wafers, sliced bananas and pudding mix. Repeat layers. Cover and refrigerate until ready to serve. Top with additional whipped topping, if desired.

Bread Pudding with Caramel Custard

1 cup firmly packed dark brown sugar
5 slices whole wheat bread
3 tablespoons margarine, softened
3 cups milk
1/8 teaspoon salt

2 eggs, beaten
1 1/2 teaspoons vanilla extract
Ice cream or frozen whipped topping,
   optional

Generously butter a 1 1/2-quart casserole dish. Sprinkle the brown sugar on the bottom of dish. Cut away crusts from bread; spread each slice with margarine. Cut each slice in quarters and arrange in dish, buttered side down, on top of sugar. Combine milk, salt, eggs and vanilla; pour over bread. Bake in 350 degree oven 1 hour or until knife inserted in center comes out clean. Serve warm or cold, with ice cream or topping, if desired.

Butter Roll

2 sticks margarine   1 (4-pack) package hot dog buns

Melt 2 sticks butter in 7x11-inch rectangular pyrex dish. Open hot dog buns and place in dish cut side down. Use just enough buns to fill dish.

Custard:

6 eggs, beaten (You may wish to use   2 cups milk
    Egg-beaters, and part egg.)   2 teaspoons vanilla extract
2 cups sugar

Combine custard ingredients; pour over buns. Bake 30 minutes at 350 degrees or until golden brown. Very unusual, but good.

Crunchy Cobbler

*Peach, pear, apple, blackberry, blueberry, strawberry, cherry
All of these are good.*

3-4 cups fresh fruit or 1 can pie filling   1/2 teaspoon vanilla extract
2 tablespoons lemon juice   6 tablespoons margarine, melted
1 cup self-rising flour   1 teaspoon cinnamon
1 cup sugar   1/2 teaspoon ginger
1 egg

Place fresh fruit or pie filling into 7x11-inch baking dish. Sprinkle with lemon juice. If you like spices, sprinkle cinnamon and ginger over fruit at this point. For crust, mix flour, sugar, egg and vanilla until lumpy. Spread or crumble over fruit. (Will be very stiff.) Drizzle melted margarine over top and bake for 30 to 35 minutes at 350 degrees. (Sometimes it is necessary to sprinkle more sugar over fruit, if very tart.)

Coincidence is God's way of remaining anonymous.

Crêpes - for Dessert

1 1/2 cups milk
1 cup all-purpose flour
2 eggs

1 tablespoon cooking oil
2 tablespoons sugar

In bowl, combine milk, flour, eggs, oil and sugar. Beat with wire whisk until well mixed. Heat a lightly greased non-stick, 6-inch fry pan. Remove from heat; spoon in 2 tablespoons of batter; lift and tilt skillet to spread batter. Return to heat; brown on one side only. Invert pan over paper towels; repeat, greasing skillet only as needed. Makes 18. Use these with fillings or sauces of your choice.
Note: If you have extra crêpes, place 2 layers of wax paper between them and freeze. Let thaw at room temperature for 1 hour before using. For purposes other than dessert, omit the sugar and add 1/4 teaspoon salt.

Custard - Baked

3 eggs
1 1/2 cups milk
1/3 cup sugar

2 teaspoons vanilla extract
Sprinkle of nutmeg or cinnamon

Combine all the ingredients, but do not beat until foamy. Place 4 (6-ounce) custard cups, or one (3 1/2 cup) casserole, or (8x8x2-inch) baking dish in larger dish and fill dish to depth of 1-inch with boiling water. Pour egg mixture into cups or dish; sprinkle with nutmeg or cinnamon, if desired. Bake in 325 degree oven for 30 to 45 minutes, or until knife comes out clean when inserted in the middle. Loosen edges and invert onto dessert plates, or spoon from casserole onto dessert plates or cups. Top with a dollop of whipped topping, or as desired.

Like interests do not establish the strongest unity between people, but rather, like faith.

Delights: (You may use sugar-free pudding mix, fat-free milk, light-cream cheese or fat-free, if desired. Very nice for those watching sugar or weight)!

Delight recipes are very simple, beautiful and delicious! They appear difficult because of the method of combination. I have listed total ingredients first, for your shopping convenience.

These recipes can be made into two pies, or a 9x13-inch dish. They can be made and refrigerated the day before needed, or tightly covered and frozen for later use.

Delight: Chocolate

1 1/2 cups all-purpose flour
1 stick margarine
1 cup chopped pecans, divided
　(optional, but so good)
1 (8-ounce) package cream cheese,
　softened
1 cup powdered sugar

1 (12-ounce) carton whipped topping,
　divided
1 (3.4-ounce) package chocolate instant
　pudding mix
1 (3.4-ounce) package vanilla instant
　pudding mix
3 cups milk
Garnish: chocolate curls, if desired

Crust: Combine flour and margarine and press into 9x13-inch baking dish. Press pecans into crust. Bake at 350 degrees for 15 minutes or until lightly browned. At this point, lightly toast remainder of pecans. Set aside.
1st layer: Combine cheese and sugar; slowly add 1 cup whipped topping. Spread over crust with spatula.
2nd layer: Mix chocolate and vanilla instant pudding mixes with 3 cups milk; slowly fold in 1 cup whipped topping. Pour over 1st layer.
3rd layer: Spread remainder of whipped topping over 2nd layer. Sprinkle with 1/2 cup toasted nuts and chocolate curls, if desired. Refrigerate. Cut into serving pieces. This recipe can be done the day before and refrigerated. (It can be tightly covered and frozen.)

It is not how much of the Spirit I have, but rather how much of me the Spirit has.

Delight: Coconut

1 1/2 cups all-purpose flour
1 stick margarine
1 cup chopped pecans, divided
  (optional, but so good)
1 (8-ounce) package cream cheese,
  softened
1 cup powdered sugar

1 (12-ounce) carton whipped topping,
  divided
1 (6-ounce) bag frozen grated coconut
  (or other), divided
1 (5 5/8-ounce) package vanilla instant
  pudding
2 cups milk
1 cup sour cream

Crust: Combine flour and margarine; press into 9x13-inch baking dish. Press 1/2 cup pecans into crust. Bake at 350 degrees 15 minutes or until lightly browned. Cool. Toast remaining pecans and the coconut until very lightly browned. Cool.
1st layer: Combine cheese and sugar; add 1 cup of the whipped topping. Spread onto crust. Spread 1/2 of the toasted coconut on this layer.
2nd layer: Mix vanilla pudding with 2 cups milk as per directions on box; fold in sour cream. Pour over last layer.
3rd layer: Mix remainder of toasted coconut, (except save out just a little for garnish). Add remainder of whipped topping; pour over 2nd layer.
Garnish: Sprinkle with the toasted pecans and coconut. Refrigerate. Cut into serving pieces. This recipe can be done ahead and refrigerated overnight, or tightly covered and frozen.

Delight: Lemon

1 1/2 cups all-purpose flour
1 stick margarine
1 cup chopped nuts, divided
  (use if desired)
1 (8-ounce) package cream cheese
1 cup powdered sugar

1 (12-ounce) carton whipped topping,
  divided
2 (3 ounce) packages instant lemon
  pudding mix
3 cups cold milk
Garnish: Finely shredded lemon peel,
  if desired

Crust: Combine flour and margarine, Press into 9x13-inch dish. Press 1/2 cup of the nuts into crust. Bake 15 minutes in 350 degree oven or until lightly browned. Cool. At this point, toast the remainder of the nuts. Cool.
1st layer: Blend cream cheese and powdered sugar; slowly add 1 cup of the topping. With spatula, spread over crust.
2nd layer: Combine milk and instant pudding; whisking in for about 2 minutes. Pour over 1st layer.
3rd layer: Spread remainder of whipped topping over 2nd layer and top with remainder of nuts or a little finely grated lemon peel.
Refrigerate; cut into serving pieces. This recipe can be done ahead of time and refrigerated, or tightly covered and frozen.

Flan

1/2 cup sugar
1/4 cup water
2 large eggs
3 large egg whites

1 (14-ounce) can low fat sweetened
  condensed milk
1 1/2 cups fat-free milk
1 tablespoon vanilla extract

Preheat oven to 325 degrees. In small heavy saucepan, combine sugar with 1/4 cup water. Simmer over low heat, stirring occasionally until syrup turns a deep amber color, about 5 minutes. Swirl the pan if coloring unevenly. Immediately pour the mixture into baking dish to be used for flan. Swirl to coat bottom and set aside while preparing custard. Combine eggs, egg whites and condensed milk and beat until blended. Add fat-free milk and vanilla, beating, but not until foamy. Pour flan into caramel-coated baking dish and set dish in a larger shallow pan, such as a roasting pan. Pour enough hot water into the larger pan so that it comes halfway the side of the dish. Bake for 60 to 70 minutes or until the custard is set around the edges, but still wobbly in center. Remove dish from water bath to rack and cool. Cover and refrigerate for at least 4 hours or overnight. To serve, run a knife around the edge of the dish and invert the flan onto a plate. This can be baked in individual custard cups if desired.

Georgia Peach Bowl

2 cups sliced peaches (preferably fresh)
1 cup blueberries
1 medium-sized cantaloupe, cubed
1 pint fresh strawberries

1 kiwi fruit, peeled and sliced
1 (6-ounce) can frozen orange juice
  concentrate, thawed (add or substitute
  any fruit desired and available)

In decorative glass bowl, layer fruit. Pour orange juice over mixture. Cover and let marinate in the refrigerator for 2 hours. Serves about 10.

God's truth is never threatened by human inquiry.

Gingerbread (Old-Fashioned)

1/2 cup margarine	1/2 teaspoon salt
1/2 cup sugar	1 teaspoon cinnamon
1 egg	1 teaspoon cloves
1 cup molasses	1 teaspoon ginger
2 1/2 cups all-purpose flour	1 cup hot water
1 1/2 teaspoons baking soda	**Lemon Sauce** (recipe follows)

Cream margarine, gradually adding sugar. Beat at medium speed until light and fluffy. Add egg and molasses. Mix well. Combine flour and next 5 ingredients; add to creamed mixture alternately with water, beginning and ending with flour, mixing after each. Pour into greased and floured 9-inch square pan. Bake at 350 degrees for 35 to 40 minutes. Cut into 9 squares. Top each square with lemon sauce.

Lemon Sauce:

1/2 cup sugar	2 tablespoons lemon juice
1 tablespoon cornstarch	1 teaspoon grated lemon peel
1 cup water	

Combine first 3 ingredients. Cook over medium heat until thick. Add lemon juice and peel. Serve over gingerbread or any time you need a good lemon sauce.

Meringues - Very special looking and delicious!
(Especially nice for dessert parties or luncheons.)

6 egg whites	1 teaspoon vanilla extract
1/4 teaspoon salt	1/2 cup nuts
1/4 teaspoon cream of tartar	2 quarts ice cream
1 1/2 cups sugar	**Sauce** (recipe follows)

Beat egg whites until foamy; add salt and cream of tartar. Beat until soft peaks form. Add sugar very slowly, beating after each addition until sugar is dissolved. Continue beating until meringue is very stiff. Add vanilla and nuts. Mix well. Draw 3 1/2-inch circles on foil; divide meringues amongst circles. Shape with back of teaspoons to form shells. Bake in 275 degree oven for 1 hour. Cool. (Makes several bakings.)

Sauce:

1 can cherry pie filling	1/2 cup orange marmalade

Heat in small saucepan. Serve meringue topped with ice cream and warm sauce. Delicious! Meringues will keep very well sealed in airtight container; so they can be done several days in advance.

Double Chocolate Meringues

2 egg whites
1/2 cup sugar

1/4 cup finely chopped nuts
(filberts, pecans or almonds)
Chocolate Rum Sauce (recipe follows)

Beat egg whites to soft peaks. Gradually add sugar, beating until very stiff peaks form and sugar dissolves. Cover baking sheets with foil. Draw six 3 1/2-inch circles on foil; divide meringue among the circles. Shape with spoon to form shells. Sprinkle nuts on top. Bake in 275 degree oven for 1 hour. Cool.

Chocolate Rum Sauce:

1 (12-ounce) package (2 cups)
semi-sweet chocolate pieces
2 tablespoons butter or margarine
1/2 cup light corn syrup

1/2 cup milk
1/2 cup rum
Chocolate ice cream

In saucepan, melt chocolate pieces and butter or margarine over low heat. Gradually stir in corn syrup and milk; stir until mixture is smooth. Cook and stir 10 minutes. Remove from heat; cool and stir in rum. Serve warm or cold. Fill each meringue with a scoop of ice cream. Top with the sauce. Makes 6 servings.

Torte: Lemon with Raspberry Sauce (Easy)
(Or strawberry)

Non-stick cooking spray
1/2 of a (9-inch) angel food cake
(Freeze remainder for later use)
1 (3-ounce) package sugar free
lemon-flavored gelatin
1/2 cup boiling water

1/2 cup frozen lemonade concentrate
1 1/2 cups frozen non-dairy creamer,
thawed
Raspberry or Strawberry Sauce
(recipe follows)

Spray an 8-inch springform pan with non-stick cooking spray. (Or deep-dish pie plate.) Cut cake into slices and press into pan. Using a large bowl, dissolve gelatin in boiling water. Stir in lemonade concentrate, then stir in non-dairy creamer. Chill for approximately 1/2 hour or until mixture mounds. Beat mixture for 4 to 5 minutes until light and fluffy. Pour over cake and refrigerate until firm or overnight.

Raspberry or Strawberry Sauce:

2 cups frozen raspberries, thawed
1/4 cup sugar

1 tablespoon cornstarch

Combine raspberries with juice, sugar and cornstarch in a small saucepan. Bring to a boil, stirring constantly. Cook 2 to 3 minutes, allowing to slightly thicken. Remove from heat, allow to cool. Remove torte from pan, slice, and spoon sauce over each serving. A delicious, very low sugar and low fat dessert!
Note: You may use other fruits. Your choice!

Trifle: Your favorite - Peach, Strawberry, Blueberry

1 box of Duncan Hines Angel Food
   Cake Mix, prepared according to
   directions (Use 1/2 of cake and freeze
   remaining half for later use.)
1/4 cup orange juice (optional)
2 cups cold milk, 2% or skim

1 (4-serving) package vanilla sugar free
   instant reduced calorie pudding mix
1 (8-ounce) carton whipped topping
2 cups (or more) fresh fruit - your choice
1 tablespoon lemon juice

Remove outside brown edges of cake, if desired. Slice cake horizontally into 3 layers. Sprinkle cake layers evenly with juice. Cut into 1-inch cubes. Pour milk into medium bowl. Add pudding mix. Beat with wire whisk 30 seconds. Let stand 2 minutes or until thickened. Gently stir in 2 cups of the whipped topping until smooth. Layer 1/2 of the cake cubes, fruit and pudding mixture in 2 1/2-quart serving bowl. Repeat layers once. Garnish with remaining whipped topping and extra fruit. Refrigerate 1 hour or until ready to serve. Store leftover dessert in refrigerator.

Trifle: Peachy Cheesecake - or Your Favorite Fruit

2 (8-ounce) packages cream cheese,
   softened
2 1/4 cups powdered sugar, divided
1 cup sour cream
2 teaspoons almond extract, divided
1 cup whipping cream

1 teaspoon vanilla extract
4 cups fresh fruit combined with
   1 1/2 tablespoons lemon juice
1 angel food cake, sliced horizontally
   into several layers
1/2 cup sugar

Blend cream cheese and 2 cups powdered sugar. Add sour cream and 1 teaspoon almond flavoring. Set aside. Beat together whipping cream, vanilla and 1/4 cup powdered sugar. Beat until stiff peaks form. Set aside. Combine fruit, 1/2 cup sugar and 1 teaspoon almond flavoring. Allow to sit to dissolve sugar. Set aside. Place a layer of angel food cake in bottom of trifle bowl. Spread about 1/3 of cream cheese mixture over cake, Pull to edges of bowl. Keep side of bowl clean. Ladle on 1/2 of fruit and juice. Repeat layers to fill bowl within 1/2 inch of top. Spread whipped cream on top. Refrigerate. Just before serving, garnish with more fruit, if desired.
Note: You may wish to use 2 cups whipped topping instead of whipping cream.

Be creative and choose the crust you would like with filling of your choice!

You may press 1/4 cup of finely chopped nuts into most any crust before baking, if desired.

With the recipes that follow, you can make your own crust for immediate use, or place in freezer for later use. If using a crust from the freezer that you have previously made, allow to thaw and place on lightly floured surface to roll out. With rolling pin, roll to about 12-inch diameter, rolling from center out. Loosely roll onto rolling pin and gently unroll into 9-inch pie plate, avoiding stretching pastry. Trim to 1/2 inch beyond edge of pie plate and turn under, building up edge. You may flute edge or shape as desired. If filling and crust are to be baked, it is not necessary to prick the crust. If crust is to be filled with pre-cooked filling, prick with fork. Bake as directed in individual recipes.

For a pre-baked crust, keep filling from soaking into crust by basting it with slightly beaten egg white before baking.

Pie Crusts (2)   (Using boiling water)

1 cup Crisco
1/2 cup boiling water

3 cups plain flour
1/2 teaspoon salt

Melt Crisco in water. Lightly work in flour and salt. Roll out.

Pie Crusts (2)

2 1/2 cups all-purpose flour
1 scant cup cold butter (or Crisco),
   cut into tablespoons

1/2 teaspoon salt
1 teaspoon sugar
1/4-1/2 cup cold water

With pastry blender, cut together dry ingredients with cold butter. Sprinkle 1 tablespoon water at the time onto dry ingredients, tossing lightly with a fork to side of bowl as it sticks together. Use just enough water to make it all stick. Divide into 2 parts. Never wad pastry. Divide in half and pour onto two pieces of plastic wrap. Holding plastic wrap, gently shape into about 5-inch flat rounds. Cover well with plastic wrap and refrigerate until chilled, or freeze until needed.

Cocoa Pastry (2 Crusts): Prepare as above except add 4 tablespoons cocoa powder and increase sugar to 4 tablespoons in dry ingredients. Cut all ingredients in half if you only need 1 crust.

Basic Two-Way Pastry

1/2 cup sugar
1/4 teaspoon salt
3/4 cup butter or margarine, room
   temperature

2 egg yolks
1/2 teaspoon vanilla extract
2 cups all-purpose flour
Grated peel of 1 lemon (optional)

Mix above ingredients, being careful not to over-mix. Roll out. Makes 1 (9-inch) tart, or pie with top crust; 2 pastry shells; 12 individual shells, or **French Jelly Cookies.** To make cookies, indent center of each cookie and fill with stiff jelly or preserves. Bake at 350 degrees until very lightly browned.

Basic Pastry (with egg)

1 1/2 cups all-purpose flour
1 teaspoon salt
1/3 cup chilled butter or margarine,
   cut into pieces

1 large egg
2-3 tablespoons ice water, as needed

Mix together flour and salt; cut butter into mixture with pastry blender until coarse crumbs form. Beat together egg and water; add to flour mixture, mixing lightly until a soft dough forms. Shape into a disk; wrap in plastic wrap and chill 1 hour or until ready to use. It may be frozen at this point to use later, if desired.

Expectations: We set those. The average person uses only 10-15% of their brain power. However well you think you can do, you can do even better.

Chocolate Crunch Pie Crust:

In heavy saucepan over low heat, melt 1/3 cup margarine and 1 (6-ounce) package semi-sweet chocolate chips; remove from heat. Gently stir in 2 1/2 cups Rice Crispy cereal until completely coated. Press onto bottom and sides of margarine greased 9-inch pie plate. Chill 1 hour. Especially delicious for chiffon and ice cream pies! **Suggestion:** If you like a thinner crust, divide into 2 pie plates and freeze one for later use. However, that crust is so good thick!

Vanilla or Chocolate Crumb Crust for 1 Pie: 1 1/2 cups vanilla wafer crumbs (about 45 wafers), 1/2 cup powdered sugar; (optional), 1/3 cup cocoa, 1/3 cup melted butter or margarine. Mix and press mixture into 9-inch pan. (Omit cocoa for vanilla crumb crust.)

Coconut Pie Crust (1): 1/2 cup butter, melted; 7-ounce package flaked coconut, 2 tablespoons flour, 1/2 cup pecans; chopped, (optional). Combine and press into pie plate firmly. Bake at 350 degrees about 10 minutes, just until edges are light brown. Especially good for chiffon or ice cream pies.

Cornflake Pie Crust (1): 2 cups crushed corn flakes, and 1/4 cup margarine. (Use a little more margarine if you have to.) Combine and press into 9-inch pie plate. Bake in 350 degree oven until lightly browned, about 13 minutes. (Low calorie) Note: For appropriate fillings, try adding 1 cup coconut!

Gingersnap Pie Crust (1): 1 1/2 cups crushed gingersnap cookies, 1/3 cup butter or margarine, melted; 1/2 cup chopped pecans, (optional). Combine and press into pie plate. Bake at 350 degrees 8 to 10 minutes.

Pecan Crust (1): 2 cups coarsely chopped pecans, 1/3 cup firmly packed brown sugar, 3 tablespoons melted butter or margarine, 2 tablespoons coffee liqueur (optional). Combine. Press firmly onto bottom and up sides of 9-inch pie plate. Bake at 350 degrees for about 10 to 12 minutes, being careful not to over cook. Gently press sides of crust with back of a spoon. Cool.

Graham Cracker-Almond Crust: Combine 1 cup Graham cracker crumbs, 1/2 cup ground or finely chopped almonds, 2 tablespoons sugar, 1/4 cup melted butter or margarine and 1/2 teaspoon almond extract. Press onto bottom and sides of 9-inch pie plate. Chill.

Banana Cream - White Chocolate Pie
(This is a very special pie, and easy.)

1 (9-inch) pie crust, baked
1 ripe banana, sliced
1 tablespoon lemon juice
1/2 cup chopped walnuts or pecans, divided
1 (3-ounce) box instant vanilla pudding mix

1 (12-ounce) can evaporated milk, chilled
2/3 cup grated or finely chopped white chocolate, divided (this will take 2 ounces, or 2 squares to make 2/3 cup)
1 (8-ounce) carton frozen whipped topping

Dip banana slices in lemon juice and arrange slices in bottom of baked pie crust. Sprinkle with 1/4 cup chopped nuts. In medium bowl, whisk together pudding mix and evaporated milk. Fold in about 1 cup of the whipped topping. Pour over bananas. In small bowl, gently fold 1/3 cup white chocolate into remaining whipped topping. Spread over pudding. Sprinkle with remaining 1/3 cup white chocolate and 1/4 cup chopped nuts. Refrigerate at least 1 hour before serving. You may wish to use sugar-free, fat-free products when possible.

Relationships: We need one another. Synergy is separate sources of energy. The sum total is greater. All relationships needed: Our God, our Creator (through Him healing that cannot be quantified); with others; with self. We control these aspects in our lives.

Banana Sunday Pie (Makes 2 pies)

2 lemons, juiced
1 can sweetened condensed milk
1 (20-ounce) can crushed pineapple,
  well drained
1 large banana, chopped

3/4 cup flaked coconut, divided
1 small jar maraschino cherries, divided
1 (12-ounce) carton Cool Whip
2 pastry shells of your choice

Mix lemon juice and milk. Stir until thick. Add all other ingredients, saving a little coconut and a few cherries for garnish. Pour into graham cracker crust or crust of your choice. Refrigerate for several hours before serving.

Blueberry and Lemon Curd Pie

1 1/2 cups heavy cream, or
  3 cups Cool Whip
1 9-inch prebaked pie crust
1 pint blueberries

2 cups lemon curd (recipe follows or
  can be purchased)
Lemon Curd (recipe follows)

Whip the cream and set aside. Fill the prebaked pie crust with the blueberries. Mix the lemon curd with the whipped cream and top the blueberries with the mixture. Serve within a few hours, or freeze. (Nice for tart shells, also.)

Lemon Curd:
1/2 cup butter
1 3/4 cups sugar
Grated rind of 2 lemons

1/2 cup lemon juice
6 eggs, beaten

In double boiler melt butter over simmering water. Stir in sugar, rind and juice. Blend in eggs and cook until very thick. Stir constantly. Pour into bowl and chill. Use in above Blueberry Lemon Pie; serve as spread for toast, or use as filling for small tarts. Makes 3 cups. Add just 2 cups to whipped cream and see if you would like more tartness before adding the other cup.

Cappuccino Pie
(Sugar-free and delicious!)

2 teaspoons unflavored gelatin
1/3 cup cold water
4 teaspoons instant coffee
1 1/2 cups cold milk, (fat-free is fine)
1 package (4 serving size)
   chocolate flavor sugar-free,
   instant pudding mix

1/2 teaspoon ground cinnamon
1 (8-ounce) carton whipped topping,
   divided
Pie crust of your choice

Sprinkle gelatin over cold water; allow to sit to dissolve for a minute. Place in microwave and heat to just below boiling; add instant coffee and stir. Allow to come to room temperature. In medium bowl combine 1st mixture with milk; whisk in pudding mix and cinnamon. When thickened, gently stir in 1/2 whipped topping; pour into pie crust and refrigerate until ready to serve. Slice into 8 servings and top each serving with a dollop of whipped topping and a little grated chocolate or cherry. Serves 8.

Chocolate Angel Pie

3 egg whites
Dash of salt
3/4 cup sugar
3/4 cup fine chocolate crumbs
   (chocolate wafers)

1/2 cup chopped pecans or walnuts
1/2 teaspoon vanilla extract
1/2 pint whipping cream, whipped or
   frozen whipped topping, thawed
Garnish: Shaved chocolate

Beat egg whites with salt until stiff, slowly adding sugar. Fold in crumbs, nuts and vanilla. Spread in a well-buttered 9-inch pie plate. Bake at 325 degrees for 35 minutes. Cool and let stand for several hours. Spread with topping; garnish with shaved chocolate.

On cream pies, you may skip the meringue and top with whipped cream or purchased whipped topping, if desired. Refrigerate meringue-topped cream pies after 1 hour of cooling. Cool on a wire rack. Cover and chill to store.

Chocolate Cream Pie

1 cup sugar
3 tablespoons cocoa
Dash of salt
5 tablespoons cornstarch or
    1/2 cup flour
3 eggs, separated

3 cups milk
1 tablespoon margarine or butter
1 1/2 teaspoons vanilla extract
Meringue (recipe follows)

Combine sugar, cocoa, salt and cornstarch or flour; add egg yolks and beat well, blending in milk. Cook on medium high heat, stirring constantly until it bubbles. Continue cooking for about 4 minutes, reducing heat if necessary, until mixture has thickened. Stir in margarine or butter and vanilla. Pour the hot filling into baked pie shell. Spread meringue over hot filling; seal to edge. Bake in a 350 degree oven until beautifully browned. Cool on a wire rack at room temperature, then refrigerate. Serve cold or at room temperature. Serves 8.

Meringue:

3 egg whites
1/4 cup sugar
1/4 cup confectioners' sugar

1/4 teaspoon cream of tartar
1/2 teaspoon vanilla extract

Beat egg whites with a pinch of salt on medium low until frothy. Add cream of tartar and increase speed to medium high. When soft peaks form, begin adding sugar gradually. Beat until firm (but not dry) peaks form. Add vanilla and beat on high for 30 seconds. Place meringue on top of filling, making sure to seal down meringue to crust.

Hints: Dark-Chocolate Cream Pie made with chocolate squares:
Make the same as above, but omit cocoa and add 3 squares (3 ounces) unsweetened chocolate, chopped and added to milk.

Milk-Chocolate Cream Pie:
Make the same as above, **except** add 3 squares chopped milk chocolate to milk, omitting cocoa.

Coconut Cream Pie: Prepare as above, except, reduce sugar to 3/4 cup, stir in 2/3 cup flaked coconut with margarine or butter and vanilla. Sprinkle 2 tablespoons flaked coconut over meringue before baking.

Lemon Meringue Pie (Old-Fashioned)
Prepare as above, except, use 2 lemons, grated rind and juice; 1 1/4 cups hot water (or milk, if you want a creamier pie); 2 tablespoons butter or margarine and top with meringue as above.

Creamy Lemon Pie (Sugar free and no cooking.)

1 (9-inch) reduced fat Graham
   Cracker Crust
2 teaspoons Knox unflavored gelatin
1/4 cup cold water
1 (12-ounce) can non-fat evaporated
   milk

1 (1-ounce) package sugar free, fat free,
   instant vanilla pudding mix
1 1/2 teaspoons sugar free dry
   lemonade mix
1 (8-ounce) carton lite, frozen
   whipped topping, divided
1/4 teaspoon dry lemonade mix

Sprinkle 1/2 envelope Knox gelatin over 1/4 cup cold water. Allow to dissolve; heat in microwave to melt. Set aside to get to room temperature. Pour evaporated milk into medium size mixing bowl; sprinkle vanilla pudding mix over milk and whisk in. Add 1 1/2 teaspoons dry lemonade mix. Allow to thicken; fold in 4 ounces of thawed whipped topping. Pour into pie crust. Chill; slice into 8 servings. Garnish each slice with dollops of the other 4 ounces of whipped topping to which you have whisked in 1/4 teaspoon of dry lemonade mix. Add a lemon twist if you like. Refrigerate and serve with pride! They will love it, and it could not be easier!

Chocolate Hershey Pie

20 marshmallows
6 small Hershey bars
1/2 cup milk

1 cup whipping cream (whipped)
1 chocolate graham cracker crust

Combine marshmallows, Hershey bars and milk in top of double boiler. Heat until chocolate and marshmallows melt. Cool and fold in whipped cream. Pour mixture into pie crust. Refrigerate. Serve cold.

French Coconut Pie

3/4 stick melted butter or margarine
1 cup sugar
3 eggs
1 teaspoon vanilla extract

1 tablespoon fresh lemon juice
1 (3 1/2-ounce) can flaked coconut
1 (9-inch) deep-dish pie shell, thawed

Mix all ingredients together and pour into the unbaked pie shell. Bake in 350 degree oven for 45 minutes or until a knife comes out clean. This is a quick, good dessert for cool days.

Coconut Buttermilk Pie (2)

3 eggs
1 1/4 cups sugar
1 cup buttermilk
1/2 stick butter, melted

1 teaspoon vanilla extract
1 cup coconut
2 unbaked pie crusts

Mix eggs and sugar; blend in buttermilk, butter and vanilla. Stir in coconut; pour into the 2 unbaked crusts and bake in 350 degree oven until done, about 35 to 45 minutes.

Cream Cheese and Fresh Fruit Pie
(Strawberry, Peach, Blueberry - Your Choice)

1 (3-ounce) package cream cheese,
    softened
1/2 cup powdered sugar
1 (12-ounce) whipped topping, divided
3-4 cups fresh fruit, divided
1 cup water, divided

1 cup sugar
3 tablespoons cornstarch
1 (9-inch) pastry shell, baked and cooled
    (or purchased)
1/4 cup chopped pecans, pressed into
    crust, optional

Blend cream cheese and powdered sugar; add 1 cup of whipped topping and spread on pastry shell. Set aside. Simmer 1 cup fruit and 2/3 cup water about 3 minutes. Mix sugar, cornstarch and the other 1/3 cup water; add to boiling mixture. Cook until clear and thick, stirring constantly. Arrange remaining well-drained fruit in pie shell, reserving about 1/2 cup for garnish, if desired. Pour cooked fruit glaze over all. Cool until firm and top with sweetened whipped cream or prepared topping.

Let the attitude of life be a continual "going out" in dependence upon God, and your life will have an ineffable charm about it which is a satisfaction to Jesus.

Making Custard Pies:

To avoid spills, you might like to place pie shell on the oven rack before adding the filling. To check for doneness, gently shake the pie. If liquid area in center is smaller than a quarter, the pie is done. The filling will continue to set after you remove pie from oven. After pie cools, cover and refrigerate. Cover and chill leftovers.

Egg Custard Pie (2)

1 1/2 cups sugar
1/4 pound butter or margarine (1 stick)
4 tablespoons cornstarch
4 eggs
2 1/2 cups milk

1 teaspoon vanilla extract
1 teaspoon nutmeg
Pinch of salt
2 unbaked pie shells

Cream sugar, butter and cornstarch. Add eggs one at a time, mixing well. Add milk, vanilla, nutmeg and salt. If you prefer, you may sprinkle nutmeg on top rather than including it in the filling. Mix. Bake in 2 unbaked pie crusts in 425 degree oven for 15 minutes. Turn oven down to 325 degrees and bake 20 minutes longer. Cool and serve.

Egg Custard (Crustless) Pie (2)

4 eggs
1 1/2 cups sugar
3 tablespoons self-rising flour

6 tablespoons butter or margarine
1 large can evaporated milk
2 teaspoons vanilla extract

Cream together eggs and sugar. Add remaining ingredients and beat well. Pour into lightly greased 10-inch pie plate. Bake at 400 degrees for 25 to 30 minutes or until done. Cool and serve.

Lemon Chess Pie (1)

Pastry for single-crust pie
4 eggs
1 1/2 cups sugar
1/4 cup margarine or butter, melted

2 teaspoons finely shredded lemon peel
2 tablespoons lemon juice
1 tablespoon cornmeal
1 1/2 teaspoons vanilla extract

Line bottom of pastry-lined 9-inch pie plate with a double thickness of foil. Bake in a 450 degree oven for 5 minutes. Remove foil. Bake for 5 minutes more. Set aside. Beat eggs lightly until combined. Stir in sugar, margarine, peel, lemon juice, cornmeal, and vanilla. Mix well. Place pastry shell on oven rack. Pour filling into shell. Cover edge of pie with foil. Bake in 350 degree oven for 20 minutes. Remove foil. Bake for 15 to 20 minutes more or until a knife inserted near the center comes out clean. Cool on a rack. Cover and chill to store. Serves 8.

Dee's Lemon Pie
(Quick, easy and delicious!)

1 (1-ounce) sugar free lemon Jell-O or
    with sugar, if you prefer
3/4 cup boiling water
1 tablespoon Real lemon, or fresh
    lemon juice

1 (8-ounce) carton Cool Whip
1 purchased graham cracker or
    chocolate crust

Dissolve Jell-O in boiling water. Set aside to get to room temperature. To whipped topping, add cooled Jell-O mixture and Real lemon or fresh lemon juice and mix well. (If you would like it more tart, add 1 teaspoon dry lemonade mix.) Pour into ready-prepared crust. Chill, slice into 8 servings; garnish with additional whipped topping in dollops on each serving. (You may add 1/4 teaspoon dry lemonade mix in topping for garnish and a thin twist of lemon on each serving, if you like.) Delicious!

Note: Lime Jell-O is good and you might like to try other flavors.

🌿 *Never run before God's guidance. Whenever there is doubt - don't!*

Lime Pie - No Bake

1 cup granulated sugar
1/4 cup cornstarch
1 1/4 cups milk
Yolks from 3 large eggs
2/3 cup fresh lime juice
(from 2 to 3 large limes)
1/2 stick (4 tablespoons) butter or
margarine

2 teaspoons finely grated fresh lime peel
1 cup sour cream
1 ready-to-fill graham-cracker crust
(save lid)
Garnish: sweetened whipped cream and
thin lime twists

Mix sugar and cornstarch in a medium-size saucepan. Whisk in milk until smooth, then yolks until blended. Stir in lime juice. Add butter and whisk constantly over medium heat 7 to 9 minutes, just until boiling. Remove from heat and stir 1 minute longer. Stir in lime peel until blended. Cover surface with plastic wrap to keep a skin from forming and refrigerate until cool, about 1 hour. Gently whisk in sour cream until well blended. Pour into pie shell. Cover with reserved plastic lid and refrigerate at least 6 hours until set, or up to 2 days. Shortly before serving, garnish with whipped cream and lime twists. Serves 8.

Peanut Butter Pie

Chocolate-Crunch Pie Crust:
1/3 cup margarine
1 (6-ounce) package semi-sweet
chocolate chips

2 1/2 cups Rice Krispies Cereal
1/4 cup finely chopped roasted peanuts
(optional)

In heavy saucepan over low heat, melt margarine and chocolate chips; remove from heat. Gently stir in rice cereal and peanuts until completely coated. Press into bottom and sides of a greased 9-inch pie plate. Chill 1 hour.

Filling:
1 (8-ounce) package cream cheese,
softened
1 (14-ounce) can sweetened condensed
milk
3/4 cup crunchy peanut butter
3 tablespoons lemon juice

1 teaspoon vanilla extract
3/4 cup finely chopped roasted peanuts,
divided (optional)
1 (8-ounce) carton whipped topping
1-2 teaspoons chocolate syrup

In large bowl beat cream cheese until fluffy; beat in condensed milk and peanut butter until smooth. Stir in lemon juice, vanilla and 1/2 cup of roasted nuts. Fold in whipped topping. Pour into crust. Drizzle syrup over top of pie and swirl with spoon. Top with the remaining 1/4 cup of roasted peanuts (optional.) Chill 4 to 6 hours.

Pecan - Angel Pie

3 egg whites
1 cup sugar
1 cup vanilla wafer crumbs

1 cup pecans, chopped
1 teaspoon vanilla extract
Topping (recipe follows)

Beat egg whites until stiff; mixing in sugar. Combine crumbs and pecans; fold into meringues. Fold in vanilla. Place in 9-inch pie plate covering bottom and sides. Bake for 30 minutes in 350 degree oven. Cool completely.

Topping:

1 cup whipping cream
2 tablespoons sugar
1 teaspoon vanilla extract

1/4 teaspoon almond extract
1/4 cup broken pecan pieces

Whip cream, gradually adding sugar, vanilla and almond extracts until peaks form. Spoon into cooked meringue shell. Sprinkle top with broken pecan pieces. Refrigerate.

Pecan Pie

1 cup sugar
3/4 cup light Karo Syrup
1 stick butter
3 beaten eggs

2 1/2 cups pecans, chopped
1 teaspoon vanilla extract
2 9-inch unbaked pie shells

Mix first three ingredients over heat and bring to a boil. Take off heat; combine next three ingredients. Pour small amount of hot mixture into egg mixture, stirring fast as you do this; then completely combine mixtures. Divide mixture into 2 (9-inch) unbaked pie shells. Bake at 350 degrees for about 40 minutes or until set. The different thing about this pecan pie is the method of combination of ingredients. It is different from most recipes, and many people seem to like it better. Serve topped with whipped cream or ice cream, if desired. Shared with me by a friend who makes such good ones! Delicious!

Praline Pecan Topping for Pecan, Pumpkin or Butternut Squash Pie

1/4 cup firmly packed brown sugar   2/3 cup pecan halves

Just before serving pie, sprinkle brown sugar and nuts on top, Broil until sugar melts and caramelizes, about 1 minute. Watch carefully not to burn. Let cool on rack. Serve warm or at room temperature. Top with whipped cream, if desired.

Praline Pie

1 (9- to 10-inch) deep dish frozen
   pie shell
2/3 cup margarine
2/3 cup light brown sugar, firmly packed
1 cup chopped nuts

1 (5.1-ounce) package instant
   vanilla pudding
2 cups milk
1 1/3 cups whipped topping, thawed
1/2 teaspoon vanilla

Bake pie shell in a 400 degree oven for 5 to 7 minutes, or until lightly browned. Combine margarine, sugar and nuts in a sauce pan and cook over low heat until sugar is melted. Pour into pie shell and bake in 450 degree oven for 5 minutes or until bubbly. Set aside and cool. Mix pudding mix with milk. Spread half over cooled praline mixture. Combine whipped topping with remaining pudding and vanilla extract. Spread over top of pie. Sprinkle with extra chopped pecans that have been lightly toasted, if desired. Cover and chill before serving. Yield: 8 to 10 slices. Delicious!

The Word of God is the abiding Reality. The abiding Reality is redemption.

Pumpkin Pie (2)

1 stick margarine, melted
1 cup pumpkin
1 cup sugar
2 tablespoons flour

3 eggs, slightly beaten
1 (12-ounce) can evaporated milk
1 teaspoon vanilla extract
2 unbaked pie shells

Topping:
1/2 cup sugar

1 1/2 teaspoons nutmeg

Combine melted margarine and pumpkin. Mix sugar and flour and add to pumpkin mixture; blend in eggs, milk and vanilla. Pour into two 9-inch pie shells. Bake in a 350 degree oven for 30 minutes. Remove from oven and let sit 15 to 20 minutes; sprinkle with topping mixture of sugar and nutmeg. Place under broiler just until sugar melts. This adds texture as well as a mild spice flavor.

Pumpkin Chiffon Pie with Ginger Snap Crust

36 marshmallows
2 cups pumpkin, cooked and mashed,
   or canned

1 teaspoon pumpkin pie spice, or
   3/4 teaspoon ground cinnamon
   and 1/4 teaspoon ground nutmeg
1 1/2 cups cream, whipped or
   3 cups whipped topping
Ginger Snap Crust (recipe follows)

Make and bake crust. Melt marshmallows in double boiler; blend in pumpkin and spice. Allow to cool thoroughly. Fold in about 1/2 of the whipped cream and pour into cooled crust. Top with remainder of whipped cream.

Ginger Snap Crust:
1 cup nuts, (walnuts or pecans),
   chopped

1 1/2 cups crushed Ginger Snaps
1/3 cup margarine or butter, melted

Combine ingredients and blend well. Spray 9-inch pie plate with vegetable spray and press crumb mixture against bottom and sides. Bake in 350 degree oven 8 to 10 minutes or until very lightly browned.

Strawberry Pie

1 prebaked pie crust of your choice
1 pint fresh strawberries
1 cup sugar
3 tablespoons cornstarch
1 cup water

3 tablespoons strawberry Jell-O
5 drops red food coloring
Frozen topping (thawed) or
  whipped cream

Stem, wash and slice strawberries. Set aside. In saucepan combine next 5 ingredients; boil 1 minute. Cool. Add strawberries to pie shell and pour Jell-O mixture over them. Refrigerate until set. When ready to serve, add desired topping. You may double recipe if you need two pies. Two pies require the whole package of Jell-O.

Sweet Potato Pie (Creamy)

1 (9-inch) unbaked pie shell
2 cups mashed sweet potatoes
1 (14-ounce) can sweetened
  condensed milk
2 eggs
1 teaspoon ground cinnamon

1/2 teaspoon salt
1/2 teaspoon ground ginger
1/2 teaspoon ground nutmeg
1 cup whipped cream for garnish
1/4 cup toasted, sliced almonds for garnish

Preheat oven to 425 degrees. In a large bowl, combine the potatoes, milk, eggs, cinnamon, salt, ginger and nutmeg. Mix well and pour into the pie shell. Bake at 425 degrees for 15 minutes. Reduce to 350 degrees and bake 35 to 50 minutes, or until a knife comes out clean. Cool on wire rack and refrigerate. Garnish with whipped cream and almonds before cutting.

There needs to be space in every family for each personality to bloom.

Most cheesecakes taste better if they have aged a day before serving. If they have a topping, make it the day after you make the cake, or on the day you plan to serve it. Most cheesecakes freeze beautifully without the topping. If previously frozen thaw in the refrigerator before adding the topping.

Beat the Heat Cheesecake - No Eggs

2 envelopes Knox gelatin
3/4 cup sugar, divided
1 cup boiling water
1 (8-ounce) cup cottage cheese,
   creamed
2 (8-ounce) packages cream cheese,
   softened

1 cup (1/2 pint) whipping cream
1 tablespoon vanilla extract
1 tablespoon fresh grated lemon peel
Graham Cracker-Almond Crust
   (recipe follows)

In a large bowl, mix gelatin with 1/4 cup sugar; add boiling water and stir until dissolved. Beating well with mixer, add remaining sugar, cheeses, cream, vanilla and lemon peel, one at a time and beating after each. Beat 5 more minutes until smooth. Turn into crust; chill until firm. Garnish with desired fruit, and almonds. Makes 12 servings.

Graham Cracker-Almond Crust:
1 cup graham cracker crumbs
1/2 cup almonds, ground or
   chopped fine

2 tablespoons sugar
1/4 cup butter or margarine, melted
1/2 teaspoon almond flavoring

Press onto bottom and sides of 9-inch springform pan; chill.

Chocolate Cloud Pie

1 (8-ounce) package cream cheese,
  softened (Neufchâtel or fat free)
1 cup confectioners' sugar
2 teaspoons vanilla extract
1/2 cup unsweetened cocoa
1/4 cup milk

1 (8-ounce) carton Lite Cool Whip
1 (6-ounce) purchased Quick Crust,
  chocolate flavored
Kahlúa (optional)
Maraschino cherries, optional
Toasted pecans, optional

In large bowl, using an electric mixer, beat cream cheese, sugar and vanilla until well-blended. Add cocoa alternately with milk, beating until smooth. Gradually add 1 cup of the Cool Whip, mixing well; fold in remaining Cool Whip. Spoon into crust. Cover; refrigerate 6 hours or until firm; slice into 8 slices. A suggested garnish is a dollop of cool whip on each slice, topped with a cherry, toasted pecans sprinkled all over pie, and drizzled with 3 teaspoons Kahlúa. This makes a yummy, real thick, pretty pie, and it cuts out perfectly.

Note: This is also nice served in sherbet dishes, without the crust, and attractively garnished.

Flight from temptation is often the only effective way to deal with it.

Lemon Cheesecake Pie
(Instant and no sugar added)

3 lemons, juice and grated rind of all
(or to taste)
1 (1-ounce) package sugar free
instant vanilla pudding mix
3/4 cup fat-free milk

1 (8-ounce) package cream cheese
(Neufchâtel)
1 (8-ounce) carton Lite Cool Whip
1 baked pie crust – your choice
(purchased Quick Crust - chocolate
flavored is good or graham cracker)

Grate rind of lemons and squeeze juice. Mix pudding mix with 3/4 cup fat-free
milk, beating just to combine. Add cream cheese, lemon juice and rind, quickly
beating to smooth consistency. Add small amount of Cool Whip, continuing to beat;
fold in remaining Cool Whip. Pour into crust. Garnish with remaining topping, putting a dollop on each serving, topped with a little grated rind or a thin lemon twist.

Variation: Kahlúa Cheesecake Pie

1 (1.4-ounce) package sugar-free
instant chocolate pudding mix
3/4 cup fat-free milk
1 (8-ounce) package cream cheese
(Neufchâtel)

2 tablespoons instant coffee, dissolved
in 1 tablespoon boiling water
3 tablespoons Kahlúa
3 cups Lite Cool Whip
1/2 cup chopped, toasted, almonds
or pecans

Mix as above; of course, omitting lemon juice and rind, and adding instant coffee
dissolved in boiling water and Kahlúa. Add 3 cups whipped topping as above.
Pour into purchased chocolate crust and refrigerate to thoroughly chill. Makes
8 servings. Garnish with additional whipped topping and toasted nuts, topped with
Maraschino cherry. Serve with pride!

🌿*Spiritual disciplines are God's way of cultivating
our lives.*

Lemon Cheesecake - Light and No Sugar Added
(2 pies or 9x13-inch dish)

Graham Cracker Crusts or following recipe:

2 cups plain flour
1 1/2 sticks margarine, melted

1 teaspoon vanilla extract
1/2 cup pecans, chopped, optional

Combine flour, margarine and vanilla. Press with fingers into 9x13-inch baking dish or 2 (9-inch) pie plates. Press nuts into crusts, if desired. Bake at 350 degrees 20 to 25 minutes or until lightly browned.

Filling:

1/3 cup boiling water
1 package sugar and fat free lemon Jell-O
1/4 cup cold water
1 package Knox gelatin
2 (8-ounce) packages cream cheese, softened

2 (1-ounce) packages sugar free, fat free, vanilla pudding (instant)
4 lemons, juice of 4, rind of 3 (save some rind for garnish)
1 (12-ounce) carton Lite Cool Whip

Dissolve Jell-O in boiling water. Sprinkle gelatin over cold water. Stir Knox gelatin mixture into hot Jell-O mixture. Set aside. Blend gelatin mixtures and cream cheese until smooth; adding lemon juice and rind. Mix pudding mix according to directions on box, but beat only 1 minute. Combine cream cheese and pudding mixtures; (adding just a little of pudding mixture into cream cheese and beating, then combine the two), beating only 1 minute. Pour into cooled crust. Let stand 5 minutes. Top with Cool Whip and garnish with reserved grated lemon rind or toasted chopped pecans. Refrigerate. This has been a favorite with many people!

Righteousness is a gift from God; we only provide the right conditions.

Piña Colada Cheesecake

Crust:

1 3/4 cups graham cracker crumbs
3 tablespoons butter, melted

2 tablespoons granulated sugar

Preheat the oven to 350 degrees. Spray a 9-inch springform pan with nonstick cooking spray (Baker's Joy). In a medium bowl, combine crumbs, butter and sugar; mix well. Press crumbs over the bottom and partway up the side of pan. Chill.

Filling:

20 ounces cream cheese, softened
3/4 cup granulated sugar
1 1/2 teaspoons vanilla extract
3 eggs

2 egg yolks
1/2 cup half-and-half or evaporated milk
3 1/2 tablespoons light rum
1 1/3 cups toasted coconut

Beat cream cheese, sugar and vanilla in a large bowl of electric mixer until light and very smooth. Add eggs and yolks one at a time, beating just to blend after each addition. Blend in the half-and-half; stir in rum and coconut. Pour batter into prepared crust. Bake until top of cake is dry to touch, about 40 to 50 minutes. The center will still wiggle a bit. Cool at room temperature for an hour; then chill.

Topping:

1 (20-ounce) can crushed pineapple,
    in juice
Canned pineapple juice

2 tablespoons cornstarch
1/4 cup granulated sugar, optional

Drain the pineapple, reserving juice. Add enough canned pineapple juice to make 1 cup liquid. Blend the cornstarch into the cool juice. Add the drained pineapple, the juice/cornstarch mixture and sugar, (if using sugar), to a saucepan and heat until the mixture bubbles and looks clear. Chill until thick; spread on cheesecake.

Joy is a quality found that has not been sought after.

Pumpkin Swirl Cheesecake

2 cups graham cracker crumbs
1/4 cup margarine, melted
2 (8-ounce) packages cream cheese
3/4 cup sugar, divided
1 teaspoon vanilla extract

3 eggs
1 cup canned pumpkin
3/4 teaspoon cinnamon
1/4 teaspoon ground nutmeg

Combine crumbs and margarine; press onto bottom and sides of 9-inch springform pan. Combine cheese, 1/2 cup sugar and vanilla, mixing at medium speed until well blended. Add eggs, 1 at a time, mixing well. Reserve 1 cup cheese mixture. Add pumpkin, remaining sugar and spices to remaining cheese mixture. Mix well. Layer half pumpkin mixture and half cheese mixture over crust; repeat layers. Cut through batter with knife several times for marble effect. Bake at 350 degrees 55 minutes. Loosen cake from rim of pan; cool before removing rim. Chill. Makes 10 to 12 servings.

Worship of God is both giving and receiving – anytime – any place. It is total involvement with Him in mind and spirit, and results in understanding and communication beyond our human capacity.

I AM

I was regretting the
    past,
Fearing the future
Then . . .
    suddenly . . .
My Lord was
    speaking.
My name is
I AM.

He paused.
I waited.
He continued.
When you live in
    the past
With its mistakes
    and regrets,
It is hard.
I AM

Not there.
My name is not
I WAS

When you live in
    the future

With its problems
    and fears,
It is hard.
I AM

Not there.
My name is not
I WILL BE.

When you live in
    this moment,
It is not hard.

I AM
    Here.
My name is
I AM

By: Helen Mallicoate

Hot Fruit

Apple-Cheese Casserole
(or Pear-Cheese Casserole)

1 stick margarine
1 cup sugar
1/2 pound Velveeta cheese, grated
3/4 cup all-purpose flour

1 can **sliced apples** (not apple pie filling) or about that amount of fresh pears

Cream margarine and sugar. Add cheese; blend, and add flour, mixing well. Place apples (or pears) in buttered casserole dish; cover completely with cheese mixture. Bake at 350 degrees for 30 to 45 minutes. Watch carefully when it begins to brown on top; do not over-cook.

Autumn Fruit Compote

1 cup apple juice
1/2 teaspoon cinnamon
4 teaspoons light brown sugar

8 ounces dried apricots
8 ounces dried prunes

Heat apple juice, cinnamon and sugar; add apricots and prunes. Simmer until fruit has plumped. Serve in compotes topped with whipped cream. Elegant! Wonderful for brunch or as a light dessert.

Cranberry-Apple Casserole

3 cups red apples, sliced or chopped,
     but unpeeled
2 cups raw cranberries
1 1/4 cups granulated sugar

1 tablespoon lemon juice
1/4 teaspoon salt
Topping (recipe follows)

Place fruit in 9x13-inch casserole; sprinkle with sugar, lemon juice and salt.

Topping:
1/2 cup brown sugar
1/3 cup flour
1/2 cup margarine, melted
1 egg yolk

1 teaspoon vanilla extract
1 1/2 cups quick oats
1/3-1/2 cup pecans, chopped

Combine brown sugar and flour; blend in melted margarine, egg yolk and vanilla. Add oats and pecans and crumble on top of fruit. Bake at 350 degrees for 30 to 45 minutes or until bubbly hot and light brown.

Cranberries Baked with Port

1 (12-ounce) bag fresh cranberries
1 cup brown sugar
2 tablespoons orange juice

Finely grated rind of 1 orange
1/4 cup port

Preheat oven to 300 degrees. In a large baking dish combine the cranberries, brown sugar, orange juice and grated orange rind; cover and bake 1 hour. Stir in the port, cover and allow to cool. Serve warm or at room temperature.

Fruit Melange

1 (10-ounce) jar orange marmalade
1/3 cup water
1/4 cup orange flavored liqueur
1 (20-ounce) can pineapple chunks,
    drained

1 (17-ounce) can apricot halves, drained
1 (6-ounce) jar maraschino cherries,
    drained
1 cup pitted prunes
1/2 cup flaked coconut

Combine first 3 ingredients in a 2 quart baking dish; blend well. Add pineapple chunks and remaining ingredients; stir. Microwave at medium-high (70% power) 8 to 9 minutes or until thoroughly heated, stirring after 4 minutes. Serve warm. Yield 8 servings.

Hot Caramel Fruit

2 (20-ounce) cans Elberta peaches
1 (pound) can dark sweet
    pitted cherries
1 (11-ounce) package dried apricots
Juice from 1/2 orange
Juice from 1/2 lemon

1/4 teaspoon finely grated orange rind
1/4 teaspoon finely grated lemon rind
1 cup firmly packed brown sugar
12 pitted dates
12 walnut halves

Drain peaches and cherries separately; reserve peach juice. Mix all other ingredients except dates and walnuts; stir in peach juice and turn into buttered baking dish and bake uncovered for 1 1/2 hours at 325 degrees, basting several times. While fruit bakes, stuff about 12 dates with walnut halves. About 15 minutes before fruit is done, arrange dates around the casserole; baste with syrup in bottom of baking dish and allow to finish baking. Yield about 10 to 12 servings. Double the recipe for a party of about 20.

Hot Fruit Casserole

1 can apple sauce
1 large can peaches or apricots
1 large can pears
1 large can chunk pineapple

3/4 cup brown sugar
1/3 cup margarine
1 teaspoon ginger
1 teaspoon cinnamon

Drain fruit; cut into pieces of desired size (not small). Combine brown sugar, margarine and spices on low heat and pour over fruit. Bake at 350 degrees for 30 minutes or until syrup bubbles. Serve warm.

Pineapple-Cheese Casserole

2 (20-ounce) cans chunk pineapple
1 cup sugar
6 tablespoons all-purpose flour

2 cups sharp cheddar cheese, grated
1 stick melted margarine, divided
1 sleeve Ritz crackers

Drain pineapple and save 6 tablespoons of juice; combine with sugar and flour. Add cheese, pineapple and 1/2 stick melted butter. Top with crackers; drizzle remainder of melted butter over crackers. Bake for 30 minutes at 350 degrees. This is especially good with pork.

Sautéed Pears with Raisins and Rum

4-6 large firm-ripe pears
1-2 tablespoons butter
2 tablespoons brown sugar
   (more if pears or not sweet)

1/2 cup raisins or currants
2-3 tablespoons rum, brandy
   or lemon juice

Core, peel and quarter the pears, then cut them into 1/4-inch slices. Melt 1 tablespoon butter in a large non-stick skillet over medium-high heat. Add the pears and sprinkle with sugar. Sauté, stirring constantly until pears begin to get tender, 2 or 3 minutes. Add the raisins and sauté for another couple of minutes to heat them through and continue to cook. Remove skillet from the heat, stir in rum, brandy or lemon juice and swirl in remaining 1 tablespoon butter to finish the flavor. Serve warm.

Sherried Fruit Compote

1 (12-ounce) box pitted prunes
1 (6-ounce) package dried apricots
1 (20-ounce) can pineapple chunks,
   undrained

1 (11-ounce) can Mandarin orange
   slices, undrained
1 (21-ounce) can cherry pie filling
1/2 cup cooking sherry

Place prunes and apricots in a 2 quart oblong baking dish. Combine remaining ingredients and pour over dried fruit. Bake in a 350 degree oven, uncovered, for 1 hour. Serve as a side dish for breakfast, lunch or dinner.

I believe true wealth is found in relationships. Picture the cross. The highest vertical point represents your relationship with God. The horizontal points represent your relationship with your family. The lower vertical point represents your relationship with your fellowman. Paradoxically, while relationships are the source of true wealth, they also are the source of many problems.

Traits of A Healthy Family

They make time for each other.
They are skilled communicators.
They are good listeners.
They are committed to one another's
    best interest.
They have a strong religious
    orientation.
They have effective crisis coping skills.
They express affirmation and
    appreciation.
They openly express feelings. (They are
    emotionally honest.)
They have structure without rigidity.
They have have a strong sense of
    family bonding, identity and loyalty.
(Belonging)
They respect each member's
    uniqueness.
The husband/wife bond is strong,
    giving clear leadership.

Main Dishes & Meats

Beef Roast - 4 to 6 pounds - Rump, Sirloin Tip, Standing Rib
with Oven-Browned Potatoes, Beef Au Jus
(served in its own juices or gravy): 325 degree oven

If you like to use a meat thermometer:
Rare - 140 degrees
Medium - 160 degrees
Well-done - 170 degrees

For accurate temperature reading, insert thermometer into thickest portion of the meat. Or, if not using thermometer, cook roast about 30 minutes per pound for medium well-done roast. The new instant-read thermometers are nice.

You may cook roast on grill or in oven. Place roast of desired size and cut on rack in roasting pan, fat side up - but trim off as much fat as possible. (It is very helpful to cover pan and rack with foil, for easy clean up; making slits in foil on rack.) Roast for desired doneness.

If desired, prepare oven-browned potatoes. Peel and quarter 5 medium potatoes (or as many as you need). Cook in boiling, salted water for 10 minutes. Drain. About 30 to 40 minutes before the roast is done, (or when the thermometer is at about 100 degrees), add 1/2 cup of water, and arrange the potatoes around the roast, turning to coat.

When meat has cooked to desired doneness, remove meat from pan. Cover with foil and let stand 15 minutes before carving. Remove potatoes to serving dish, (keeping warm), adding roast later.

After removing roast and potatoes from pan, remove pan drippings; skim fat, or put in freezer allowing fat to rise, to be more successfully removed. Add 2 cups of boiling water to pan, stirring and scraping crusty bits from bottom. Add pan drippings and 3 teaspoons instant beef bouillon (1 1/2 teaspoons per cup of water). If you would like it a deeper brown, add a little Kitchen Bouquet. Season to taste. Also, if you like your gravy thickened a little, add 1/4 cup flour dissolved in small amount of the gravy and then added to pan, simmering to thicken. If your family likes lots of gravy, add water to drippings from roast to make as much gravy as you like. Add 1 1/2 teaspoon instant beef bouillon per cup of liquid. Place a tablespoon of flour for each cup of liquid, plus 1 more, into large non-stick frying pan. Make a roux, mixing flour with a little water until a paste is formed, pressing with spatula on bottom of pan to avoid lumps. Gradually add more water until all is added. Cook until thickened, adding Kitchen Bouquet to obtain desired color; adjust seasonings, adding more beef bouillon if desired.

Slice roast across grain; serve roast and potatoes with just a little gravy drizzled over them. Serve additional gravy on the side. A favorite!

Beef - 500-Degree Eye-of-Round
(Desired Size)

Marinade, if desired:

1 tablespoon lemon juice	1 1/2 teaspoons instant beef bouillon
2 tablespoons Worcestershire sauce	1 tablespoon brown sugar
1/2 cup soy sauce	2 cloves garlic, more if desired
1 cup water	1 can mushrooms, if desired (drained)

Combine all ingredients and marinate roast several hours, turning often, before cooking. After roast is cooked, (following directions below), remove from pan; add marinade and 1 can of mushrooms and allow to boil just a few minutes, scraping bits from pan. Wonderful gravy for serving on the side!

If you do not want to marinate:
Preheat oven to 500 degrees. Place eye-of-round in roasting pan. Cook at 500 degrees 5 minutes per pound. Turn oven off and leave in oven for about 2 hours. Remove from oven and cover with foil; let stand 15 minutes before carving. Will be deliciously pink!

Beef - Prime Rib with Horseradish Jus

1 (8- to 10-pound) beef standing rib roast	Freshly ground pepper
4 cloves garlic, minced	1/2 cup brandy, or 1/2 cup water plus 3/4 teaspoon instant beef bouillon
Salt	2 teaspoons horseradish

Have butcher French the rib bones. Rub roast all over with garlic, salt and pepper, to taste. Lightly oil roasting pan; place roast in pan and roast at 350 degrees about 1 1/2 hours, or when instant-read meat thermometer inserted in center of roast registers 140 degrees. Remove roast from oven. Place on warm serving platter. Let stand 15 to 30 minutes. Pour off fat from roasting juices and reserve juices. Over high heat, add brandy, if desired, or water and beef bouillon to roasting pan. (Ignite brandy, if using it). Swirl juices in pan while scraping. When flames die down (if using brandy), liquid should be sufficiently reduced to about 1 to 2 tablespoons. Add reduced brandy, or reduced broth to reserved roasting juices. Stir in horseradish. Carve roast at table and pour spoonful of horseradish jus over each serving.

Beef Pot Roast

1 (2 1/2- to 3-pound) beef chuck
   pot roast
2 tablespoons cooking oil
3/4 cup water, dry wine, or tomato juice
1 tablespoon Worcestershire sauce
1 teaspoon instant beef bouillon granules
1 teaspoon dried basil, crushed

Potatoes, medium or tiny new
Carrots
Onions, cut into wedges
Celery, bias-sliced into 1-inch pieces
1/4 cup flour
1/2 cup cold water

Trim fat from roast. Brown roast on all sides in hot oil; drain fat. Combine water, Worcestershire sauce, bouillon and basil. Pour over roast. Bring to boil; reduce heat. Cover and simmer for 1 hour. If using new potatoes, remove a narrow strip of peel from the center of each new potato, or peel and quarter each medium potato. Add potatoes, carrots, onions, and celery to meat. Cover; simmer 45 to 60 minutes or until tender, adding additional water if necessary. Remove meat and vegetables from pan.

For gravy:

Measure pan juices; skim fat. If necessary, add water to equal 1 1/2 cups. Combine flour and 1/2 cup cold water. Stir into juices; return to pan. Cook and stir until thickened and bubbly. Cook and stir 1 minute more. Season to taste. Makes 8 to 10 servings.

Beef - Zesty Short Ribs

2 to 4 pounds beef short ribs, cut into serving-size pieces

Sauce:

1/3 cup chili sauce
1/3 cup catsup
1/4 cup honey

3 tablespoons lemon juice
2 tablespoons prepared mustard
   or to taste

Trim off as much fat as possible from ribs. Place in large pan or Dutch oven and just cover with water. Cover and simmer 1 1/2 hours or until tender; drain. Combine sauce ingredients; baste ribs and broil 4 to 5 inches from heat for 10 to 15 minutes or until heated through. Turn often and baste. Heat remaining sauce and serve with ribs.

Beef Fajitas

1 pound beef eye of round, rump,
    sirloin tip roast, or some good cut
1 teaspoon ground cumin
1/4 teaspoon salt
1/4 teaspoon pepper

1 large clove garlic, minced
3 tablespoons vegetable oil, divided
1 large Vidalia onion, thinly sliced
1 large green bell pepper, thinly sliced

Freeze or partly freeze beef; slice into 1/4-inch thick strips, 1 inch wide and 2 inches long. Toss with cumin, salt, pepper and garlic. Heat 2 tablespoons of oil in fry pan. When hot, add beef strips; sear on both sides and remove. Add remaining oil to pan and lower heat. Saute onions and pepper until soft. Combine with beef and serve with hot flour tortillas and tomato salad.

Beef Tips on Rice

2 tablespoons shortening
2 pounds beef tips
1 (10 1/2-ounce) can beef consommé
1/3 cup Burgundy wine
2 tablespoons soy sauce
1/4 teaspoon onion salt

1/4 teaspoon garlic salt
1/4 teaspoon seasoning salt
2 tablespoons cornstarch
1/4 cup water
Hot cooked rice

Brown beef tips in shortening; stir in consommé, wine, soy sauce and salts. Heat to boiling and reduce heat. Cover and simmer for one hour, or until meat is tender. Blend corn starch and water. Stir gradually into meat mixture. Cook and stir until mixture thickens – about 2 minutes. Serve on rice.

Work hard to provide the highest quality culture and environment for your children. They deserve it.

Country-Fried Steak with Gravy

Salt
Pepper
Flour
1-2 pounds cubed steak
Oil for frying

1 (10 3/4 ounce) can cream
   of mushroom soup
1 soup can of water
1 small can mushrooms, if desired

Combine salt, pepper and flour; dredge cubed steak in mixture. At this point you may cook thoroughly on both sides, drain and serve, or just brown on both sides in oil; remove and drain. Place in oven-table bake dish. Combine soup, water and mushrooms and pour over steak (adjust liquid if necessary); cover tightly and bake in 325 degree oven for about 1 hour. Serve with rice and hot biscuits. A favorite!

Oven Beef Stew

2 pounds beef stew (cut in bite-size
   pieces and browned in skillet)
1 can mushroom soup
1 can sliced mushrooms and the liquid

1 package Lipton onion soup mix
1 cup water (adjust liquid as needed)
1/2 cup red wine

Mix all ingredients; pour into casserole and cover with lid or foil. Bake in 300 degree oven for 4 hours or until desired taste and consistency. Serve on egg noodles or rice. Just toss a salad and serve French Bread. Wonderful to serve on busy days!

Meat Loaf Glaze
(Use on meat loaf, when desired.)

1/2 cup ketchup or chili sauce
4-6 tablespoon brown sugar

2-3 teaspoons cider vinegar

Place ingredients in a small mixing bowl and blend thoroughly. Cover meat loaf before baking. Makes enough to cover a 9-inch meatloaf.

Barbecued Meat Loaves (Individual Loaves)
(This recipe has spicy seasoning in loaves.)

1 1/2 pounds ground chuck
4 slices day old bread (diced)
1/4 cup lemon juice
1/4 cup minced onion
2 teaspoons seasoned salt
   (or plain, if preferred)
1 egg, slightly beaten

1/3 cup ketchup
1/3 cup brown sugar
1 teaspoon dry mustard
1/4 teaspoon allspice
1/4 teaspoon ground cloves
6 thin lemon slices

Preheat oven to 350 degrees. In large bowl, combine meat, bread, lemon juice, onion, salt and beaten egg. Mix well and shape into 6 individual loaves. Place in 9x13-inch baking pan. Bake 15 minutes; drain off grease if there is any. In small bowl combine remaining ingredients except lemon slices. Cover loaves with sauce and top each with a lemon slice. Bake 30 minutes longer, basting occasionally with sauce from pan. These can be prepared ahead of time.

Barbecued Meat Loaf with Rudy's
Sage Sausage, and Sauce

1 1/2 pounds ground chuck (lean)
1/2 pound Rudy's ground sage sausage
   (or your favorite pork sausage with
   sage seasoning)
1 cup dried bread crumbs

1 teaspoon salt
1/2 teaspoon pepper
1 egg
1/2 cup milk

Sauce:
1 tablespoon Crisco Canola oil
2 cups V-8 juice (or 1 (1.5-ounce)
   can V-8 juice and finish to
   2 cups with water or milk)

2 tablespoons flour
1/4 cup water
3/4 cup barbecue sauce (your favorite)

Combine all meat loaf ingredients, mixing well. Bake in 350 degree oven 30 minutes. Cover with sauce. Bake 45 minutes longer.

Meat Loaf (with Pork)

1 1/2 pounds ground beef
1/2 pound ground pork
1/4 cup finely chopped onions
2 tablespoons finely chopped celery,
    optional
2 teaspoons salt
1/2 teaspoon poultry seasoning

1/4 teaspoon pepper
1/4 teaspoon dry mustard
1 tablespoon Worcestershire sauce
4 slices soft bread, without crusts, cubed
1/2 cup milk
2 eggs
1 cup chili sauce, divided

Preheat oven to 350 degrees. Coat baking pan with vegetable cooking spray. Mix meats well and stir in next 7 ingredients. Soak bread cubes in milk, add eggs and beat well. Combine meat and egg mixture. Form 2 loaves and place in pan. With a knife score the tops of loaves and spread each loaf with 1/2 cup chili sauce, or **Meat Loaf Glaze** listed on page 170. Pour 1/2 cup boiling water around loaves. Bake uncovered 1 hour, or until done, at 350 degrees. Yield: 8 to 10 servings.

Meat Loaf

1 1/2 pounds ground beef
1 cup bread crumbs
2 eggs
1 tablespoon Worcestershire Sauce

1 medium onion, chopped
1/2 teaspoon salt
1/4 teaspoon pepper
1/2 (15-ounce) can tomato sauce

Sauce:

1/2 (15-ounce) can tomato sauce
2 tablespoons brown sugar
2 tablespoons vinegar

2 tablespoons prepared mustard
1 cup water

Combine all meat loaf ingredients and form loaf; place in oven-to-table bake pan. Combine sauce ingredients and pour over meat loaf; bake in 350 degree oven until done, about 45 minutes to 1 hour. (From a wonderful cook.)

Listen to children; make eye contact; be patient and kind.

Meatzza

1 1/2 pounds lean ground beef
1 teaspoon salt
1 teaspoon pepper
1 teaspoon oregano
1 1/2 teaspoons dry mustard
2 teaspoons minced instant onion
1/2 teaspoon minced instant garlic

1 egg
1/4 cup dry bread crumbs
1 small can sliced, drained mushrooms,
　if desired
1 scant cup pizza sauce,
　1/2 (15-ounce jar)
4 ounces mozzarella, sliced or grated

Mix all ingredients, saving 1/2 cup pizza sauce and cheese for topping. Pat mixture into non-stick skillet. Cook 20 minutes over low heat, covered. Top with pizza sauce to within about 1 inch of edge; sprinkle cheese over sauce. Uncover and cook an additional 20 minutes. Cut into pie-shaped wedges and serve. Delicious! (This is an old recipe that our family enjoyed many times when the children were young.)

Pizza

2 pounds lean ground beef
1 (15-ounce) can tomato sauce
1 (4-ounce) can sliced mushrooms,
　drained
2 teaspoons oregano (less, if desired)

1/2 teaspoon garlic salt
1 can biscuits or prepared pizza crust
Parmesan cheese
Mozzarella cheese, shredded

In a large skillet slowly cook meat; drain well. In a bowl combine tomato sauce, mushrooms, oregano, garlic salt and meat; mix well. Place biscuits on cookie sheet, pressing to flatten; spread each with about 1/2 cup meat mixture. Sprinkle each with about 2 teaspoons Parmesan cheese; top with mozzarella. Bake 5 to 8 minutes in 400 degree oven. Yield: 10 servings. A good, simple recipe, loved especially by the younger set.

We need to have a Christian sense of self-worth. We don't have to be first, number one, on top, the best, etc.

Pizza Burgers

1 egg, slightly beaten
1/4 cup rolled oats
2 tablespoons ketchup
1/4 teaspoon dried Italian Seasoning,
  crushed
1/4 teaspoon garlic powder
1/4 teaspoon onion powder

1/4 teaspoon salt
3/4 pound lean ground beef
4 ounces reduced-fat mozzarella cheese,
  sliced
4 whole wheat buns or Kaisers rolls,
  split and toasted

Combine egg, oats, ketchup and all seasonings. Mix well. Add ground beef and mix well; shape into 4 3/4-inch thick patties. Place patties on broiler rack. Broil 3 to 4 inches from heat for 12 to 14 minutes or until well done, turning once. Top with cheese; broil 1 minute more. Serve on hot buns with lettuce, tomatoes, additional ketchup and other condiments, if desired.

Suggestion: Serve with creamy pasta salad.

Making Meatballs of Equal Size:
1. Lightly pat meat mixture into a 1-inch-thick rectangle. Cut the rectangle into the same number of squares as meatballs in the recipe.
2. Gently roll each square into a ball.

Meatballs and Spaghetti

2 pounds ground chuck
6 slices loaf bread, processed into crumbs
4 eggs
1 onion, chopped fine
1 1/2 teaspoons salt

1 teaspoon ground cinnamon, optional
1 teaspoon ground cloves, optional
1-2 tablespoons vegetable oil
Parmesan cheese
Purchased spaghetti sauce or recipe below

Sauce:
1 (28-ounce) bottle ketchup
  (more if needed)

1/2 box (about 1 cup) firmly packed
  brown sugar
1/2 cup cider or white vinegar

In large mixing bowl, combine ground chuck, bread, eggs, onion, salt, cinnamon and cloves. Form into 2-inch-diameter meatballs, (or whatever size you like); brown meatballs in vegetable oil, about 20 minutes. When done, drain on paper towels. (At this point meatballs may be frozen or added to sauce.) Cook spaghetti according to package directions.

Meanwhile, in a saucepan, combine spaghetti sauce (recipe above, or purchased), and meatballs. Cover and simmer 15 minutes just to heat meatballs. Serve over spaghetti; top with Parmesan cheese, if desired.

To make sauce: In large saucepan, combine ketchup, sugar and vinegar; cover and simmer 15 minutes.

Porcupine Meatballs

1 1/2 pounds ground beef
1/2 cup rice
1 teaspoon salt
1/2 teaspoon pepper

1 tablespoon onion, minced
1 small can tomato soup
1/2 soup can of water

Combine first 5 ingredients. Shape into small balls. Brown in non-stick skillet; drain. Place in casserole and add tomato soup and water. Cook 45 minutes on 325 degrees. An old family favorite; especially when the children were young. This old favorite came out of the *Presto Cooker Cookbook* at the time that it came out!

Thirty-Minute Meal

1-1 1/2 pounds very lean ground beef
1 chopped onion
1 (10 1/2-ounce) can tomato soup, undiluted

1 small cabbage, chopped
2 tablespoons cooking oil

Heat oil; brown onion and ground beef; drain. Add tomato soup and stir until hot. Add cabbage, chopped as you like it for boiled or steamed cabbage. Cover and stir occasionally until cabbage is desired tenderness - just tender-crisp. Be careful not to over-cook. While this is cooking, prepare your favorite cornbread for a quick and complete meal.

Chili Rice

1 pound lean ground beef
1 (16-ounce) can crushed, undrained tomatoes
2 cups water
1 teaspoon salt
1/4 cup sugar

1 teaspoon black pepper
1 teaspoon or more chili powder
1/2 can Ro-tel tomatoes or 1 can if you like it hot
1/2 cup raw rice
1/2 cup chopped onion

Brown ground beef and drain; add all other ingredients. Stir and simmer for 20 to 30 minutes, or to desired consistency.

Lasagna

1 1/2 pounds very lean ground chuck
1 1/2 tablespoons olive oil
2 cloves garlic, crushed
1 onion, chopped
1 (16-ounce) can tomatoes
1 (16-ounce) can tomato paste
1/4 cup brown sugar
1 1/2 teaspoons salt

1/2 teaspoon pepper
1/2 teaspoon oregano
1 (8-ounce) package lasagna noodles
1 (8-ounce) carton cottage cheese or
    ricotta cheese
1 large package mozzarella cheese
Parmesan cheese

Brown meat in olive oil and drain excess fat, if necessary. Add garlic, onion and all other ingredients except lasagna noodles and cheeses. Cover and simmer 30 minutes. Cook noodles as directed on package and drain. Layer noodles, sauce, cottage cheese, mozzarella cheese and Parmesan cheese. Repeat layers, ending with sauce and a sprinkle of Parmesan. Bake 30 minutes at 350 degrees. (Add a little water, tomato juice or ketchup and water mixed, if there is not plenty of liquid. You do not want lasagna to be dry. Be sure to always cover noodles with sauce.)
Note: If you are in a rush, you may use purchased spaghetti sauce. A medium jar should be enough. I sometimes use angel hair or regular spaghetti instead of lasagna.

Shepherd's Pie

2 tablespoons margarine
1 large onion, finely chopped
1 clove garlic, mashed
1 pound lean ground round steak
    (or 3 cups left over chopped roast)
1 cup water

1 1/2 teaspoons beef bouillon
Salt and pepper
1/4 cup chopped parsley
1 egg
2 cups well-seasoned mashed potatoes
1/2 cup grated Parmesan cheese

Preheat oven to 400 degrees. Sauté onion and garlic in margarine until onion is translucent. Add ground beef and cook until no longer pink. Add water and beef bouillon; cook 20 minutes. Season to taste with salt and pepper; stir in parsley. Beat egg thoroughly and stir into the mashed potatoes. Place meat mixture in shallow, greased baking dish and top with potatoes. Sprinkle with cheese and bake 20 minutes in preheated oven.

Stir Fry - Beef

Marinade:

1 tablespoon wine
2 tablespoons soy sauce

2 teaspoons cornstarch

1/2 pound lean beef, sliced thin and cut into bite-size pieces (easier to slice partially frozen)
1/2 cup sliced mushrooms (4 ounces)

1 (6-ounce) package frozen pea pods (or vegetable of your choice)
2 tablespoons cooking oil
1 teaspoon salt
2 cups cooked rice or noodles

Marinate beef for 5 minutes. Heat oil. Add beef, including marinade, and sauté over high heat until meat color changes. Add pea pods and mushrooms. Cook for 2 minutes, stirring constantly. Serve hot over rice or noodles.

Dry Rub for Steak or Burgers

2 cloves garlic, mashed
1/4 teaspoon salt

1 1/2 pound top round or flank steak (or burgers)

Chop or mash garlic and salt, making paste.

Spice Rub

1 1/2 teaspoons cumin
1 teaspoon chili powder

1/2 teaspoon oregano
1/8 teaspoon ground red pepper

Combine all ingredients in bowl. Pat onto both sides of steak or burgers. Oil and heat grill. Grill 8 to 9 minutes per side for medium rare for steak. Transfer to cutting board. Cover and let stand 5 minutes. Slice and garnish with lime wedges. Makes 6 servings.
Note: Try adding 1 package dry Ranch Dressing Mix to 1 pound hamburger meat for delicious hamburgers!

Georgia Bulldog Hamburgers

1 pound lean hamburger meat
1 medium Vidalia onion, chopped
1 cup grated sharp cheddar cheese

1/3 cup A-1 Bold Steak Sauce
Garlic salt and pepper to taste

Mix all ingredients and shape into 4 patties.　Grill.　Serve with buns, lettuce and tomatoes.

Zesty Hamburgers

1 pound very lean ground beef
　or turkey
4 teaspoons prepared horseradish
2 teaspoons Dijon mustard

1 teaspoon paprika
1/4 teaspoon pepper
1/8 teaspoon salt, optional
4 hamburger buns

Combine first 6 ingredients; mix well.　Shape into four patties.　Pan-fry, grill or broil. Serve on buns.

I believe true wealth is found in relationships. Picture the cross. The highest vertical point represents your relationship with God. The horizontal points represent your relationship with your family. The lower vertical point represents your relationship with your fellowman.
Paradoxically, while relationships are the source of true wealth, they also are the source of many problems.

Family Reunion Ham Loaf

3 pounds ground smoked ham
3 pounds ground pork
3 eggs, slightly beaten
1 (12-ounce) can evaporated milk

1 (10 3/4-ounce) can condensed
   tomato soup
1 cup cracker crumbs

For ham loaf, combine all ingredients and mix thoroughly. Pack into two 5x9-inch loaf pans. Bake in 325 degree oven for 2 hours. You may bake this in individual loaves if desired. (This may be made ahead of time, frozen and baked when needed.) This is a tried and true recipe from a friend!

Epicurean Sauce:
1 pint whipping cream
1/4 cup mayonnaise
1/2 cup horseradish

4 teaspoons prepared mustard
2 teaspoons salt
1/4 cup chopped parsley

Whip cream until stiff. Fold in other ingredients until well blended. Serve on the side with ham loaf, chilled or at room temperature.

Individual Ham Loaves - with Spice

2 eggs, beaten
3/4 cup cracker or bread crumbs
1/2 cup milk
1/2 cup, plus 2 tablespoons grated
   Parmesan cheese, divided
1/4 cup finely chopped onion

1 teaspoon Worcestershire sauce
1 teaspoon garlic salt
1 teaspoon Italian seasoning, divided
2 pounds ground pork
1/4 cup ketchup

In large bowl, combine eggs, crumbs, milk, 1/2 cup cheese, onion, Worcestershire sauce, garlic salt and 1/2 teaspoon Italian seasoning. Add pork and mix well. Shape into 10 individual loaves; place on a rack in a greased large shallow baking pan. Spread ketchup over loaves; sprinkle with remaining cheese and Italian seasoning. Bake at 350 degrees for 45 to 55 minutes or until no pink remains. Yield: 10 servings.

Pennsylvania Dutch Scalloped Ham and Potatoes

1 1/2 pounds tenderized ham
   (1-inch thick), cubed
1 teaspoon salt
2 tablespoons flour
2 cans mushroom soup

1/4 teaspoon paprika
1 quart sliced raw potatoes
2 tablespoons butter
1 1/2 cups milk, scalded

Place ham in casserole. Mix salt, flour and paprika. Cover ham with potatoes mixed with seasonings and dot with butter. Add milk, cover and bake 1 1/2 hours at 300 degrees. Remove lid and continue baking 15 minutes to brown potatoes. Serves 6.

Smoked Ham with Pineapple

Trim any fat from serving-size slices of ham. Spray frying pan with Pam. Place ham slices in frying pan; sprinkle top with small amount of brown sugar. Cook ham on medium heat; turn when brown, remove ham and lightly brown 1 pineapple slice for each serving. Return ham to skillet, placing pineapple slice on top of each serving. Add small amount of pineapple juice. When serving drizzle small amount of juice on each serving.

Party Casserole

2 (6-ounce) boxes Uncle Ben's Wild Rice
1 1/2 pounds bulk medium hot Jimmy
   Dean sausage (or hot, if desired)
1 large onion, chopped
3 stalks celery

4 1/2 cups cooked chicken or turkey
1 small can mushroom pieces
1 medium jar pimiento or
   sun-dried tomatoes
1 can water chestnuts, sliced

Cook rice as directed. Brown sausage and drain. Sauté onion and celery. Mix all ingredients and bake in 350 degree oven for 40 minutes.

Delicious Pork Chops

6 pork chops

Sauce:

2 tablespoons oil
1/2 cup ketchup
1 tablespoon lemon juice

1 tablespoon Worcestershire sauce
1 tablespoon soy sauce
1 tablespoon brown sugar

Preheat oven to 350 degrees. Arrange chops in single layer in casserole. In small bowl, mix oil, ketchup, lemon juice, Worcestershire sauce, soy sauce, and brown sugar, using a wire whisk or fork. Spread half of mixture over chops. Bake uncovered 30 minutes. Turn chops and spread with remaining sauce. Bake uncovered 30 minutes longer. Yield: 4 servings.

Deviled Pork Chops

6 thick pork chops
Salt and pepper
2 cups chili sauce
1 teaspoon dry mustard

2 teaspoons Worcestershire sauce
1 teaspoon lemon juice
1 medium onion, grated

Preheat oven to 350 degrees. Sprinkle chops with salt and pepper. Place in baking dish. Cover with sauce made from remaining ingredients. Let stand 30 minutes to marinate. Cover and bake until tender, approximately 1 hour. Check during cooking; if too dry, add small amount of water. (Served many years ago at the Frances Virginia Tea Room in Atlanta. Ladies wore hats and white gloves!)

Pork Chops and Gravy - Slow Cooker

1/2 cup all-purpose flour
1 1/2 teaspoons dry mustard or to taste
1/2 teaspoon salt
1/2 teaspoon garlic powder

6 (1-inch thick) lean pork chops
1 (10 3/4-ounce) can condensed chicken
 broth, undiluted
2 tablespoons vegetable oil

Combine first 4 ingredients and dredge chops in mixture. Combine remaining flour mixture and chicken broth in 3 1/2-quart slow cooker. Pour oil in large skillet over medium heat and brown chops on both sides. Place in slow cooker. Cook, covered on high 2 to 2 1/2 hours or until tender. If you need to leave them cooking longer while you are away, just cook on low. Serve with hot rice or mashed potatoes.

It is only when you cast yourself to the ground and trust God that He can grow a beautiful, happy new life.

Our Favorite Pork Roast

Pork Tenderloin or boneless Boston Butt - the size you need. Salt and pepper.
Sauce (recipe follows)

Preheat oven or grill to 450 degrees. Salt and pepper pork lightly, (the sauce is salty); place on rack in baking pan. (It is so much easier if you will cover the rack and the pan well with foil for easy clean up. Cut slits in foil on rack for drainage.) Place in oven and reduce heat to 325 degrees; cook until meat thermometer reaches 170 degrees. (Lay a piece of foil loosely over top of roast if browning too fast.) Remove from oven and let roast stand at least 10 minutes. Just before serving time, slice diagonally across grain and place on serving platter. Dip sauce onto each slice and serve remaining sauce on the side. This is a sauce and not a gravy. If you desire gravy, make as usual, using drippings and browned bits on foil. (Just pour liquid you are using onto foil and let it sit a few minutes and it will all turn loose. Add instant ham or chicken bouillon to liquid, if needed. If not as brown as you like, add a little Kitchen Bouquet.)

Sauce:

1 cup ketchup	4 tablespoons Worcestershire sauce
1 cup water	4 tablespoons soy sauce
6 tablespoons lemon juice	4 tablespoons brown sugar

Combine all ingredients and heat to dissolve sugar. This will keep well in refrigerator.

Garlic-Rosemary Pork Roast

1 (3 1/2 pound) lean boneless double pork loin roast, tied	2 tablespoons chopped fresh chives
4 cloves garlic, crushed	2 tablespoons chopped fresh parsley
2 tablespoons chopped fresh or dried rosemary	Vegetable cooking spray

Untie roast and trim fat. Retie roast. Rub garlic over surface of roast. Combine rosemary, chives, and parsley; sprinkle evenly over roast. Cover and chill 2 to 4 hours. Place roast on rack of a broiler pan coated with vegetable cooking spray. Insert meat thermometer into thickest part of roast, if desired. Place roast in a 450 degree oven. Reduce heat to 325 degrees and bake 2 hours or until meat thermometer registers 160 degrees. Let roast stand 10 minutes. Remove string from roast, and slice diagonally across grain into thin slices.

Grilled Pork Tenderloin
(Marinated for 12 Hours)

1/2 cup soy sauce
1/2 cup white wine
4 green onions, chopped
2 cloves garlic, pressed

1/2 teaspoon ground black pepper
Grated fresh ginger to cover bottom of
marinating dish
1 (2-pound) pork tenderloin

Combine soy sauce, wine, onions, garlic and pepper. Pour over grated ginger. Add tenderloin and coat all sides. Marinate, refrigerated, at least 12 hours. Preheat oven to 325 degrees, if baking; or drain tenderloin, reserving marinade, and cook over hot coals until internal temperature reaches 160 degrees. If baking, cook, uncovered, until tenderloin reaches 160 degrees on thermometer, about 1 hour. While pork is cooking, strain marinade and boil for about 5 minutes. To keep pork moist after cooking, pour marinade over tenderloin and cover with foil. Makes 6 servings.

Fresh Small Pork Spareribs
with Tangy Barbecue Sauce

Small pork spareribs (as many as needed)

Cook ribs slowly on grill until brown and tender. Cool, cut into serving pieces. Place in oven-to-table serving dish and add your favorite barbecue sauce or Tangy Barbecue Sauce, double or triple sauce recipe if needed. Cover tightly with lid or foil and place in 300 degree oven for about 1 hour. Serve.

Tangy Barbecue Sauce:
1/2 cup A-1 Sweet & Tangy
Steak Sauce
1/4 cup minced onion

1 clove garlic, minced
3/4 teaspoon liquid hot pepper seasoning

In small bowl, combine all ingredients. Use as a basting sauce for ribs during the last 15 minutes of cooking, or add to ribs and bake in oven as directed above.

The only true nobility is to be better today than you were yesterday.

Apricot-Glazed Chicken

2 boneless skinless chicken breast
   halves
1/4 cup light apricot preserves
1 1/2 teaspoons light soy sauce

1 teaspoon Dijon mustard
1 teaspoon honey
1 teaspoon margarine, melted

Coat broiler pan with baking spray; place chicken on pan. Combine remaining ingredients; brush half over chicken. Broil 5 to 6 inches from heat for 5 minutes. Turn chicken over; brush with remaining apricot mixture. Broil until juices run clear. Yield: 2 servings.

Athenian Chicken

3 large boneless, skinless chicken
   breasts, cut into strips (Chicken will be
   easier to cut if partially frozen.)
1 tablespoon chili powder
1/2 lime, juiced

2 cups cooked brown rice
1 large tomato, cut in 1/4-inch slices
1/4 cup small stuffed green olives, halved
1 (8-ounce) package Feta cheese, grated
10 buttery crackers, crumbled

In medium bowl mix chili powder and lime juice. Add chicken, stirring to coat. Refrigerate until ready to use. Spray 13x9-inch casserole dish with vegetable spray. Place rice in dish, completely covering bottom. Arrange tomato slices on rice. Sprinkle olive halves evenly over tomato and rice. Arrange chicken strips lengthwise on top. Cover with foil and bake at 350 degrees about 45 minutes or until almost tender. Remove foil and sprinkle Feta cheese over chicken and top with cracker crumbs. Cook until fork can be inserted in chicken with ease. Makes 8 servings.

Spiritual disciplines are not laws or virtues in themselves; they only put us in the place so God can use us, and bring us into fellowship with Him.

Baked Chicken with Durkee Sauce

1 chicken, cut-up (about 3 pounds) or your favorite pieces

Sauce:

1/4 cup Durkee Famous Sauce
1/2 cup mayonnaise
2 tablespoons lemon juice
1 tablespoon honey

1 teaspoon Worcestershire sauce
1 1/2 teaspoons rosemary leaves,
   crushed or dill weed, optional

Place chicken (about 3 pounds), in 9x13-inch baking pan. Pour sauce over chicken, turn to coat. Bake at 375 degrees for 45 to 55 minutes or until done, turning once and brushing occasionally with baste. **Grilled:** Dip chicken pieces into sauce to coat. Reserve remaining sauce. Grill chicken 6 inches from heat source; turn and brush every 5 minutes with remaining sauce for 30 minutes or until done. (Also great as a sauce for broiled or grilled fish steaks.)

Buttermilk Chicken

4 to 6 chicken breasts (skinless and
   boneless)
1 3/4 cups buttermilk, divided
3/4 cup flour

1/2 teaspoon salt
1/4 teaspoon pepper
1/4 cup margarine
1 can cream of mushroom soup

Preheat oven to 425 degrees. Dip chicken into 1/2 cup buttermilk. (Add additional buttermilk, if needed.) Roll chicken in mixture of flour, salt, and pepper. Melt margarine in 9x13-inch pan. Place chicken in pan. Bake 25 minutes, uncovered. Turn chicken and bake for 15 minutes more. Turn chicken again and pour mixture of 1 1/4 cups buttermilk and mushroom soup over chicken. baking 15 minutes more.

Sin manifests itself in our heart and mind; the acts that follow are because of what we allow to happen in our heart and mind.

Chicken Breasts in Smoked Beef

6 chicken breast halves, deboned
(Sometimes chicken breast are large;
cut these in half again, if you like
smaller servings.)
1 package smoked beef
(containing 12 slices)

Bacon (1/2 slice per serving)
1 can mushroom soup
1 cup sour cream
Paprika

Wrap each chicken breast in smoked beef and then 1/2 slice bacon. Place in casserole dish with loose ends down. Combine soup and sour cream and pour over chicken. Sprinkle each serving with paprika. Bake at 300 degrees for 2 hours. This freezes well. Serve with rice. (If you use 1 whole half-chicken-breast, wrap it in two slices smoked beef. If you half it, use 1 slice of smoked beef.)

Chicken Parisianne

4 chicken breast halves, skinned
and deboned
1 can mushroom soup

1 (4-ounce) can mushrooms,
with liquid
1 cup sour cream
1/2 cup cooking sherry

Place chicken in baking dish. Combine all other ingredients and pour over chicken. Sprinkle each serving with paprika. Bake in 350 degree oven for 1 hour. Serve over rice, if desired.

Chicken Spaghetti

2 fryers or about 6 chicken
breast halves
2 bell peppers
1 large onion
1 stick margarine

1 (8 1/2-ounce) can English Peas,
optional
1 can Ro-tel tomatoes
2 pounds Velveeta cheese
1 pound thin spaghetti

Boil chicken and save broth; remove chicken from bones and cut into bite-size pieces. Cook spaghetti in broth; drain, reserving 2 cups. Cook pepper and onion in margarine. Cut up cheese and put in broth. Add other ingredients. Bake until bubbly at 350 degrees (about 30 to 40 minutes). This recipe will make two 9x13-inch casseroles. Wonderful to freeze one before baking to have later!

Chicken Thighs

3 pounds chicken thighs (about 12)
1/4 cup soy sauce
1 clove garlic, crushed or
    1/2 teaspoon dried minced garlic
1 teaspoon grated fresh ginger, optional

Salt and pepper to taste
1 teaspoon sugar
2 tablespoons dry sherry
1 tablespoon honey
2 tablespoons olive oil

Rinse and dry chicken. In a large bowl combine all ingredients except oil. Place chicken in mixture and turn to coat. Cover and chill overnight. Heat oven to 350 degrees. Pour chicken, marinade and oil into large enough baking dish for thighs to fit in one layer and not touch. Bake 35 to 40 minutes, basting once or twice, until cooked. Remove chicken from oven, brush with marinade and serve.

Swiss Baked Chicken

8 chicken breast halves
8 slices Swiss cheese
1 (10 3/4-ounce) can cream of chicken
    soup, undiluted

1/4 cup dry white wine
1 cup herb-seasoned stuffing mix,
    crushed
1/4 cup melted butter or margarine

Arrange chicken in greased 13x9-inch baking dish. Top each chicken breast with cheese slice. Combine soup and wine, mixing well. Spoon sauce over cheese evenly. Bake 45 minutes in 350 degree oven; sprinkle with stuffing mixed with melted butter or margarine. Bake another 5 to 10 minutes until brown. This dish can be prepared ahead of time, refrigerated and baked prior to serving.

Tangy Baked Chicken

4 boneless, skinless, chicken
    breast halves
1/4 teaspoon black pepper
1/8 teaspoon ground red pepper

1/4 cup reduced-calorie Catalina salad
    dressing
1 tablespoon Dijon-style mustard
1 teaspoon Worcestershire sauce

Rinse chicken; pat dry with paper towels. Combine black and red peppers; rub onto chicken breasts. Combine salad dressing, mustard and Worcestershire sauce. Lightly brush both sides of chicken breasts with some of the dressing mixture. Place chicken in a shallow baking dish or pan. Bake, uncovered in a 375 degree oven for 20 to 25 minutes or until chicken is no longer pink. In a small saucepan heat any remaining dressing mixture just to boiling; serve with chicken. Makes 4 servings.

Garlic Baked Chicken

1 chicken, cut up
Olive oil to coat
Salt and pepper to taste
2 medium onions, halved and sliced

3 medium potatoes, peeled and cut in
   half (If you have new potatoes, peel
   off strip around middle)
15 garlic cloves
1 cup white wine
Parsley for garnish

Preheat oven to 375 degrees. Rub chicken with olive oil and then salt and pepper. Place chicken, vegetables and garlic in 9x13-inch baking dish. Pour wine over all; cover and bake 1 1/2 hours. Makes 6 to 8 servings.

Orange Baked Chicken

4 chicken legs with thighs,
   skin removed
1 teaspoon salt
1/8-1/4 teaspoon pepper

3 tablespoons orange juice concentrate
1 tablespoon honey
1 teaspoon prepared mustard

Place chicken in greased baking pan. Sprinkle with salt and pepper. Bake uncovered, at 375 degrees for 25 minutes. In a small bowl, combine orange juice, honey and mustard. Brush over chicken; bake 15 minutes longer. Brush again; bake 10 minutes longer or until juices run clear.

We can be used as instruments of God's Grace to lift each other up, so that together we can be in His Presence and glorify Him.

Chicken Dressing

Egg Bread:

2 eggs, lightly beaten
2 cups buttermilk
3 tablespoons shortening
2 1/2 cups cornmeal

2 teaspoons salt
1 teaspoon soda
3 teaspoons baking powder

Combine in order given and pour into well greased pan or skillet. Bake in 375 degree oven about 30 minutes or until lightly browned.

Dressing:

2 cups chopped onions
2 cups chopped celery
1 stick margarine
Sage, to your taste
1/2 teaspoon salt, or to taste

1/2 teaspoon pepper, or to taste
3 eggs, lightly beaten
1 cup milk
Chicken broth as needed

Place onions and celery, with margarine sliced over them, in microwave and steam until tender crisp. Combine seasonings with onion, celery, and finely crumbled egg-bread. Add beaten eggs, milk and enough chicken broth to form soft mixture. Bake in 350 degree oven for about 45 minutes, or until lightly browned. This is a family favorite.

Chicken à la Russell

1 pound ground pork sausage with sage
3/4 cup all-purpose flour
1 teaspoon dried thyme
1 teaspoon salt
1 teaspoon crushed black pepper
8 skinned and boned chicken breast
    halves

1/3 cup vegetable oil
1 (.9-ounce) envelope béarnaise sauce mix
1 (14-ounce) can artichoke hearts,
    drained and halved
1/3 cup chopped pecans

Brown sausage in large skillet, stirring until it crumbles. Drain sausage; set aside. Discard drippings. Combine flour, thyme, salt, pepper; dredge chicken in flour mixture. Heat oil in skillet over medium heat. Add chicken to skillet; brown well on both sides. Drain chicken; set aside. Prepare béarnaise sauce according to package reduced calorie directions; keep warm. Spread sausage in a lightly greased 9x13-inch baking dish. Top with chicken, artichokes, bèarnaise sauce, and chopped pecans. Bake at 325 degrees for about 30 minutes or until done. Yield: 8 servings.

Chicken Almondine

1 can cream of chicken soup
1/2 can water
1/2 cup mayonnaise
1 tablespoon lemon juice
1 tablespoon Durkee's sauce
1 cup chopped celery

1 medium onion, minced
3/4 cup minute rice
1 1/2 cups cooked, chopped chicken
1/2 cup slivered almonds
1 cup crushed potato chips or
  buttered crackers

Combine all ingredients in order given except potato chips or crackers. Pour into lightly oiled casserole dish. Top with chips or crackers and cook in 375 degree oven for 35 to 40 minutes.

Chicken- Broccoli Casserole

2 packages frozen broccoli,
  cooked and drained
2 cups cooked chicken, cut up
2 tablespoons butter or margarine
1/8 teaspoon salt
Pepper to taste

1 tablespoon lemon juice
1 can low sodium cream of mushroom soup
1/2 cup lowfat milk
1/2 cup light mayonnaise
1/2 cup white wine
1/3 cup grated lite cheddar cheese

In a large baking dish, arrange the broccoli; place chicken on top. Drizzle with butter; sprinkle with salt, pepper and lemon juice. Mix together the remaining ingredients, except cheese, and pour over the chicken. Top with cheese. Bake at 325 degrees for 35 to 40 minutes.

The process of being made broken bread and poured out wine means that we have to be the nourishment for other souls until they learn to feed on God.

Chicken Casserole Delight

1 (6-ounce) package long-grain and
   wild rice (I use only 1/2 of the
   seasoning mix)
2 3/4 cups chicken broth
1 large onion, chopped
1/2 cup chopped celery
Butter, enough for sautéing
2 full cups cooked chicken, chopped
   (2 pounds raw chicken, cooked)
1 (10-ounce) can sliced water
   chestnuts, drained

1 (4-ounce) jar pimientos, drained
1 (6-ounce) can mushrooms, drained
1 (10 3/4-ounce) can cream of celery
   soup, undiluted
1 cup mayonnaise
2/3 cup crushed potato chips or
   2/3 cup cracker crumbs mixed,
   with 1/2 cup
Parmesan cheese for topping
Paprika for garnish

Cook rice in chicken broth until done, (expect to have a little broth left in rice after it has cooked done, your casserole will need this liquid). Set aside. Sauté onions and celery in butter. Mix chicken, rice, onion, celery, water chestnuts, pimientos, mushrooms, soup and mayonnaise in a 2-quart casserole dish. At this point casserole may be refrigerated or frozen and baked later. When ready to cook, sprinkle top with crushed potato chips and paprika, or crumbs mixed with Parmesan and sprinkled with a little margarine and paprika. Bake at 350 degrees for 30 minutes, or until heated through and bubbly. Excellent with fruit salad and rolls for a luncheon. Serves 10 to 12.

There is not anything that can take the place of one ingredient crucial to success - work.

Chicken Casserole with Rice

1 (10 3/4-ounce) can cream
  of chicken soup
1/2 soup can of water
3/4 cup mayonnaise (or half
  mayonnaise, half fat-free sour cream)
1 tablespoon lemon juice
1 tablespoon Durkee's Sauce
3 hard-boiled eggs, chopped

1 medium onion, chopped
1/2 teaspoon salt
1 can sliced water chestnuts
3/4 cup minute rice
1 cup chicken broth
2 cups chopped chicken
1 cup cracker crumbs or cornflakes
1 tablespoon margarine, melted

Combine soup, water, mayonnaise, lemon juice, Durkee's Sauce, eggs, onion, salt, chestnuts, rice, and broth. Mix well; fold in chicken. Pour into slightly oiled 1 1/2 to 2 quart casserole; top with cracker crumbs or cornflakes tossed with melted margarine. Bake in 350 degree oven 35 to 40 minutes or until bubbly and lightly browned.

Creamed Chicken and Ham

1/4 cup butter or margarine
1/2 cup chopped onion
1/4 cup all-purpose flour
1 tablespoon prepared mustard
1/2 teaspoon salt
Dash pepper
1 (14-ounce) can (1 2/3 cups)
  evaporated milk

1 cup water
1 (3-ounce) can (2/3 cup) sliced
  mushrooms, undrained
1 cup cubed cooked chicken or turkey
1 cup cubed cooked ham
1/2 cup sliced ripe olives

Melt butter in large saucepan; add onion and cook until tender. Blend in flour, mustard, salt, and pepper. Add milk, water, and liquid from mushrooms. Bring to boil and cook 2 minutes, stirring constantly. Stir in mushrooms, chicken, ham and olives; heat. Serve on biscuit waffles (in this book), toast, chow mein noodles, rice, etc.

Identify items in your life that lead you to bondage; you should be free.

Curried Chicken-Broccoli Casserole

1 chicken, boiled, deboned and cut
    into bite-size pieces (or 4 chicken
    breast halves)

1 (10-ounce) package broccoli florets
1 (8-ounce) package Monterey Jack
    cheese, grated

Sauce:
4 tablespoons margarine
1/4 cup chopped onion
1/4 cup flour
1 teaspoon salt
1/2 teaspoon curry powder
Dash pepper

1 (13-ounce) can evaporated milk
1 (4-ounce) can sliced mushrooms,
    drain and save liquid
Water - add to mushroom liquid to
    make 1/2 cup

Melt margarine; add onion and sauté. Add flour, salt, curry powder and pepper; blend, slowly adding milk and mushroom-liquid/water mixture. Add mushrooms; cook until it begins to thicken. In casserole, layer broccoli, chicken and then sauce. Top with shredded Monterey Jack cheese. Bake in 375 degree oven for 20 to 30 minutes or until bubbly. Delicious!

Poppy Seed Chicken

4 chicken breast halves, cooked,
    deboned and chopped
1 can cream of chicken soup
1 (8-ounce) carton sour cream

1 cup chicken broth
1 stick margarine
1 1/2 cups Ritz crackers, crushed
1 tablespoon poppy seed

Place cut up chicken in bottom of oiled casserole. Mix cream of chicken soup, sour cream and chicken broth together. Spread over chicken. Mix butter, cracker crumbs and poppy seed together and sprinkle on top. Bake at 350 degrees for 30 minutes.

Defensiveness is a tell-tale sign of the world's mind-set.

Upper Crust Chicken

10 white bread slices (day-old)
2 cups chopped, cooked chicken
1 cup chopped celery
2 cups (8 ounces) shredded sharp
    cheddar cheese, divided

1 cup mayonnaise
2 eggs, slightly beaten
1/2 teaspoon salt
1/2 teaspoon poultry seasoning
1 1/2 cups milk

Trim crust from bread, reserving crust. Cut bread slices diagonally into quarters. Cut reserved crust into cubes. Combine bread cubes, chicken, celery and 1 3/4 cups cheese; mix well. Spoon into slightly oiled, 9x13-inch baking dish. Arrange bread quarters over chicken mixture. Combine mayonnaise, eggs and seasonings. Mix well. Gradually add milk, mixing until blended. Pour over bread. Sprinkle with remaining cheese. Cover. Refrigerate several hours or overnight. Bake, uncovered, at 375 degrees, 30 minutes or until lightly browned. Garnish with celery leaves, if desired. Makes 8 servings. (An old, well-liked, do-ahead dish.)

Chicken Pie
(Easy)

1 (3-pound) fryer, boiled, deboned
    and chopped or
    2 to 3 cups chopped chicken

1 1/2 cups chicken broth
1 can cream of celery soup
3 hard-boiled eggs, chopped

Place chicken in 9x13-inch casserole dish. Cut up eggs and sprinkle over chicken. Combine chicken broth and celery soup and pour over chicken.

Topping:
1 cup self-rising flour
3 tablespoons mayonnaise
1/4 teaspoon pepper

1 cup milk
1/2 stick margarine

Mix flour, mayonnaise and pepper, gradually adding milk and mix well. Pour over casserole. When crust forms, drizzle margarine over crust and finish baking until bubbly and brown.

We should teach our children to prepare to take care of themselves.

Chicken Divan Pot Pie
(In A Pie Plate)

3 tablespoons butter
3 tablespoons flour
1/4 teaspoon pepper
1/2 cup chicken broth (more, if needed)
1/4 cup milk

4 ounces (1 cup) shredded American cheese
2 cups cooked and diced chicken
1 (10-ounce) package frozen chopped
   broccoli, thawed, and drained well
2 regular frozen pie crusts

Heat oven to 425 degrees. Place cookie sheet in oven to preheat. In a medium saucepan, combine butter, flour and pepper. Cook over low heat until mixture becomes thick and bubbly. Gradually stir in broth and milk and stir until mixture begins to thicken; add cheese and stir until melted. Stir in chicken and broccoli. Pour mixture into pie shell. Remove second crust from pie pan and center frozen crust upright on top of filled pie. Let thaw 10 to 20 minutes; crimp edges. Cut 2 to 3 slits in top crust. Place pie on preheated cookie sheet. Bake for 30 to 35 minutes until beautifully browned. Yield: 6 servings.

Chicken Pot Pie

1 cup chopped onion
1 cup celery
1 cup carrots
1/3 cup melted butter
1 1/2 cups all-purpose flour
2 cups chicken broth

1 cup half-and-half
1 teaspoon salt
1/4 teaspoon pepper
4 cups chopped chicken
Parsley
Pastry (recipe follows)

Sauté onion, celery and carrots in butter until tender-crisp. Add flour to sautéed mix. Combine broth and half-and-half. Gradually stir in chicken broth and half-and-half; cook while stirring over medium heat until thick and bubbly. Stir in salt and pepper; fold in chicken. Pour mixture into a shallow 2-quart casserole. Top with pastry. Cut slits to allow steam to escape. Bake in 350 degree oven for about 40 minutes or until bubbling at slits and beautifully browned.

Pastry: You may like to use purchased pastry or use the following recipe.

1 1/2 cups all-purpose flour
1 teaspoon salt
1/3 cup chilled butter, cut into pieces

1 large egg
2-3 tablespoons ice water

Mix together flour and salt; cut butter into mixture with knives or pastry blender until coarse crumbs form. Beat together egg and water; add flour to mixture, mixing lightly until a soft dough forms. Shape into a disk; wrap in plastic and chill one hour or until ready to use. On lightly floured surface, roll the pastry to fit top of casserole. Place on top of pie, trim and seal edges. (Roll out trimmings; cut leaves and flowers, if desired.) Spray very lightly with vegetable cooking spray.

Chicken and Noodles

9 cups water
4 tablespoons, plus
   1 teaspoon chicken bouillon
1 (6-ounce) package noodles
1/2 stick margarine
1 cup chopped celery
6 tablespoons flour
1/2 teaspoon curry powder

1/2 teaspoon pepper
3 eggs, hard-boiled and chopped
1/2 (2-ounce) jar chopped pimiento
   (more, if desired)
2-3 cups chicken or ham, cooked
   and chopped
Salt or more bouillon, to taste, if needed

Bring water to a boil; add chicken bouillon. Add noodles and cook until noodles are tender. Reduce heat to simmer. In small skillet, melt margarine; add celery and sauté until tender; add flour and stir. Gradually add enough liquid from noodles to blend to desired consistency. Add to large mixture. Add all remaining ingredients and adjust salt, pepper, or bouillon, if necessary. Simmer for 5 minutes and serve.

Help your children to practice the art of prioritizing, along with you, early on in their lives. Help them to realize what "we" are doing. It will become a way of life for them, teaching them a method of organization, making their lives less stressful, so much happier, and more rewarding.

Grandmama's Easy Chicken and Dumplings

12 cups water
6 tablespoons chicken bouillon
   (You may use chicken broth if you
   like, and have that, but I would remove
   fat and enrich it with bouillon.)
1 (12-ounce) package Mary Hill frozen
   dumplings

3 eggs, hard-boiled and chopped
1/4 teaspoon curry powder
1/2 teaspoon pepper
2 full cups boiled, chopped chicken
Tabasco sauce, if desired
Parsley, if desired

In large pot, bring water to a boil; add chicken bouillon. Reduce heat to medium boil, add dumplings, breaking each strip into thirds or desired size for dumplings. Cook until dumplings are translucent; add eggs, seasonings and chopped chicken. Return to a boil. Adjust seasonings (salt, pepper or bouillon), if needed. (I do not use any salt when I use bouillon.) Some people like Tabasco sauce in them. Serve. Delicious! This might be our family's most favorite dish! Wonderful for family, or to take to someone, especially when people are sick. Most people love them! If you keep frozen, chopped, chicken in your freezer for ready-use, you can fix this in about 45 minutes. Another advantage is, you can fix as few or as many as desired by adjusting ingredient portions. Just keep your freezer stocked with chopped chicken and frozen, purchased, Mary Hill dumplings!

Suggestion: When allowed to sit for a while, the dumplings will absorb more of the liquid. Add some hot water and chicken bouillon to season, if needed. If warming over, take out the amount needed and warm in microwave.

Note: There are 12 layers of frozen dumplings in 1 Mary Hill (12-ounce) package. If you would like to make half this much, let the dumplings thaw just enough to take off 6 layers, and return the package (in a zip-lock bag) to the freezer for later use. You will need to half the amount of the other ingredients.

What a tangled web we weave when we practice to deceive. (Shakespeare)

Fried Chicken - Southern Style

Chicken, the pieces you like, as
much as you need
Salt and pepper to taste

Buttermilk - enough to cover chicken
in a bowl
Self-rising flour for dredging
Oil for frying

Wash chicken; add salt and pepper to each piece. Use a little more than you would usually use, since it will be marinated. In a bowl, cover chicken with buttermilk. Allow to marinate for short period of time. Remove a piece at the time from buttermilk and dredge well in flour. Fry in medium hot oil until juices run clear when stuck with fork, and chicken is golden brown. A favorite!

Southern-Style Oven-Fried Chicken

3 1/2 cups fresh white bread crumbs
(Use electric chopper)
1 teaspoon black pepper
1 teaspoon garlic powder (optional)
1/2 teaspoon salt

2 large egg whites
1/4 cup buttermilk
2 teaspoons Dijon-style mustard (optional)
6 chicken breast halves

Stir together bread crumbs and seasonings. Set aside. Whisk together egg whites, buttermilk and mustard. Set aside. Dip each breast in buttermilk mixture and then into bread crumbs, coating well. Firmly press the crumbs into the chicken. Place each breast, not touching, on an oiled non-stick jelly-roll pan. Bake in 350 degree oven for 40 to 50 minutes, or until brown, turning once.

Oven-Fried Chicken with Parmesan

12 deboned chicken breasts halves
(may be halved again)
2 cups Ritz crackers, crushed
3/4 cup grated Parmesan cheese
1/4 cup chopped parsley

1/4 teaspoon garlic salt
1 1/2 teaspoons salt
1/2 teaspoon pepper
1 cup melted butter

Blend cracker crumbs with cheese and seasonings. Dip chicken in melted butter and then dry crumb mixture. Bake uncovered in 350 degree oven for 40 to 50 minutes.

Diet Oven-Fried Chicken

1 cup egg substitute
1 cup no-fat milk
2 cups all-purpose flour

Black pepper and salt
2 pounds chicken breast halves
   or thighs, skin removed

Mix egg substitute and milk. Dip chicken in milk, then dredge in flour and seasoning mixture twice. Place on baking pan lined with tinfoil that has been sprayed with vegetable oil. Spray chicken generously. Bake in 350 degree oven about 50 minutes or until brown.

Breast of Chicken Tarragon

6 chicken breast halves, de-boned
Flour (enough to roll chicken in)
2 tablespoons margarine
1/4 teaspoon salt

1/2 teaspoon tarragon
1/2 cup white wine
1 can undiluted chicken broth
Rice

Roll chicken in flour. Shake off excess flour. Melt 2 tablespoons margarine in skillet. Sauté chicken until brown on one side; sprinkle with 1/4 teaspoon salt and 1/2 teaspoon tarragon. Turn; sauté other side. Add 1/2 cup white wine and 1 can undiluted chicken broth. Serve over rice. (Rice may be cooked in chicken broth, if desired.)

Chicken Breast in Wine

1 tablespoon butter or margarine
2 tablespoons slivered almonds
4 large chicken breast halves, deboned
1 small clove of garlic, minced
4 ounces mushrooms, sliced
1/2 teaspoon salt

1/4 teaspoon pepper
2 chicken bouillon cubes, or
   2 teaspoons instant bouillon
1/2 cup white wine
1 cup hot water
1 tablespoon cornstarch

In skillet, over low heat, brown almonds in butter. Remove almonds and set aside. Add chicken breasts and brown on all sides. Stir in next five ingredients and 1 cup of hot water. Reduce heat to low, cover and simmer 25 minutes; add wine. In cup blend cornstarch in tablespoon of water until smooth. Gradually stir into hot liquid in skillet and cook until thick. Serve over plain rice and sprinkle with almonds. Serves 4.

Chicken Chow Mein

2 chicken breast halves
  (cut into bite-size pieces)
2 tablespoons margarine
1 can golden mushroom soup
1/2 cup water
1 beef bouillon cube
1 tablespoon soy sauce
1 tablespoon Worcestershire sauce

1/2 teaspoon curry powder
1/2 teaspoon poppy seed
1/2 cup chopped celery
1/2 cup chopped onion
1 chopped green pepper, optional
1 (8-ounce) can water chestnuts, sliced
3 tablespoons dry white wine
1 (3-ounce) can chow mein noodles

In skillet brown cut up chicken in margarine. Stir next 7 ingredients into chicken and cook 15 minutes. Add celery and onion and cook 10 minutes. Add pepper, water chestnuts and wine; cook 2 or 3 minutes. This dish can be frozen. Serves 4. Serve from skillet or dish and top with chow mein noodles.

Chicken with Fruited Rice

1/4 cup olive oil
2 cloves garlic
8 chicken breast halves, skinned
  and boned
1 pound Italian sausage
2 cups white wine

1/2 pound fresh mushrooms
1 teaspoon salt
1/4 cup water
2 tablespoons cornstarch
Fruited Rice (recipe follows)

In large skillet over medium heat, add olive oil and cook garlic until golden. Remove garlic and discard. Cook chicken and sausage in pan drippings until brown on all sides. Discard all but 2 tablespoons of drippings. Return chicken and sausage to skillet. Stir in wine, mushrooms and salt. Heat to boiling. Reduce heat to low, cover and simmer 30 minutes or until chicken is tender, basting occasionally. Remove chicken and sausage to serving dish. Blend water and cornstarch and gradually stir into hot liquid in skillet. Cook, stirring, until thickened.

Fruited Rice:
1 cup uncooked rice
1/2 cup dried fruit bits

1/2 cup boiling water

Cook rice as directed on package. In measuring cup, cover fruit with boiling water. Add fruit to rice when done. Spoon some sauce over chicken and serve other sauce from gravy boat.

Curried Chicken with Mashed Potatoes

3-4 pound stewing chicken, or
   3 or more chicken breast halves
1 stalk of celery
1 medium onion
1 carrot
Parsley
1 teaspoon salt

4 tablespoons butter or margarine
4 tablespoons flour
2 cups chicken broth
1 teaspoon salt
1/4 teaspoon pepper
1/4 teaspoon curry powder
3 cups mashed potatoes

Cover chicken with cold water, throw in celery, onion, carrot, parsley and 1 teaspoon salt. Cover and cook slowly until chicken falls away from bones easily. Cool in broth until cool enough to handle. Remove from stock; strip meat from bones and chop into bite-size pieces. Chop and use vegetables, if desired. Melt butter in large skillet, stir in flour smoothly, remove from heat and stir in chicken broth. Stir over a low heat until sauce is smooth and thick as gravy. Season with salt, pepper and curry powder to taste. Pour over chicken and serve over hot mashed potatoes or rice. (An old family favorite. Over 40 years old!)
Note: Also good over toasted buns as hot open-faced sandwich.

Glazed Lemon Sherried Chicken

2 tablespoons butter
8 boneless, skinless chicken thighs
2 tablespoons fresh lemon juice
1/2 cup dry sherry, divided

1/4 cup chicken broth
1 tablespoon grated lemon peel
Lemon slices and watercress for garnish

In nonstick fry pan, place butter and melt over medium heat. Add chicken and cook, turning in about 8 minutes or until brown on all sides. Add lemon juice, 1/4 cup of the sherry and chicken broth. Cover, reduce heat to low temperature and simmer about 15 minutes or until fork can be inserted in chicken with ease. Remove chicken to serving platter and keep warm. To fry pan, add remaining sherry and lemon peel. Bring to a boil, reduce heat and cook until sauce coats back of a spoon. Drizzle sauce over chicken and garnish with lemon slices and watercress. Makes 4 servings, or more.

Quick Cacciatore

5-6 teaspoons olive oil
1 pound skinless and boneless
    chicken thighs
2/3 cup chopped onion

1 (14 1/2-ounce) can Italian-style
    stewed tomatoes, undrained
2/3 cup chicken broth
Salt and ground black pepper to taste

Heat oil in a large non-stick skillet over medium-high heat. Add chicken; brown 2 minutes on one side. Turn chicken and add onions to skillet. Cook 2 minutes longer or until chicken is browned and onions are golden, stirring occasionally. Stir in remaining ingredients; reduce heat to medium-low. Cover and simmer 10 to 15 minutes until chicken is tender and sauce has thickened slightly, stirring occasionally. Serve chicken with sauce over your favorite pasta. We love this!

Skillet-Simmered Chicken and Onions

1 tablespoon vegetable oil,
    more as needed
2 large onions, thinly sliced
3 pounds chicken thighs or
    8 chicken breast halves

Salt and pepper to taste
2 cups chicken broth
1 (14.5-ounce) can stewed tomatoes

Heat the oil in a large skillet. Add the onions and sauté until translucent, 5 to 8 minutes. Add the chicken, salt and pepper; brown on both sides, about 8 minutes. Add the broth and stewed tomatoes; simmer 20 minutes or until the chicken is very tender. Add more broth if needed to keep the mixture soupy. Serve hot over rice or mashed potatoes. Serves 8.

Troubles nearly always make us look to God; His blessings are apt to make us look elsewhere. (Isaiah 45:22)

Note: If using a frozen turkey, allow 1 day of thawing in the refrigerator for each 4 pounds of frozen turkey.

Turkey - Roasted

If you have purchased a frozen turkey, allow to thaw as directed on covering or as above. Rub with oil and salt. Place in roaster and add 2 quarts of water; cover and close vent. Put in 500 degree oven. For 20-pound turkey, leave oven on for about 1 hour. Turn off oven. Leave in oven over night. Do not open oven until next morning.

Turkey with Cranberry Apricot Conserve

1 (10- to 12-pound) baked or
   smoked turkey
3 cups fresh or frozen thawed cranberries
2 cups dried apricots, quartered
1 1/2 cups firmly packed dark brown sugar

1 cup golden raisins
1/4 cup grated fresh ginger, optional
1/4 cup cranberry or orange juice
1/2 teaspoon ground cinnamon

Heat turkey according to package directions. Combine remaining ingredients in a large saucepan. Bring to a boil over medium heat, stirring constantly until dark brown sugar dissolves. Boil, uncovered, 5 minutes. Cover and let cool to room temperature. Serve with turkey. Yield: 14 to 16 servings.

Worship is giving God the best that he has given you. Be careful what you do with the best that you have.

Baked Turkey Breast

5-6 pound turkey breast
1/2 teaspoon black pepper, optional
1/2 teaspoon garlic powder, optional

1 teaspoon ground thyme, optional
No-cholesterol margarine

Preheat oven to 400 degrees. Line baking pan and rack with foil, slitting foil on rack for drainage. This is only for easy clean up. Thaw turkey breast as directed; wash and dry. Rub with margarine and seasonings. Insert meat thermometer in thickest part. Lay a piece of foil loosely over the top of turkey so it will not get too brown. Put turkey in oven; turn temperature down to 325 degrees. Bake until thermometer reaches 180 degrees. It takes about 20 minutes per pound. When it has finished baking, remove from oven and turn oven to broil, if it is not brown. Spray turkey with vegetable oil and run under broiler just long enough to brown. (I never have to do this.) Serve with gravy and your favorite Cranberry Sauce. I very often do these on covered grill. Turn the grill on "high". Place the turkey on a rack in baking pan on opposite end from heat; start timing and turn the grill down to "low". When my grill registers "low", that is about 325 degrees. Lay a piece of foil over top of turkey to keep it from getting too brown on top. It will take about 20 minutes per pound from the time it is put into grill. It is a good thing to use the meat thermometer to make sure meat is done. The "instant-read thermometers" are nice.

Yellow Gravy for Turkey or Baked Chicken
(A real favorite of our grandchildren, and they named it.)

5 tablespoons margarine
5 tablespoons flour
3 cups water

5 teaspoons chicken bouillon
1/8 teaspoon curry powder
Black pepper to taste

Melt margarine in skillet; blend in flour. (It is easy to avoid lumps if you use your spatula to blend, stirring from bottom with straight end, and then pressing mixture against bottom.) Gradually add water, cooking on medium heat; add chicken bouillon, curry powder and black pepper. Cook, stirring constantly, until thick. Add water, if necessary to get desired thickness. Check seasoning. Our grandchildren use this as a dip.

Note: To make giblet gravy, add cooked and chopped meat from neck of turkey, chopped boiled egg and some chopped liver and gizzard, (or the parts you like). Adjust water and seasonings to taste. Add more chicken bouillon to taste, if needed.

Turkey and Mushroom Casserole
(Easy, Lowfat, Low Calorie)

1 tablespoon olive oil
1 cup chopped onions
1 tablespoon chopped garlic
1 cup long-grain brown rice
1 (14 1/2-ounce) can chicken broth
1/4 cup water
1/4 teaspoon sage
1 tablespoon plus 1 teaspoon margarine

1/4 teaspoon salt
1/4 teaspoon pepper
1 pound mushrooms, shiitake or
    white button, sliced
3 cups diced, left over turkey breast
1 can mushroom soup
1/2 cup white wine
1/4 cup chopped parsley

Heat oil in medium saucepan on medium heat. Add onions, cook 5 minutes; add garlic, cook 1 minute. Stir in rice. Slowly add chicken broth, water and sage. Bring to boil. Reduce heat to low; cover and simmer 40 minutes. Meanwhile melt 1 tablespoon of margarine in large nonstick skillet over medium heat. Add mushrooms; cook until tender and liquid has evaporated, about 10 minutes. Stir in salt and pepper. Heat oven to 400 degrees, Grease bottom of shallow 2-quart baking dish with remaining 1 teaspoon margarine. Spoon rice into dish and top evenly with turkey. Spoon mushrooms over turkey. Whisk together soup and wine, pour over top of mushrooms. Bake until sauce is hot, 25 to 30 minutes. If top is becoming too brown, cover loosely with foil during last 15 minutes of baking. Sprinkle top with parsley. Makes 6 servings.

Turkey Chili

1 1/2 pounds ground turkey
1 cup chopped onion
1 tablespoon minced garlic
4 cups crushed tomatoes
4 cups pinto beans (canned)

1/4 cup chili powder
1 teaspoon salt
1 teaspoon cumin
1/4 teaspoon pepper

Brown ground turkey with onion and garlic in saucepan; Stir in remaining ingredients. Heat to boiling and reduce heat; boil gently for 30 minutes, adding water to desired consistency. Serves 12.

Turkey Chili - White

1 tablespoon olive oil
1 pound ground turkey
1 1/2 cups chopped onion
2 cloves garlic minced
1 jalapeño pepper minced
1 (4-ounce) can chopped mild
   green chiles
1 teaspoon ground cumin
1/2 teaspoon dried oregano

1/4 teaspoon cayenne pepper
1/4 teaspoon salt
1 cup chicken bouillon
1 (19-ounce) can white kidney beans
   (cannellini, or Great Northern white beans)
1/4 cup fresh cilantro, coarsely
   chopped (optional)
1/2 cup Monterey Jack cheese

In 3-quart saucepan, add olive oil and brown the ground turkey. As turkey begins to get brown, add the onions and garlic. Sauté until onion is tender. Add jalapeño pepper, chiles, cumin, oregano, cayenne pepper and salt. Cook 1 minute. Stir in bouillon and beans. Bring to a boil. Reduce heat and simmer, uncovered, 20 to 25 minutes or until slightly thickened. Stir in cilantro. To serve, ladle into bowls and top each with 2 tablespoons of Monterey Jack cheese.

Turkey Curry

1/4 cup margarine
2 cups diced celery
1 cup chopped onions
1/4 cup all-purpose flour
2 teaspoons salt
2 cubes chicken bouillon

1 tablespoon curry powder (or to taste)
4 cups milk
1 (5 3/4-ounce) can pitted ripe olives,
   halved and drained (about 2 cups)
4 cups diced, cooked turkey or chicken

In large skillet over medium heat, in hot margarine, cook celery and onions until limp. Stir in flour, salt, bouillon and curry powder; heat, stirring, until blended. Slowly stir in milk and cook over medium heat, stirring until thickened. Stir in olives and the turkey and heat through, stirring occasionally. Makes 6 to 8 servings. Serve on hot rice or mashed potatoes.

Spiritual disciplines set us free into habit patterns for spiritual growth.

Turkey Cutlets with Lemon and Olives
(These cutlets are from the tenderloins.)

2 pounds turkey breast cutlets
1/3 cup olive oil
1/2 cup lemon juice

1 cup dry white wine
1 cup pitted black olives
Freshly ground black pepper to taste

Wash and pat dry turkey cutlets. Slice them on bias into flat scallops about 1/4 inch thick and set aside. Heat oil in large skillet. Sauté turkey scallops 1 to 2 minutes on each side. Remove cooked scallops and sauté remaining ones if your skillet would not hold them all. Put all scallops into skillet and reduce heat and squeeze lemon over turkey, adding wine and olives. Sprinkle with pepper. Cook for about 1 minute and serve. Delicious with wild rice!

Smoked Turkey - Pasta Primavera

1 (12-ounce) package fettuccine, uncooked
1 1/2 pounds fresh broccoli, cut into florets
2 medium zucchini, thinly sliced
6 green onions, thinly sliced
1 sweet red pepper, cut into thin strips
1 (6-ounce) can pitted ripe olives, drained and sliced

4 cups chopped, cooked smoked turkey
2/3 cup grated Parmesan cheese
1/2 teaspoon salt
1/2 teaspoon freshly ground pepper
2 cups cherry tomatoes, halved
Lettuce leaves
Basil Sauce (recipe follows)

Cook fettuccine. Rinse with cold water and drain. Combine fettuccine and next 9 ingredients. Add Basil Sauce and cherry tomatoes; toss gently. Cover and chill. Serve in lettuce-lined bowl.

Basil Sauce:

1/3 cup chopped fresh basil
1 clove garlic
1/4 teaspoon dry mustard
1/4 teaspoon salt

1/4 teaspoon lemon juice
2 teaspoons white wine vinegar
1/3 cup mayonnaise
1/3 cup sour cream

Combine basil and garlic in container of a chopper or blender; process 30 seconds or until basil is finely chopped. Add mustard, salt, lemon juice, and white wine vinegar; process 20 seconds, stopping to scrape down sides. Stir in mayonnaise and sour cream. Yield: 2/3 cup.

Smoked Turkey Salad

1 tablespoon olive oil
1 tablespoon plus 2 teaspoons
   vegetable oil
2 tablespoons plus 2 teaspoons
   red wine vinegar
2 large cloves garlic, pressed
3/4 teaspoon crushed, dried
   oregano leaves
1 teaspoon salt
1/2 cup tomato juice
8 drops Tabasco sauce

1/2 teaspoon lemon juice
1/4 teaspoon Worcestershire sauce
1 head romaine lettuce, torn
   into bite-size pieces
1 pound smoked turkey breast,
   cut into strips or slices
1 green pepper, cut in half, seeded,
   and sliced into rings
1 red onion, thinly sliced
3 large tomatoes, cut into wedges

Mix first 10 ingredients in plastic container or jar. Close and shake well. Arrange bed of lettuce on large round serving dish. Beginning at outer edge of serving dish and working inward, spirally arrange remaining ingredients, beginning with sliced or strips of turkey, next pepper rings, next sliced onion rings and last tomatoes wedges in the center. Pour dressing over all. Serve with hot buttered pasta sprinkled with Parmesan cheese, and crusty French bread. Delicious!

The severest discipline of a Christian's life is to learn how to keep "beholding as in a glass the glory of the Lord."

Cornish Hens with Crabmeat Stuffing

4 (1 1/2-pound) Cornish game hens
1 lemon, cut in half
Salt and pepper to taste
1/2 cup margarine
1 clove garlic, peeled and chopped
2 tablespoons chopped fresh parsley
1/4 cup chopped green onions

1/4 cup chopped celery
1 cup crabmeat
1/2 teaspoon salt
Freshly ground black pepper to taste
1 cup fine bread crumbs
1/3 cup half-and-half

Preheat oven to 350 degrees. Rinse the hens inside and out and pat dry. Rub the hens with the lemon and sprinkle with salt and pepper to taste. Melt margarine in a skillet. Sauté the garlic, parsley, green onions and celery in the butter until tender. Stir in the crabmeat, salt and black pepper to taste. Add bread crumbs and half-and-half, gradually, stirring until mixed. Stuff the hens with the crabmeat mixture. Truss the hens, tying the legs close to the body. Place hens in a baking pan, breast side up, and roast about 1 hour, checking internal temperature at about 45 minutes, or until hens reach an internal temperature of about 155 degrees. Baste frequently with pan drippings.

Note: Substitute imitation crabmeat for fresh crabmeat, if desired.

In sanctification the regenerated soul deliberately gives up his right to himself to Jesus Christ, and identifies himself entirely with God's interest in other men.

Cornish Hens with Orange Glaze or Raspberry Sauce

4 Cornish hens
Salt and pepper to taste
1/4 cup sherry
2 tablespoons margarine, melted

2 teaspoons lemon juice
Orange Glaze (recipe follows) or
Raspberry Sauce (recipe follows)

Preheat oven to 450 degrees. Split Cornish hens in half. Rub hens with salt and pepper. Mix sherry, margarine and lemon juice; brush mixture on hens. Place in uncovered roaster and cook uncovered for 15 minutes. Reduce heat to 350 degrees and roast one hour uncovered, basting several times with glaze or sauce. Your choice: Orange Glaze or Raspberry Sauce.

Orange Glaze:

1 cup of orange marmalade

1/3 cup Heinz 57 sauce

Mix together in saucepan and heat.

Raspberry Sauce:

1 tablespoon margarine
1/2 cup red raspberry jam
  (Simply Fruit)
1 tablespoon lemon juice

1/4 cup cold water
1/2 cup water
1/2 cup sherry
1 tablespoon cornstarch

Combine in saucepan, margarine, jam, lemon juice and water; simmer 5 minutes. Add sherry and pan juices from hens. Thicken with cornstarch mixed with water. Stir until thickened. Serve over hens. Yield: 8 servings.

"Take no thought about your life." "Be careful about one thing only", says our Lord - "your relationship to me." (Matt. 6:25)

Baked Quail or Dove Breast

12 doves
Flour for dusting
Olive oil

2 teaspoons chicken bouillon
1 cup water
Salt and pepper, if needed

Dust birds with flour. Place small amount of olive oil and 2 cloves of garlic in Dutch oven and lightly brown birds, stirring them around to let them brown just a little. Add 2 teaspoons chicken bouillon and 1 cup of water and cover tightly. Bake in 350 degree oven for about 1 1/2 hours, or until very tender. Serve with hot rice. Serves 4 to 6.

Charles' Grilled Dove Breasts

Marinate dove breasts in Zesty Italian Dressing for about 1 hour. Wrap each dove breast in a slice of smoked bacon, securing with toothpick. Grill away from coals on covered grill for about 15 minutes. Turn and cook another 10 to 15 minutes.
Texas Style: Same as above but put a jalapeño pepper on one side and slice of onion on the other, securing with bacon. This does add some zing!

Duck

Put duck in cooking bag; add tarragon, orange juice, onion, and apple. Cook until very tender; discard onion and apple, saving juices. Place duck and juices in pan in oven to brown, adding orange juice concentrate and brown sugar to juices for sauce to serve over duck. Baste duck with juices.

Consecration means the continual separating of myself to one particular thing.

Duck and Wild Rice Casserole

4 ducks
1 3/4 cups duck stock
1 box Uncle Ben's long grain and
    wild rice with seasonings

1 small onion, diced
1/2 cup mayonnaise
2 cans cream of celery soup
1 can water chestnuts, optional

Cook slow, simmering 6 to 8 hours the day before you are planning to serve. Add to duck, salt; pepper; onion; celery; apple, and refrigerate. Save the stock, discarding celery and apple, and taking the duck off bone. The day you plan to serve, prepare the casserole. Cut the duck into bite-size pieces and add the remaining ingredients together in casserole and bake at 350 degrees for about 1 hour. Serves 10.

Venison Stew

2 pounds venison (approximately)
1 (10-ounce) package McKenzie
    Petite Lima Beans
2 cans cream-style corn
2 cans chopped tomatoes
3 potatoes, chopped
2 large onions, chopped

3 carrots, chopped
1 1/2-2 cups chopped celery
1 cup ketchup
1/2 cup Real Lemon
Tabasco sauce to taste
Garlic to taste
Salt and pepper to taste

Put venison in crock pot and cook overnight, or in cooking bag in oven and cook until **very** tender. Cut into bite-size pieces. To the venison and broth add the remaining ingredients. Simmer for about 1 hour or until vegetables are tender and flavors have melded.

Venison Stroganoff

1 pound venison roast, cut in strips	1 cup tomato juice
3 tablespoons flour, more if needed	1 1/2 cups water
Salt and pepper	1 teaspoon sugar
1 onion, sliced	1 small can sliced mushrooms
1-2 tablespoons olive oil	1/2 cup sour cream

Dredge venison in flour, salt and pepper mixture. Brown venison and onion lightly in small amount of olive oil. Add tomato juice, water and sugar; cover and simmer until very tender. Ten minutes before serving, add mushrooms and sour cream. Serve over noodles. This serves 4. Double or triple as needed.

Being born again is a perennial, perpetual, and eternal beginning; a freshness all the time in thinking and in talking and in living, the continual surprise of the life of God. Staleness is an indication of something "out of joint" with God.

Fried Catfish

or whatever kind of fish available that are good for frying -
(With a good Southern recipe for sweet potatoes to go with them)

6 pan-dressed farm-raised catfish
   (3/4 to 1 pound each)
1 cup buttermilk
Salt to taste
Pepper to taste

1 1/2 cups self-rising cornmeal
1/2 cup self-rising flour
1 1/2-2 quarts peanut oil for deep drying

Thaw fish if frozen. Place fish in a deep container. Add buttermilk, salt and pepper. Stir to coat fish evenly. Let fish marinate in refrigerator 4 to 6 hours (or overnight). Drain marinade from fish. Roll fish in meal-flour mixture, coating evenly. Heat oil in deep fryer to 370 degrees. Place a few fish at a time in cooker. Fry until fish are golden brown. Drain cooked fish on absorbent paper. Transfer fish to pan with a wire rack. Place in a warm oven to keep fish crisp.

(Recipe for Hushpuppies in Breads in this book.)
Note: Try frying sweet potatoes in the same grease after fish and hushpuppies. They are delicious! Wash the number of potatoes you need and cook them on HIGH in the microwave for 3 minutes. Rearrange and cook about 3 minutes more. Of course this time will vary with the number of potatoes you place in oven at one time. You may need to bake more than once if you need many. The potatoes need to get heated through and through, but do not need to be soft. After cooking, peel and slice into rounds about 3/8-inch thick. Drop into hot grease and fry until brown on edges and cooked through. Remove and drain well on paper towel. While hot sprinkle with Brown Sugar Twin mixed with cinnamon to taste. Serve with fish. This is an old Southern specialty we need to pass on to our children, as they are delicious! This is a fun cook-out idea.

Oven-Fried Catfish

2 tablespoons lemon juice
1 cup low-fat or skim milk
1 1/2 cups cornmeal
3/4 teaspoon cayenne pepper, or
   to taste

4 teaspoons grated lemon peel
1/2 teaspoon dried thyme, optional
Salt and pepper
6 catfish fillets (about 2 pounds)
Paprika (optional)

Preheat oven to 400 degrees. Stir lemon juice into milk and let stand a few minutes, until thickened and slightly textured. Mix cornmeal, cayenne pepper, lemon peel, thyme, and spread onto a large plate. Salt and pepper each catfish fillet. Dip the fillets in the milk mixture, then coat thoroughly with the cornmeal mixture and transfer to foil-lined, oiled, baking sheet. Sprinkle with paprika, if desired. Bake for 20 minutes, then reduce heat to 350 degrees and bake for about 5 minutes more, until the crust is golden and the fish flakes easily.

Baked Fish - Your Favorite

1 large can tomato sauce
1 medium onion
1 cup mushrooms, chopped
1 stick margarine

1/2 cup lemon juice
1/2 cup Vermouth, optional
Salt and pepper

Preheat oven to 350 degrees. Place fish in baking pan; combine above ingredients and pour over fish and bake for 30 to 40 minutes, or until flaky. Bake uncovered.

Broiled or Grilled Fish - Your Favorite

Baste Recipe:
1/2 cup mayonnaise
1/4 cup Durkee's sauce
2 tablespoons lemon juice
1 tablespoon honey

1 teaspoon Worcestershire sauce
1 1/2 teaspoons rosemary leaves,
    crushed, or dill weed, optional

Dip pieces of your favorite baking fish into baste to coat. Continue to brush with baste until fish is flaky. (Grill or bake.)

Baked Fish with Italian Sauce

2 (1-pound) packages fish fillets, thawed
1 (8-ounce) can spaghetti sauce
    with mushrooms

1 tablespoon instant onion
1 (4-ounce) package mozzarella
    cheese (1 cup)

Arrange fillets in single layer in well-greased baking pan. Sprinkle with salt. Mix spaghetti sauce and onion; pour over fillets. Bake, uncovered, at 350 degrees until fish flakes easily with fork, about 25 to 30 minutes. Sprinkle with cheese; return to oven until cheese melts, about 3 minutes. This is a very old recipe, but one that we have enjoyed.

Pan-Broiled Fish with Delicious Sauce

2 catfish filets
  (a size for 1 serving each)

Margarine
Sauce (recipe follows)

Pan broil catfish in small amount of margarine in non-stick fry pan, turning once and cooking until flaky. Remove from skillet to warm serving plates.

Sauce:

Ketchup
Lemon juice
Horseradish sauce
Pepper

2 drops liquid smoke or to taste
Margarine, melted
Water (small amount)

Mix first 5 ingredients to taste. Then add margarine and water. Cook in skillet where fish were browned to desired consistency. Pour on serving plates on each side of filets. Serve with hot grits, slaw and crusty bread. Though designed for 2, this recipe can easily be adjusted for as many as you like.

Crab Cakes

1 pound fresh or frozen crabmeat
1 egg
1 cup bread crumbs, seasoned
  with lemon pepper
1/4-1/3 cup mayonnaise
1 teaspoon dry mustard (to taste)

1 teaspoon Worcestershire sauce
1/2 teaspoon salt
1/4 teaspoon pepper
1 tablespoon minced onion
1 tablespoon minced bell pepper, optional
Oil for frying

Clean shell and cartilage from crabmeat. Mix egg, bread crumbs, mayonnaise, mustard, Worcestershire sauce, salt and pepper. Mix in onion and bell pepper, if desired. Add crabmeat and mix gently, but thoroughly. Shape into 6 cakes. Fry in skillet with just enough oil to prevent sticking, about 5 minutes on each side, until golden. Garnish with parsley and slice of lemon.

Hot Crab Salad

1/2 cup green pepper, chopped
1/4 cup onion, chopped
1 cup celery, chopped
1/2 cup mayonnaise
1/2 cup sour cream
1 teaspoon Worcestershire sauce

2 tablespoons butter, melted
1 clove garlic, chopped
13 ounces crabmeat, shell and
  cartilage removed
1 cup croutons

Combine all ingredients except crabmeat and croutons. Mix well. Fold in crabmeat last; bake 20 minutes in 350 degree oven. Top with croutons and cook 5 more minutes.

Flounder with Crab Stuffing (or any large fish)

1/2 cup chopped onion
1/3 cup chopped celery
1/3 cup green pepper
2 cloves garlic, chopped
1/3 cup cooking oil, or less
2 cups soft bread crumbs
2 eggs, beaten

1 tablespoon parsley
1 teaspoon salt
1/2 teaspoon pepper
1 pound crabmeat, fresh or frozen
1 3/4 pound flounder, pan dressed

Sauce:
1/3 cup lemon juice
3/4 cup margarine, melted

2 cloves garlic
Paprika

Cook onion, celery, green pepper and garlic in oil until tender. Combine bread crumbs, eggs, parsley, salt, pepper, cooked veggies and crabmeat. Mix thoroughly. Stuff flounder loosely. Brush with sauce; sprinkle with paprika and bake at 350 degrees for 25 to 30 minutes until fish flakes.

Low Country Boil

Seasoning - shrimp or seafood
    seasoning bag
Shrimp - 1/3 pound per person
    (unpeeled, headless, fresh)
Hillshire Polish Sausage - 1/4 pound
    per person

New potatoes - 4 small per person
Corn on the cob - 1 or 2 half ears
    per person
Vidalia onions - 1/2 per person, or less

Combine water and seasoning in large pot; bring to a boil. Add vegetables and sausage; return to boil and cook 10 to 15 minutes or until potatoes are tender. Add shrimp and stir constantly until shrimp turn pink. Drain mixture; remove and discard seasoning bags. Serve immediately with lemon wedges and cocktail sauce. (Vary amounts of ingredients if you think necessary.) You may use this same recipe and use shrimp as the only meat for shrimp boil.

Loosen the bonds that hinder life with Christ.

Baked Oysters with Garlic Butter

8-12 raw oysters   1 tablespoon butter
1 clove garlic, finely minced

Preheat oven to 375 degrees. Place raw oysters in shells on a cookie sheet and bake 20 to 25 minutes, or until the shells open slightly or liquid starts oozing out. Do not overbake, or the flesh will toughen. Meanwhile, simmer the garlic and butter together in a small pot on the stove for a minute or two, or microwave 30 seconds, to mingle the flavors. Do not let the garlic brown. Dip the cooked oysters in butter. Designed for one, this recipe can easily be adjusted for as many as you like. **Suggestion:** Serve with crusty bread and a simple salad.

Fried Oysters

Fried oysters work best when they are plain and simple. Skip the egg; forget the batters. Stick to flour, meal, or whatever combination suits your palate (the more meal, the coarser the crust). You can add more pepper or spices if you like. Make sure the oil is heated to 375 degrees (use deep-fat thermometer), and don't cook the oysters too long or they will be tough.

Vegetable oil for deep-fat frying   1/2 teaspoon salt
1/2 cup flour   1/2 teaspoon cayenne pepper, to taste
1/2 cup meal (corn, cracker, etc.)   1 quart oysters
1 teaspoon white pepper   Lemon wedges, optional

In a Dutch oven or deep-fat fryer, heat oil to 375 degrees. On a plate, mix together the flour, meal, white pepper, salt and cayenne pepper. Drain oysters then roll them in the mix. Fry in hot oil 3 or 4 minutes, or until light brown. Remove and drain on paper towels. Douse with lemon juice, if you like.

Obedience keeps us in the light as God is in the light. Freshness does not come from obedience, but from the Holy Spirit.

Oyster Stew

1 pint fresh oysters
1/4 cup melted margarine
1 quart milk

1 1/2 teaspoons salt
1/8 teaspoon black pepper
Paprika, optional

Drain oysters, reserving liquid. Remove any remaining shell particles; add liquid. (Add small amount of water, if needed.) Add margarine, milk, salt and pepper; heat thoroughly, but do not boil. Garnish with paprika. Serve at once with crackers. Yield: 6 servings.

Pacific Salmon Loaf with Cucumber Sauce

1 (15 1/2-ounce) can Black Top
   Salmon, drained and flaked
1/2 cup dry bread crumbs
1/2 cup chopped onion
1/4 cup chopped pepper

1 teaspoon salt
1/2 cup mayonnaise
1/4 cup celery, chopped
1 egg, beaten
Cucumber Sauce (recipe follows)

Combine ingredients, except Cucumber Sauce, mixing lightly. Shape into loaf in shallow baking dish. Bake at 350 degrees 40 minutes. Serve with **Cucumber Sauce**. **Note:** This is a good sauce recipe and is also delicious with any fish.

Cucumber Sauce:
1/2 cup sour cream
1/2 cup mayonnaise
1/2 cup finely chopped cucumber

2 tablespoons onion, chopped
1/2 teaspoon dill weed

Combine ingredients; mix well. Yield: 6 to 8 servings

Baked Whole Salmon

Preheat oven to 350 degrees. Coat whole salmon on all sides with mayonnaise. Salt and pepper lightly. Place in baking dish and bake 35 to 45 minutes or until golden brown and flaky.

Baked Salmon Steaks

4 salmon steaks
1 tablespoon oil
Salt and pepper to taste

Fresh dill or 1 teaspoon dried dill
1 lemon, sliced

Brush both sides of fish with oil, salt and pepper; place in baking dish. Top each with a sprinkle of dill and slices of lemon. Cover and bake 15 to 20 minutes or until flaky.

Salmon or Tuna Mousse

(A beautiful salad loaf for the mainstay of lunch or supper)

2 envelopes unflavored gelatin
1/2 cup boiling water
1/4 cup lemon juice
1 cup mayonnaise
1 cup sour cream
3 (6-ounce) cans chunk light tuna
   (in spring water)

1/2 cup chopped, pared cucumber
1/2 cup thinly sliced celery
1/4 cup finely chopped onion
1/4 cup sliced, stuffed green olives
1 1/2 teaspoons prepared horseradish
1/4 teaspoon paprika

Dissolve gelatin in boiling water in saucepan. Add lemon juice; whisk in mayonnaise and sour cream. Add tuna and remaining ingredients. Stir well and pour into plastic wrapped-lined, lightly oiled, loaf pan. Chill until firm; unmold and remove plastic wrap. Serves 8.
Note: Serves 25 to 30 as an appetizer when spread on crackers or party rye, but can also be used as a mainstay for a meal. Especially for parties, use a fish mold.
For salmon mold: Use 1 (1-pound or 14.75) can pink salmon.

Salmon Patties

1 (16-ounce) can salmon, drained,
   skinned, flaked
1 egg, beaten
1/3 cup buttermilk
1/3 cup finely chopped onion
1/4 cup chopped parsley, optional
Juice of 1 lemon

1/3 cup cornmeal, or finely crushed
   saltines
1/4 teaspoon baking soda
Salt and pepper to taste
Vegetable oil for frying
Saltines (optional) A friend coats hers in
   finely crushed saltines before frying.

Remove skin from salmon and crumble into mixing bowl. Add all other ingredients; stir until well-blended. Shape into 6 patties. (My friend also refrigerates hers before frying.) Fry in 1 1/2 to 2 inches of oil in heavy skillet for about 10 minutes or until brown on both sides. Drain well.

Scallop Curry - Fish dish in a flash

(Scallops are one of nature's fast foods; they require no shelling, scaling, filleting or deveining! Maybe we should consider them more often.)

1 tablespoon margarine
2 tablespoons vegetable oil
1 pound scallops, rinse in cold water, dry on paper towels
1 teaspoon curry powder, or to taste

1/4 cup dry vermouth or white wine
1 tablespoon lemon juice
2 tablespoons finely chopped parsley
2 cups cooked rice
Lemon wedges

Heat the butter and oil in a medium skillet. Add the scallops and cook, stirring 2 minutes. Sprinkle with the curry and mix well. Cook about 2 minutes more or until done, watching carefully so they don't toughen. Remove the scallops and keep warm in a serving dish. To the same skillet, add wine, lemon juice and parsley. Stir, scraping bottom of the skillet to incorporate any browned bits. Pour sauce over scallops and serve over cooked rice. Garnish with lemon wedges.

Seafood Casserole

(May be prepared ahead of time.)

2 (10 1/2-ounce) cans condensed cream of shrimp soup
1/2 cup mayonnaise
1 small onion, grated
3/4 cup milk
Salt, white pepper, seasoned salt and cayenne pepper
2 1/2 cups cooked white long grain rice, dry and fluffy

3 pounds raw shrimp, cleaned and cooked
1 (7 1/2-ounce) can crabmeat, drained
1 (5-ounce) can water chestnuts, drained and sliced
1 1/2 cups celery
3 tablespoons parsley, chopped
Paprika
Slivered almonds

Blend soup with mayonnaise in a large bowl. Stir until smooth. Add onion, then milk. Add seasonings (use a heavy hand, because the rice is bland and so is the seafood.) When mixture is well seasoned, combine with rice and other ingredients except paprika and almonds. Check seasoning; add a few tablespoons of milk if mixture seems dry; it should be moist. Turn into a large, shallow, buttered casserole; sprinkle with paprika and scatter almonds generously over top. Bake, uncovered, at 350 degrees for about 30 minutes, or until hot and bubbly. Freezes well. Serves 10 to 12.

Garlic-Buttered Shrimp

1 pound unpeeled large fresh shrimp
1/4 cup butter or margarine
1/4 cup olive oil
2 tablespoons minced fresh parsley
1 tablespoon lemon juice

1/2 green onion, minced
1 large clove garlic, minced
Salt and pepper to taste
4 ounces linguine or your favorite pasta

Peel and devein shrimp, leaving tails intact if you prefer. Set aside. Place butter in large, shallow baking dish. Microwave on high, uncovered 30 seconds, or until melted. Stir in olive oil, parsley, lemon juice, onion, garlic and salt and pepper. Arrange shrimp in one layer in dish, tails toward the center. Cover with heavy-duty plastic wrap, and marinate in refrigerator at least 1 hour. Remove from refrigerator and microwave, covered, on high for 2 minutes. Rearrange shrimp and continue to microwave until shrimp are pink and firm, checking at 30-second intervals. Cook pasta, drain, place on platter and top with shrimp mixture. Yield: 3 servings.

Shrimp Au Gratin

1/3 cup margarine
1/3 cup flour
1 cup chicken broth
1 cup whipping cream or half-and-half
1 cup (4 ounces) shredded Swiss
  cheese
2 1/2 tablespoons dry sherry

1 teaspoon Worcestershire sauce
1/4 teaspoon salt
1/8 teaspoon white pepper
1/8 teaspoon hot sauce
3 pounds boiled shrimp
3 tablespoons grated Parmesan cheese
Angel hair pasta, cooked

Melt butter; add flour. Gradually add chicken broth and whipping cream. Cook, stirring constantly. Add Swiss cheese and next 5 ingredients, stirring until cheese melts; add shrimp. Spoon into 3-quart baking dish; sprinkle evenly with Parmesan cheese. Bake at 350 degrees for 40 minutes or until heated through and bubbly. Serve over hot angel hair pasta. Yield: 6 servings.
Note: This dish can be prepared ahead. Do not bake. Cover and refrigerate up to 8 hours, then bake.

It is necessary in life that we have a moral rudder.

Shrimp Casserole

1 medium onion
1/2 stick margarine
1-2 pound raw shrimp
1 teaspoon salt, optional

2 teaspoons soy sauce
1 teaspoon paprika
1 can mushrooms
White Sauce (recipe follows)

Brown onion in margarine. Add all other ingredients and cook slowly while making white sauce.

White Sauce:
2 tablespoons margarine
2 tablespoons flour
1 cup milk

1 cup sour cream
1/2 cup Sauterne
Parmesan cheese

Combine margarine and flour on very low heat, blending well. Slowly add other ingredients, except Parmesan cheese, cooking slowly until slightly thickened. Add shrimp mixture, sprinkle with cheese and serve. Serves 8 to 10.

Camouflaged Trout (or Bass)

1 whole trout or bass
1/2 cup white wine
1/4 cup lemon juice

2 tablespoons soy sauce
1/4 teaspoon onion powder
1 heaping teaspoon horseradish

Salt and pepper the inside of the fish and place in a baking dish. Mix the other ingredients together and pour over the fish. Bake in oven at 350 degrees for 30 minutes or until the fish flakes easily. Turn the fish over once while in oven.

The important thing in life is not what the world holds for you, but what you bring to it.

Many of us refuse to grow where we are put, consequently we take root nowhere.

Service is the overflow of superabounding devotion; there is no call of God to this. It is my own little bit, and is the echo of my identification with the nature of God.

Never be hurried out of the relationship of abiding in Him.

God is in the commonplace things and people around us.

We sometimes allow our minds to mirror outer problems and disturbances; when it might be more effective and rewarding to seek to activate God's peace that we have in our hearts.

Some things, even catastrophes, can cause a fundamental re-ordering of your priorities.

Pastas

Easy Cheese & Pasta

8 ounces (3 1/4 cup) wagon wheel
  or rotelle pasta, or less
1 cup frozen peas
1 cup frozen corn kernels

4 ounces (about 1 cup) shredded
  cheddar cheese
1 cup cherry tomato halves
1/2 cup prepared mild salsa

Fill a large saucepan two-thirds full of water; bring to a boil. Add pasta; cook until nearly done, 6 to 7 minutes. Add peas and corn; cook until pasta is tender but firm, about 1 minute longer. Drain; return to saucepan. Add cheddar cheese; toss until cheese melts. Add cherry tomatoes and salsa. Toss and serve immediately.

Dill Pasta Salad

3 cups cooked spiral pasta
  (green, orange and white)
1/2 cup thinly sliced celery
1 cup par-boiled broccoli florets
1/2 cup thinly sliced carrots

1/4 cup thinly sliced green onion
1 teaspoon dill weed
1/2 to 3/4 cup ranch dressing
Salt and pepper to taste

Prepare pasta according to package directions. Drain. Combine all ingredients and chill.

Fresh Garden Salad

1 (7-ounce) package elbow macaroni
  (2 cups uncooked)
1 cup McKenzie frozen petite green
  peas, thawed
2 cups diced cooked ham
1 cup diced cheddar cheese

1 medium tomato, chopped
1/2 cup diced green pepper
1/4 cup minced onion
3/4 cup bottled Italian dressing
Salt and pepper to taste

Prepare macaroni according to package directions. Drain. Run very hot water over peas for a few minutes. Combine all ingredients. Cover and chill. Yield: 6 to 8 servings.

Macaroni and Cheese

2 cups elbow macaroni (8 ounces)
1 medium onion, chopped, optional
2 tablespoons butter or margarine
2 tablespoons all-purpose flour
Dash black pepper

2 1/2 cups milk
2 cups (8 ounces) shredded sharp
   cheddar cheese
1 cup toasted wheat germ, optional
Paprika, optional

Preheat oven to 350 degrees. Cook macaroni according to package directions; drain well. For cheese sauce: In a saucepan, cook onion in butter until tender but not brown. Whisk in flour and pepper; add milk all at once. Cook and stir until slightly thickened and bubbly. (Save a little of the shredded cheese for top if you do not wish to top with wheat germ.) Add shredded cheese; stir until melted. Stir macaroni into cheese sauce. Transfer to a 1-quart casserole and sprinkle top with wheat germ or reserved shredded cheese. Bake, uncovered, for 20 to 25 minutes.

Mock Pasta Alfredo - Diet

1 1/2 cups 1% cottage cheese,
   or fat-free
1/2 cup skim milk
2 garlic cloves, minced

2 tablespoons all-purpose flour
1 tablespoon lemon juice
1 teaspoon dried basil

Blend all ingredients in blender. Heat to thicken and serve over your favorite pasta.

Favorite Pasta

6 ounces pasta - your favorite shape
8 ounces shredded mozzarella cheese,
   divided
8 ounces ricotta cheese
2 eggs, beaten

2 tablespoons Parmesan cheese
1/2 pound ground turkey
1 tablespoon olive oil
1 (32-ounce) jar spaghetti sauce

Cook your favorite pasta according to package directions. Combine 4 ounces of the mozzarella, the ricotta, eggs and Parmesan cheese. Brown ground turkey in olive oil; combine sauce and meat. Layer pasta first, cheese mix and then meat mixture. Top with mozzarella. Bake at 350 degrees 30 to 40 minutes.

No Cook Tomato Sauce with Pasta

2 cups chopped ripe tomatoes
1/4 cup olive oil
1/2 cup chopped green or red onions
1/4 cup chopped fresh basil
1/4 cup chopped fresh parsley
1/4 cup sliced black olives

1/4 teaspoon dried red pepper flakes
Salt and pepper to taste
Morton's Nature's Seasons Seasoning
  Blend
Your favorite pasta

Mix all ingredients except pasta. Cook your favorite pasta as directed on box; drain. Serve pasta with tomato sauce.

Parmesan Pasta Salad

1 (8-ounce) package rainbow
  rotini pasta
3 tablespoons olive oil
2 cups broccoli florets
2 cups sliced zucchini

1 teaspoon chopped garlic
1 teaspoon dried basil
Salt and pepper to taste
1 cup grated Parmesan cheese

Cook pasta in boiling water according to package directions. Heat oil in a skillet and lightly sauté broccoli and zucchini with the chopped garlic until just tender crisp. Once vegetables are sautéed, mix in basil, salt and pepper. Combine vegetable mixture with pasta in large mixing bowl. Allow to cool. When cool, toss in Parmesan cheese.

Pasta and Cheese Casserole

2 pounds ground beef
2 medium onions, chopped
1 garlic clove, crushed
1 (14-ounce) jar spaghetti sauce
1 (16-ounce) can stewed tomatoes

1 (3-ounce) can sliced mushrooms,
  undrained
8 ounces pasta shells
1 1/2 pints sour cream
1/2 pound provolone cheese
1/2 pound mozzarella cheese

Brown ground beef; drain off excess fat. Add onions, garlic, spaghetti sauce, stewed tomatoes and undrained mushrooms. Mix well and simmer 20 minutes or until onions are tender. Meanwhile, cook pasta shells; drain and rinse. Pour half of meat sauce in casserole; cover with shells and top with slices of provolone and half of sour cream. Repeat, topping with mozzarella. Cover casserole. Bake at 350 degrees for 35 to 40 minutes. Remove cover and continue baking until mozzarella browns slightly.

Pasta with Roasted Garden Vegetables

3 tablespoons extra-virgin olive oil
Nature's Seasons Seasoning Blend
(by Morton)
1 each red, green and yellow bell pepper,
cut into 1/2-inch strips
2 red or sweet white onions, cut into
quarters or eighths (depending on size
of the onion)
3 yellow squash, cut into 1/2-inch slices
2 small zucchini, cut into 1/2-inch slices

1 small eggplant, cut into 1-inch
chunks, optional
6 large garlic cloves, peeled and halved
3 plum tomatoes, cut vertically into
quarters or eights
Salt and freshly ground black pepper,
if needed
1 pound penne, radiatore, or your
favorite pasta
1/3 cup grated Parmesan cheese

Preheat oven to 425 degrees. Prepare 15x10-inch roasting pan by lining with foil. (Optional, the foil just makes easy clean up.) Place olive oil in large bowl; add Nature's Seasons Seasoning Blend (by Morton). Add vegetables (except tomatoes) and toss to coat evenly. (Add more oil and Seasons Blend, if needed.) Spread vegetables evenly in roasting pan; roast until browned a little and just tender crisp, adding oiled, seasoned tomatoes last 5 minutes of cooking time. Remove from the oven; season with salt and pepper, if needed. Meanwhile, cook pasta. Ladle out 1/2 cup of the pasta cooking liquid and reserve. Drain pasta. Gently toss pasta, vegetables, reserved cooking liquid (if needed), and Parmesan cheese in large flat serving bowl. Sprinkle with additional Parmesan, if desired. Wonderful!

Losing your grip on life can be a blessing if we turn to God and trust Him.

Microwave Rice

This is the basic method for microwaving rice to serve six: In a 2-quart casserole or glass measure, mix 2 cups cold water, 1 cup rice and 1 teaspoon salt. Cover and microwave on high (100 percent power) until boiling, about 6 minutes. Stir, recover and microwave 5 more minutes. Stir, recover and microwave 3 minutes. Add 1 tablespoon butter, cover, and let stand 5 to 10 minutes.

Brown Rice

1 cup rice
2 (10 1/2-ounce) cans beef broth
　(You may use 1 can beef broth
　and 1 can French Onion Soup)
1 small can mushrooms

1/2 cup onions or 1 tablespoon dry
　Lipton onion soup mix (Omit
　onions if you use onion soup mix)
1/2 stick butter or margarine

If using fresh onions, place butter and onions in casserole and cook in oven until onions are tender. If using French Onion Soup or dry Lipton onion soup mix, just add all ingredients; season to taste and cook for 1 hour or longer at 300 degrees.

Brown Rice for 12-15 - Quick

1 (14-ounce) box Minute Rice
3 cans beef broth, plus enough water
　to make the amount of liquid that
　instructions on rice box call for

3 tablespoons onion soup mix
1 (8-ounce) can mushrooms with liquid
1 tablespoon Kitchen Bouquet sauce

Combine all ingredients and cook in microwave or regular oven until done.

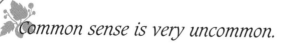
Common sense is very uncommon.

Green Rice Casserole

1 1/4 cups (5 ounces) shredded
   Monterey Jack or Swiss cheese,
   divided
1 cup ricotta cheese
1 cup mayonnaise or salad dressing
1/2 teaspoon garlic salt

1/4 teaspoon pepper
3 cups cooked rice
1 (10-ounce) package frozen chopped
   broccoli, thawed and drained
1 cup frozen English peas, thawed
1/4 cup sliced green onions, optional

Combine 1 cup Monterey Jack cheese and next 4 ingredients in a large bowl; stir in rice, broccoli, peas, and, if desired, green onions. Spoon rice mixture into a lightly greased 2-quart casserole. Bake uncovered at 375 degrees for 20 minutes. Sprinkle casserole with remaining 1/4 cup Monterey Jack cheese and bake 5 additional minutes. Yield: 8 servings.

Jade Green Fried Rice

1 cup uncooked white rice
5 ounces frozen chopped spinach,
   thawed and drained well
1 1/2 ounces ham, finely chopped
2 tablespoons chopped onions

1 tablespoon soy sauce
1 teaspoon salt
3 tablespoons peanut oil
2 eggs, beaten

Cook rice according to package directions. Set aside. Combine spinach, ham, onions, soy sauce and salt. Set aside. In skillet or wok over medium-high heat, add 1 1/2 tablespoons of oil. Add beaten eggs and cook until set. Remove from pan and coarsely chop. Set aside. Heat remaining oil in skillet or wok. Add cooked rice and heat through. Add spinach mixture. Stir-fry for 2 to 3 minutes. Add chopped eggs and toss to distribute evenly. Serve immediately. Makes 6 servings.

Success unshared is failure.

Red Beans and Rice

1-2 pounds lean ground beef
2 (8-ounce) cans Ro-tel tomatoes, diced
3-4 cans kidney beans
Worcestershire sauce to taste
1/2 teaspoon cayenne pepper, optional
1 tablespoon garlic salt
1/2 teaspoon cumin seed

1 pound smoked sausage, sliced
   diagonally, optional
1 medium onion
2 (14 1/2-ounce) cans chopped tomatoes
Bay leaves
Tabasco sauce, optional
1/2 teaspoon black pepper
1/2 teaspoon oregano

Brown ground beef; drain. Add remaining ingredients. Simmer in crock pot - the longer, the better. Serve over rice.

Rice Casserole

2 cups raw rice, salt and cook
1 can green chiles
1 cup sour cream

1 cup sharp cheddar cheese, grated
1 cup Monterey Jack cheese, grated

Stir together and place in casserole; heat and serve. (Microwaves well.)

Wild Rice Casserole

2 (6-ounce) packages long-grained
   and wild rice mix
1 (8-ounce) jar process cheese spread
1 (8-ounce) can sliced water chestnuts,
   drained

1 (6-ounce) jar sliced mushrooms, drained
1 (2-ounce) jar diced pimiento, drained
1 (2.8-ounce) container fried onion rings,
   crushed

Cook rice according to package directions; drain. Stir in cheese spread, water chestnuts, mushrooms, and pimiento. Spoon into lightly greased 7x11-inch baking dish. Bake, uncovered, at 325 degrees for 20 minutes. Uncover and sprinkle with crushed onion rings and bake 10 additional minutes. Yield: 8 servings.

Garlic Grits Casserole (for 50)

8 cups quick-cooking grits
22 cups water
3 pounds sharp cheddar cheese,
   cut into small pieces
4 sticks margarine

Milk to make 1 cup when added
   to each egg
8 eggs, beaten
3 teaspoons garlic powder, or to taste
8 cups coarse, fresh bread crumbs

Add grits to boiling water and cook until done, keeping stirred. Stir cheese and margarine into hot, cooked grits. Add milk mixed with eggs. Add garlic. Top with bread crumbs and spray lightly with buttery cooking spray. Bake at 350 degrees about 30 minutes.

Lawana's Grits Casserole

6 cups water
1 1/2 cups grits (regular) with
   2 teaspoons salt
1 1/4 sticks margarine

3 tablespoons chili peppers or
   1/4 teaspoon cayenne
3 tablespoons pimiento, chopped
3 eggs
1 pound cheddar cheese, grated - divided

Add grits to salted boiling water and cook until done, keeping stirred. Add butter, cayenne or chili peppers, pimiento, eggs and 3/4 cup of the cheese, mixing well. Pour into buttered, 2 1/2-quart baking dish; top with remaining cheese and bake in 350 degree oven 1 hour and 15 minutes or until lightly browned and bubbly.

No day is dark when we live in the light of God's love.

Hot Tomato Grits

2 slices bacon, chopped
2 (14 1/2-ounce) cans ready to serve
   chicken broth
1/2 teaspoon salt
1 cup quick-cooking grits

2 large tomatoes, peeled and chopped
2 tablespoons canned chopped green
   chiles
1 cup (8 ounces) sharp cheddar cheese

Cook chopped bacon in a large heavy saucepan until crisp. Drain. Gradually add broth and salt; bring to a boil. Stir in grits, tomatoes and chiles; return to a boil, stirring often. Reduce heat, and simmer, stirring often, 15 to 20 minutes. Stir in cheese; cover and let stand 5 minutes or until cheese melts. Yield: 6 servings.

Nassau Grits

1 cup grits
8-10 pieces bacon or ham, optional
1/2 bell pepper
1-2 onions
1 can diced tomatoes
1/2 teaspoon basil

1/2 teaspoon oregano
1 teaspoon salt
1/2 teaspoon pepper
Garlic, optional
2 tablespoons Worcestershire sauce
Tabasco sauce to taste

Cook 1 cup grits as per directions on box. Cook 8 or 10 pieces of bacon. Drain. Use 2 tablespoons bacon drippings to sauté bell pepper and onions. Drain. Add crumbled bacon, bell pepper and onions to cooked grits. Add diced tomatoes and sprinkle with basil, oregano, salt, pepper and garlic (optional). Stir. Add Worcestershire and Tabasco sauce; stir. Serves 6 to 8. Freezes well.

Southern Grits Soufflé

4 cups water
1 stick butter
1 teaspoon salt (garlic salt is good)

1 cup regular grits (not instant)
1 (12-ounce) jar Cheez Whiz
4 large eggs

Cook first 4 ingredients according to directions on grits package. Beat cheese and eggs for 10 minutes with electric mixer. Add a little of grits mixture at the time into egg mixture, stirring constantly. Completely combine the 2 mixtures. Pour into large oblong pyrex casserole and place in water bath (dish placed in larger pan of water) and cook in 350 degree oven for 1 hour. Serve with eggs or preferably as an accompaniment to your dinner entrée.

Salads

Frozen Cherry Salad

1 can cherry pie filling
1 can Eagle Brand condensed milk
1 (20-ounce) can pineapple tidbits,
　　drained

1/3 cup lemon juice
1 cup nuts, chopped
1 (12-ounce) whipped topping, thawed

Combine all ingredients, folding in whipped topping last. Cover tightly and freeze. This is a delicious and pretty salad and will keep in freezer for several weeks. You may freeze in paper-cup-lined muffin tins and remove to ziplock bag when frozen to save space, if you like. Serves 12 to 15.

Frozen Cranberry Salad - (with very little sugar)

1 (8-ounce) package cream cheese,
　　softened
1 teaspoon lemon juice
2 tablespoons sugar
2 tablespoons mayonnaise

1 (8 to 12-ounce) container whipped
　　topping, thawed
1 (8-ounce) can crushed pineapple, drained
1 (16-ounce) can whole cranberry sauce
1/2 cup coarsely chopped pecans

Combine cream cheese, lemon juice, sugar and mayonnaise, beating on low speed with mixer until thoroughly blended. Add about 1 cup of the whipped topping; blend well. Add remaining ingredients, folding in remainder of whipped topping last. Pour into lightly greased mold, individual molds, or dish and freeze. Keep tightly covered in freezer. Keeps well. Serves 12 to 15.

Frozen Cranberry Salad

1 (8-ounce) carton non-dairy whipped
　　topping, thawed
1 (14-ounce) can Eagle Brand
　　condensed milk
1/4 cup lemon juice

1 (16-ounce) can whole cranberry sauce
1 (20-ounce) can crushed pineapple,
　　drained
1 cup pecans, chopped

Combine thawed whipped topping, milk and lemon juice in large bowl. Stir in cranberry sauce, pineapple and nuts. Freeze in lightly oiled mold. Serves 12.

Frozen Fruit Salad

1 (3-ounce) package cream cheese
3 tablespoons mayonnaise
1 banana, mashed
1 tablespoon lemon juice
1 (20-ounce) can crushed pineapple,
  with most of juice drained off

1 cup miniature marshmallows
1 small jar maraschino cherries, drained
  and chopped
1/2-1 cup nuts, optional
1 (8-ounce) carton Lite Cool Whip,
  thawed

Blend cream cheese, mayonnaise, banana and lemon juice. Add other ingredients, folding in whipped topping last. Freeze in your choice of lightly oiled container, mold, or individual molds. Keep tightly covered in freezer. Serves 12.

Frozen Watergate Salad

1 (8-ounce) package cream cheese
3/4 cup sugar
2 bananas, mashed
2 tablespoons lemon juice
3 tablespoons mayonnaise
1 (20-ounce) can crushed pineapple,
  including juice

1 (10-ounce) package frozen
  strawberries, thawed
1 cup nuts, chopped
1 (12-ounce) carton whipped topping,
  thawed

Blend cream cheese and sugar; add bananas, lemon juice and mayonnaise. Add other ingredients, folding in whipped topping last. Freeze in your choice of lightly oiled dish or mold. Keep tightly covered in freezer and it will keep well for weeks.

Frozen Strawberry Yogurt Salad

2 tablespoons honey
2 (8-ounce) cartons strawberry yogurt
1 (8-ounce) carton whipped topping,
  thawed, or 1 cup whipping cream,
  whipped

1 (20-ounce) can pineapple tidbits,
  drained
1 (10-ounce) package frozen sliced,
  strawberries, thawed and undrained
Lettuce

Fold honey and yogurt into whipped topping; fold in pineapple and strawberries. Spoon mixture into 8 lightly oiled 1/2 cup molds. Cover tightly and freeze. Remove from freezer and let stand a few minutes before serving on lettuce. Yield: 8 servings.

Ambrosia Salad

2 (3-ounce) packages orange Jell-O
1 cup boiling water
1 cup cold water
Sections from 4 to 6 oranges, coarsely
    chopped
1 (20-ounce) can pineapple tidbits,
    drained

1 small jar maraschino cherries, chopped
2 cups Angel Flake coconut
1/2-1 cup chopped nuts
1 (12-ounce) carton whipped topping,
    thawed

Dissolve Jell-O in boiling water; add cold water. Chill until slightly thickened. Add fruit, coconut, and nuts; fold in whipped topping. Congeal in dish or molds as desired.

Just for today, I will make a conscious effort to be agreeable. I will look as good as I can, dress becomingly, speak softly, and act courteously. I'll try not to improve anybody but myself.

Apricot-Pineapple Salad

1 (16- or 17-ounce) can apricots or peaches, drained and chopped (reserve juice) or 2-3 cups fresh or frozen peaches, reserving juice
1 (20-ounce) can crushed pineapple, drained (reserve juice)
1 (11.5-ounce) can peach or apricot nectar (You will find this at grocery with other juices - looks like a coke can)

2 small packages apricot or peach Jell-O (sugar free, if desired)
1 cup boiling water
1 cup cold water
1 cup miniature marshmallows
Topping (recipe follows)
Garnish - sliced almonds or chopped pecans, optional

Drain fruit; reserve juice from each fruit and combine with nectar . Measure out 1 cup of this combined juice; set aside for salad topping. Dissolve Jell-O in boiling water. Add the 1 cup of cold water and the remaining fruit juice. Chill until slightly thickened. Fold in fruit and marshmallows. Pour into 9x13-inch dish or molds. When congealed, spread with topping and garnish with almonds or pecans, if desired.

Topping:

1 (3-ounce) peach or apricot Jell-O (sugar free, if desired)
1 cup of combined fruit juice (reserved from salad)

1/2 cup mayonnaise
1/2 cup plain vanilla yogurt or sour cream
2 cups Lite Cool Whip, thawed

Heat remaining cup of combined juice to boiling; remove from heat and dissolve peach or apricot Jell-O in it. Allow to cool. In the meantime, combine mayonnaise, yogurt or sour cream, and whipped topping. Combine cooled Jell-O mixture with whipped topping mixture and spread on congealed salad. Garnish with a few sliced almonds or chopped pecans, if desired. This is a good salad! Serves 12.

Blueberry Salad

2 (3-ounce) packages blackberry or
   black cherry Jell-O
1 cup boiling water
1 cup cold water

1 (8-ounce) can crushed pineapple,
   undrained
1 (16-ounce) can blueberries,
   undrained
Topping (recipe follows)

Dissolve Jell-O in boiling water, add the 1 cup of cold water, cool. Add the blueberries and pineapple. Congeal.

Topping:

1 (8-ounce) package cream cheese
1 (8-ounce) carton sour cream
1/2 cup sugar, or 6 packets or
   2 teaspoons Sweet & Low

1/2 teaspoon vanilla extract
1/2 cup chopped pecans

Mix cream cheese, sour cream, sugar or Sweet & Low, and vanilla extract. Spread on top of congealed mixture. Top with chopped nuts.

Buttermilk Salad

2 (3-ounce) packages Jell-O -
   your favorite flavor
1 (20-ounce) can crushed pineapple,
   undrained

2 cups buttermilk
1 (12-ounce) carton Lite Cool Whip
1/2-1 cup finely chopped nuts,
   optional

Place Jell-O and pineapple in small saucepan. Stir over low heat until melted; cool. Refrigerate until slightly thickened. Add buttermilk a little at a time, blending well. Fold in topping; add nuts, if desired. Place in your choice of dish, mold or molds.
Note: This makes a beautiful shade of pink salad when made with peach or apricot Jell-O. If made with sugar-free Jell-O, pineapple in its own juice, fat-free buttermilk, and Lite Cool Whip, it is very low calorie.

Cherry Congealed Salad

2 (3-ounce) packages of cherry Jell-O
  (sugar free, if desired)
1 cup boiling water
1 cup cold water, divided
1 envelope Knox gelatin

1 (21-ounce) can cherry pie filling
1 (8 1/4-ounce) can crushed
  pineapple, drained
Topping (recipe follows)

Dissolve Jell-O in 1 cup boiling water; sprinkle Knox gelatin over 1/4 cup of the cold water, allowing to dissolve. Add to hot water/Jell-O mixture; add remaining cold water. Add cherry pie filling and pineapple. Stir; pour into desired dish or mold and let congeal.

Topping:
1 (8-ounce) package cream cheese
1 (8-ounce) carton sour cream
1/2 cup sugar, or 6 packets
  or 2 teaspoons Sweet & Low

1 teaspoon vanilla extract
1/4 cup chopped nuts

Blend cream cheese, sour cream, sugar and vanilla; spread on top of salad and top with nuts.

Cranberry Crunch Salad

2 (3-ounce) packages raspberry Jell-O
2 cups boiling water
1 can whole cranberry sauce
1 cup finely chopped celery, or
  1 cup unpeeled chopped green apple

1 (20-ounce) can crushed pineapple,
  with juice
1 cup chopped pecans or walnuts

Dissolve Jell-O in boiling water; add cranberry sauce and stir until melted. Add other ingredients and congeal. Delicious!

Cranberry-Cherry Salad Mold

1 (16-ounce) can dark sweet cherries
1 (6-ounce) package cherry Jell-O
1 (16-ounce) can whole cranberry
  sauce

3/4 cup finely diced celery
1/2 cup chopped pecans
1/2 cup unpeeled diced apple

Drain cherries, reserve liquid and add enough water to make 2 cups. Heat to boiling; remove from heat, add Jell-O and stir to dissolve. Chill until it begins to thicken. Add remaining ingredients. Pour into 6-cup mold or 13x9-inch dish sprayed with non-stick vegetable spray. Chill 4 to 6 hours or overnight.

Fruit for Salad: Use pears - A wonderful fruit, plentiful in the Southeast and probably the most wasted! Be sure to make fruit bowls often while you have fresh pears. Combined with pineapple, including juice, and other fruits, they stay a beautiful white and will keep in the refrigerator up to a week. We love the hard, but crunchy kind that are sweet. They are great for many dishes, such as cobblers, baking, hot fruit casseroles, pear ambrosia, pear cakes, pear relish, pear pickles, pear honey, etc. We put them in the freezer for winter fruit bowls and the grandchildren love them.

When peeling fresh fruit like pears, peaches, etc., make up a large pan of water (about 1 gallon), add 1 tablespoon of salt and 2 tablespoons of vinegar. Chop or slice your fruit into it and fruit will not darken; drain fruit in colander. Remove fruit to large bowl or pan; add Fruit Fresh and sprinkle with Sweet & Low or sugar, if desired. Fruit is then ready to be sealed in freezer bags, or to use immediately. When I remove them from the freezer, they change color, but not a bad color and the taste is the same.

Fruit Bowl

This will keep at least a week in refrigerator.

8 cubed pears or more
　(about 2 quarts, depending on
　amount needed)
1 (20-ounce) can chunk or
　tidbit pineapple, including juice

1 (11-ounce) can Mandarin oranges,
　drained
1 (10-ounce) jar maraschino cherries,
　drained and halved

Prepare pears as suggested above. Add pineapple, including juice; Mandarin oranges (or fresh oranges), and cherries. Toss and place in refrigerator to chill thoroughly. The pears make it so much better, and they are pretty and white. To serve, dip fruit up out of juice. You can prepare fruit ahead of time as this fruit will keep refrigerated up to a week! No dressing is needed! Vary your fruits to please your family, and the amount to meet your need. (Do not use bananas unless serving at once.) Use as a breakfast fruit, salad, dessert, snack and as gifts! This is a family favorite!
Note: If you are not familiar with Fruit Fresh, it can be purchased in grocery, usually with freezing supplies. It protects color and adds flavor to fruits, and is rich in vitamin C.

Pear Ambrosia - No Sugar Added

7 pounds crispy, firm, pears, shredded
2 (20-ounce) can crushed, or
　tidbit pineapple, drained

1 (12- or 6-ounce) package frozen,
　grated, fresh coconut
1 (10-ounce) jar maraschino cherries,
　drained and chopped (optional)

Combine ingredients and place in desired size freezer cartons.

Pear Honey

8 cups chopped pears
6 cups sugar
1 large can crushed pineapple,
   including juice
1 lemon rind and juice

1 whole orange, rind included
   (grate peel or grind whole orange)
1 (10-ounce) jar maraschino cherries,
   drained and chopped

Combine all ingredients, except cherries, and refrigerate over night. The next day place in saucepan or Dutch oven and cook until thick. When about done, add chopped cherries. Put into sterilized jars and seal.

Pear Relish

7 pounds pears
2 medium onions
4 bell peppers

Pimiento or red sweet pepper
3 pounds sugar
5 cups vinegar (or less - test by tasting)

Shred pears, onions, peppers; add other ingredients and cook, simmering, 30 minutes or longer - until the consistency of relish. Put into sterilized jars and seal. This is so good on vegetables and meats! It is also easy to make; especially with the convenience of food processors.

Fruit Salad (Different and Easy)

Combine your favorite chopped fruits, celery and nuts. Be sure to use 1 large can of pineapple tidbits, reserving juice.

Dressing:
1 small package instant vanilla or white
   chocolate pudding mix
Reserved pineapple juice and enough
   milk to make 2 cups

1 (8-ounce) carton Lite Cool Whip,
   thawed

Mix pudding and liquid according to directions on pudding box; fold in Cool Whip, fruits, celery and nuts. Delicious!

Grapefruit Salad

1 (8-ounce) package cream cheese
1 cup sugar
2 1/2 envelopes Knox gelatin
1 cup water

1 (20-ounce) can crushed pineapple, undrained
1 (16-ounce) can grapefruit sections, undrained

Cream sugar and cream cheese. Dissolve gelatin in 1/2 cup cold water. Heat other 1/2 cup water to boiling and add to gelatin mixture. Add pineapple and grapefruit to cream cheese mixture. Stir in gelatin mixture and congeal as desired.
Suggestion: 3 drops of red food coloring may be added to first mixture if you would like a beautiful pink grapefruit salad. You also may use 1 can pink grapefruit sections instead of white, if desired.

Lemon-Black Walnut Salad

1 (6-ounce) package lemon gelatin
2 cups boiling water
2 cups small marshmallows
1 (8-ounce) package cream cheese
1 large carrot, grated

1 (20-ounce) can crushed pineapple, undrained
1 cup black walnuts, chopped (You may use pecans or plain walnuts)
1 cup whipping cream, whipped, or 2 cups whipped topping, thawed

Dissolve gelatin in boiling water. Place marshmallows and cream cheese in bowl and slowly add gelatin mixture, stirring until melted and well mixed. Chill until partially set. Add carrot, pineapple, nuts and whipped cream or topping. Mix well and pour into mold slightly oiled with mayonnaise. Serves 12 to 16.

Mandarin Orange Salad

2 (11-ounce) cans Mandarin oranges, drained
1 (20-ounce) can pineapple tidbits, drained

1 cup Angel Flake coconut
1 cup miniature marshmallows
1 cup sour cream

Mix all ingredients and chill for several hours to blend flavors.

Orange Salad

2 (3-ounce) packages orange Jell-O,
  sugar-free, if desired
1 package Knox gelatin
1 cup boiling water
1 1/2 cup cold water
1 (6-ounce) can frozen orange juice
  concentrate, thawed

1 (20-ounce) can crushed pineapple,
  undrained
2 (11-ounce) cans Mandarin oranges,
  drained
Topping (recipe follows)

Dissolve both gelatins in boiling water; add cold water, orange juice concentrate, pineapple and oranges. Refrigerate. When firm, add topping.

Topping:

1 small package lemon Jell-O,
  sugar-free, if desired

1 (8-ounce) package cream cheese,
  Neufchâtel, if desired (softened)
1/2 (8-ounce) carton Lite Cool Whip

Blend dry Jell-O with cream cheese; add in Cool Whip a little at a time until of a lighter consistency. Fold in remainder of Cool Whip; spread on salad. Garnish with just a little grated orange rind or a few finely chopped nuts.

Peach Aspic

1 envelope plain gelatin
2 (3-ounce) packages peach gelatin
1 cup boiling water
2 (11.5-ounce) cans peach nectar
3 tablespoons lemon juice
Grated rind of 1 lemon

1/4 teaspoon ground cloves, optional
1/4 teaspoon ground cinnamon, optional
1 1/2 cups fresh mashed peaches,
  sweetened with 1/4 cup
Sugar or sweetened to taste with
  Sweet & Low

Dissolve both gelatins in boiling water. Add all other ingredients except crushed peaches. Refrigerate until the consistency of thick syrup; add crushed peaches and pour into a 6-cup ring mold or an 11x7x2-inch dish. Chill until set. Serve with mayonnaise, or 1/2 mayonnaise and 1/2 fat-free sour cream, with a sprinkle of celery seed or nuts. Spices are especially nice for fall.

Peach Fluff

2 (3-ounce) packages peach
flavored gelatin
1 (8-ounce) can crushed pineapple,
drained (reserve juice)
3-4 cups finely chopped fresh
peaches (about 3 large)
2 cups buttermilk

1 (8-ounce) container whipped
topping, thawed
1/2 cup chopped nuts, if desired
Vegetable cooking spray
2 envelopes Sweet & Low or
sugar to taste for peaches

Combine gelatin and pineapple in medium saucepan over low heat. Dip peaches in pineapple juice; then add juice to saucepan, stirring until gelatin dissolves. Remove from heat and cool; stir in buttermilk. Place in refrigerator until the consistency of thick syrup; fold in thawed whipped topping, peaches, and nuts if desired. Pour mixture into an 8-cup ring mold or pyrex dish lightly coated with vegetable cooking spray. Garnish with peaches and mint leaves, if desired.

Peach Pickle Salad - A Southern Specialty

1 pint chopped peaches, fresh,
frozen or canned, drained -
(reserve juice, if any)
2 (11.5-ounce) cans of peach nectar
from concentrate, plus peach juice,
if any, and enough water to make
3 cups of liquid
1/4-1/2 cup vinegar (to desired tartness)
2 tablespoons whole cloves

3 cinnamon sticks
2 small packages peach Jell-O
(sugar-free, if desired)
1 envelope Knox gelatin
6 packages Sweet & Low
1 cup celery, finely chopped
1/2 cup nuts, finely chopped
Sour cream/mayonnaise/celery
seed dressing

Peel and chop peaches; sprinkle with about 3 shakes of Fruit Fresh. Drain; reserving juice. Refrigerate. Boil 3 cups of nectar with vinegar, cloves and cinnamon sticks for about 15 minutes on medium heat. Strain off spices and discard. Add water, if necessary, to again measure 3 cups. Heat to boiling; remove from heat and add Jell-O, and Knox gelatin, stirring until dissolved. Add Sweet & Low; stir. Chill until slightly thickened. Add peaches, chopped celery and nuts. Congeal in mold, molds, or as desired; serve with dollop of sour cream/mayonnaise dressing, 1/2 of each and a light sprinkle of celery seed. Garnish with nuts.

Raspberry-Wine Salad with Cream Cheese Fluff Topping (Festive)

1 (6-ounce) package raspberry
flavored gelatin
2 cups boiling water
1 (16-ounce) can whole-berry
cranberry sauce
1/2 cup dry red wine

1 (8-ounce) can crushed pineapple,
undrained
1/3 cup chopped walnuts
Cream Cheese Fluff Topping
(recipe follows)

Combine gelatin and boiling water; add cranberry sauce, stirring until sauce melts. Stir in wine. Cover and chill until slightly thickened. Fold in pineapple and walnuts; spoon into a lightly oiled 6 cup ring mold or 7x11-inch pyrex dish. Cover and chill until firm. Unmold (or cut into squares) onto lettuce. Yield: 8 to 10 servings. Serve with a walnut topped dollop of Cream Cheese Fluff.

Cream Cheese Fluff Topping:
1 (3-ounce) package cream cheese,
softened
3 tablespoons milk

1/2 teaspoon grated orange rind
1 cup whipped topping, thawed

Combine all ingredients except topping; beat at medium speed with electric beater. Fold in whipped topping.

Red, White & Blueberry Salad

1 (3-ounce) package raspberry gelatin
3 scant cups boiling water, divided
2 envelopes plain gelatin
1/2 cup cold water
1 cup sugar
1 cup half-and-half

1 (8-ounce) package cream cheese,
softened
1 teaspoon vanilla extract
1/2 cup chopped nuts
1 (3-ounce) package black cherry gelatin
1 (15-ounce) can blueberries, undrained

Dissolve raspberry gelatin in 2 scant cups boiling water. Pour into a 9x9x2-inch square dish or a 2 quart oblong dish and chill until firm. Soften plain gelatin in 1/2 cup cold water. Combine sugar, gelatin/water mixture and half-and-half; heat until hot enough to dissolve softened gelatin (do not boil). Add softened cream cheese and vanilla to this mixture and beat until smooth. Add nuts and pour over raspberry layer. Chill until firm. Dissolve black cherry gelatin in scant cup of boiling water. Add blueberries, undrained. Pour over congealed cream cheese layer. Chill until firm. May reverse red and blue layers if you prefer the red on top. Serves 12.

Stir-Up Orange Salad - Quick, Easy and Delicious!

1 (8-ounce) carton Lite Cool Whip
1 (3-ounce) package orange Jell-O
1 (20-ounce) can pineapple tidbits,
   drained

1 (16-ounce) carton cottage cheese
1/2-1 cup chopped pecans, optional

Blend whipped topping and dry Jell-O lightly. Fold in pineapple, cottage cheese and nuts. Refrigerate. Serve by dips. (Use sugar-free Jell-O, pineapple in own juice, fat-free cottage cheese, and this is a good diet salad and rich in calcium.)

Strawberry-Pretzel Salad

3/4 cup margarine
2 cup pretzels, crushed
1 cup sugar
1 (8-ounce) package cream cheese,
   softened

2 cups whipped topping, thawed
2 cups water
1 (6-ounce) package strawberry Jell-O
2 (10-ounce) packages frozen
   strawberries

Crust: Melt margarine in 9x13-inch baking dish. Stir in crushed pretzels. Spread evenly in bottom of dish. Bake in 350 degree oven for 10 minutes. Cool.
1st layer: Cream sugar and cream cheese. Add whipped topping. Spread over crust. Refrigerate 30 minutes.
2nd layer: Dissolve Jell-O in 2 cups boiling water. Add frozen strawberries. Cool until it begins to thicken. Pour on top of cream cheese layer and refrigerate until congealed.

Many of us probably put too much emphasis on material things, and more importantly, far too little emphasis on the things that have real meaning and eternal values.

Strawberry Salad

2 packages strawberry Jell-O
2 cups boiling water
1 envelope Knox gelatin, softened in
  1/4 cup cold water
2 (10-ounce) packages frozen
  strawberries, including juice

1 (20-ounce) can crushed pineapple,
  including juice
2-3 bananas, mashed
1 cup nuts, chopped
Topping (recipe follows)

Bring water to boil; remove from heat and dissolve Jell-O and Knox gelatin mixture in it. Add strawberries, pineapple, bananas and nuts. Mix until strawberries are thawed. Pour into 9x13-inch pyrex dish and congeal.

Topping:

1 (8-ounce) package cream cheese,
  softened
1 cup powdered sugar

1 cup whipped topping, thawed
1/2 cup chopped nuts, if desired

Blend in order given and add topping on salad. Garnish with nuts, if desired.

Waldorf Salad

2 large Red Delicious apples,
  chopped, unpeeled
1 large Granny Smith apple,
  unpeeled and chopped
2 tablespoons lemon juice
1/4 cup golden raisins

1 stalk celery, diagonally sliced
1/2 cup mayonnaise
1/2 cup sour cream
1 tablespoon honey
1 teaspoon grated orange rind
1/4 cup slivered almonds, toasted

Mix apples well with lemon juice and add raisins and celery. Combine mayonnaise and next 3 ingredients; stir in 1/4 cup mayonnaise mixture to apples. Transfer salad to serving bowl and sprinkle with almonds. Garnish with celery leaves, if desired. Serve with remaining mayonnaise mixture. Yield: 6 servings.

Chicken Salad - with A Touch of Carrot

3 cups cooked chicken, chopped
1 cup diced celery
1 (20-ounce) can tidbit pineapple,
   drained
1/4 cup shredded carrot
1/2 cup mayonnaise

1/4 cup sour cream
1 1/4 teaspoons curry powder
   (more or less)
1 teaspoon lemon juice
1/2 teaspoon salt
1 cup toasted pecans, coarsely broken

Combine chicken, celery, pineapple, and carrot. In a small bowl combine dressing ingredients: mayonnaise, sour cream, curry powder, lemon juice and salt; blend. Add dressing ingredients to chicken and fruit mixture; toss. Top with toasted pecans.

Chicken Salad - With A Different Dressing

Chicken, cooked and chopped -
   the amount you need

Celery, chopped - the amount you like

Combine the amount that you need of the dressing ingredients below to bind your salad together and to please your taste: (These combinations give a very good flavor.) Four parts mayonnaise and 1 part Durkee's is a good ratio. - (From a friend)

Durkee's Dressing
Mayonnaise
Curry powder

Ginger
Pickle

Add these dressing ingredients to chicken and celery; toss.

Chicken Salad Plus

8 ounces chicken Rice-a-Roni,
   cooked
6 ounces marinated artichoke hearts,
   drained and cut into bite-size pieces,
   reserve oil
6 green onions, chopped

1 cup celery, chopped
8 ounces pitted ripe olives, sliced
1 1/2 cups mayonnaise, with artichoke
   oil added to this
4 chicken breast halves, cooked,
   boned and diced

Toss all ingredients together and refrigerate overnight.
Variation: Add sliced water chestnuts, frozen green peas, nuts or whatever your family likes.

Waldorf Chicken Salad

3 cups cooked chicken, cubed
1 cup celery, diced
2 apples, cored and diced
1 (20-ounce) can pineapple tidbits, drained

1 1/2 cups grapes, halved
  (red or white)
1 cup, coarsely chopped and lightly
  toasted almonds, pecans or walnuts

Dressing:
1/2 cup mayonnaise
1/2 cup fat-free sour cream
2 tablespoons lemon juice

2 tablespoons honey
1 teaspoon poppy seed
1 cup Cool Whip

Combine chicken, celery and fruits; combine dressing ingredients. Pour dressing over chicken combination and toss; top with lightly toasted nuts.

Chicken Salad Ring

2 envelopes unflavored gelatin
1 cup cold water
1 (10 3/4-ounce) can cream of
  celery soup, undiluted
1 cup mayonnaise
2 tablespoons lemon juice

2 tablespoons grated onion
1/2 teaspoon salt
2 cups cooked chicken, chopped
1 cup celery, chopped
1/2 cup sweet pickle relish
1 (2-ounce) jar diced pimiento, drained

Sprinkle gelatin over cold water in a large saucepan; let stand 1 minute. Cook over low heat, stirring until gelatin dissolves; remove from heat. Stir soup and next 4 ingredients into gelatin mixture. Chill until mixture is slightly thickened. Fold in chicken, celery, pickle relish and pimiento. Spoon into a lightly oiled, 6-cup mold; cover and chill until firm. Unmold onto lettuce leaves and garnish with lemon slices, if desired. Yield: 8 servings.

Deviled Eggs

6 hard-cooked eggs
1/4 cup mayonnaise or salad dressing
1 teaspoon vinegar
1/2 teaspoon mustard

1/2 teaspoon salt
Dash of pepper
Pimiento strips for garnish

Halve hard-cooked eggs lengthwise; remove yolks. Mash yolks with fork; mix mayonnaise or salad dressing, vinegar, mustard, salt and pepper. Refill egg whites; chill. Trim with thin pimiento strips.

Ham and Rice Salad

2-3 cups baked or canned ham,
  chopped or cubed
3 cups cooked rice
1 cup sweet relish, drained
3 hard-cooked eggs, chopped

1/2 cup chopped onion
1 (2-ounce) jar pimiento, finely chopped
1/3 cup chopped green pepper
3/4 cup mayonnaise
3/4 cup sour cream

Combine all ingredients and refrigerate for several hours or overnight to blend flavors. Yield: 8 to 10 servings.
Note: This is a nice way to use left-over ham and is also easy to half or double recipe according to the number of servings desired.

Hot "N" Crunchy Turkey Salad (Microwaved)

1 cup thinly sliced celery
3 tablespoons chopped onion
2 1/2 cups cooked turkey, chopped
1/2 cup chopped cashews, divided
  (pecans, or almonds)
1/3 cup sour cream

1/3 cup mayonnaise
1 tablespoon lemon juice
1/4 teaspoon salt
1/8 teaspoon pepper
Paprika

Place celery and onion in 1-quart casserole. Microwave 2 to 4 minutes or until vegetables are tender-crisp. Stir in turkey, 1/4 cup cashews, sour cream, mayonnaise, lemon juice, salt and pepper. Microwave at medium (70%) 3 to 5 minutes or until heated. Sprinkle with remaining cashews and paprika.
Yield: 3 to 4 servings.

Crab & Shrimp Salad

1 can crabmeat
1 can shrimp
1/2 cup celery, diced
1/4 cup chopped black olives

1/4 cup cocktail sauce
Mayonnaise to taste
Dash of paprika, if desired

Mix all ingredients together; add mayonnaise to taste. Add a dash of paprika, if desired. Serve with crackers.

Crab House Tuna Salad

1 can chunk light tuna, about
   6 ounces
2 tablespoons mayonnaise
1 teaspoon lemon juice
1/2 teaspoon black pepper

1/8 teaspoon white pepper
1/8 teaspoon granulated garlic
1/2 teaspoon celery salt
2 tablespoons finely chopped onion
2 tablespoons finely chopped celery

Drain the tuna and break into chunks. Place mayonnaise, lemon juice, black and white pepper, garlic and celery salt into a bowl and blend well. Add the tuna, onion and celery and mix well. Refrigerate up to 3 days. Makes 2 servings.
Note: This unique seasoning blend gives Crab House Tuna Salad its zip.

Nothing that other saints do or say can ever perturb the one who is built on God.

Asparagus Salad - Congealed

2 envelopes Knox gelatin plus
   1/2 cup cold water
1 cup cold water
3/4 cup sugar
1/2 cup white vinegar
1/2 teaspoon salt

1 medium can green asparagus,
   coarsely chopped
1 small onion, grated
1 (2-ounce) jar pimiento, chopped
1 cup celery, chopped
1/2 cup pecans, chopped

Sprinkle Knox gelatin over the 1/2 cup cold water to dissolve. Combine the 1 cup water, sugar, vinegar and salt in saucepan and bring to a boil; remove from heat and combine gelatin mixture with this. Allow to cool until it begins to thicken; add remaining ingredients and congeal. Serve with mayonnaise/sour cream dressing, (1/2 mayonnaise, 1/2 sour cream and a sprinkle of celery seed.)
Note: You may like to substitute chopped water chestnuts for the pecans.

Bean Salad - Easy

1 can French-style green beans
1 can Chinese vegetables
1 can LeSueur English peas (petite)
Onions, thinly sliced
1 cup celery, diagonally sliced

1/2 cup sugar (or 6 packets Sweet & Low
   or 2 teaspoons)
1/2 cup apple cider vinegar
Salt and pepper to taste

Drain green beans, Chinese vegetables and English peas; add celery. Place a thin layer of sliced onions in dish; add other vegetables; add another thin layer of onions. Mix sugar, vinegar; salt and pepper in small saucepan and heat to dissolve sugar. Pour over vegetables. Marinate in refrigerator overnight. Keeps well. (If you use Sweet & Low, do not heat; just mix.)

Beet Salad - Pickled Beets and Onions - Congealed

2 (3-ounce) packages raspberry Jell-O
2 cups boiling water
3/4 cup cold water

1 jar pickled beets and onions,
   chopped (include juice)
1 tablespoon horseradish

Dissolve Jell-O in boiling water; add cold water. Add other ingredients; stir and pour into mold and refrigerate. Serve with a mixture of 1/2 mayonnaise, 1/2 fat-free sour cream, and a sprinkle of black pepper.

Broccoli Salad

1 head broccoli (broken into tiny
  florets)
1 cup raisins
1 medium red onion, sliced and
  separated

8 slices bacon, cooked crisp and
  crumbled
1/2 cup roasted peanuts or pecans,
  optional

Dressing:
1 cup mayonnaise
1/4 cup sugar

2 tablespoons red wine vinegar, or
  plain vinegar

Mix broccoli, raisins, onion and bacon. Blend dressing ingredients and pour over salad just before serving. Add nuts last over top, optional. Some people prefer to leave out the bacon and use nuts instead. Also, some use 1/2 broccoli and 1/2 cauliflower.

Cabbage and Cucumber Salad - Hot, Sweet and Sour

1 cucumber, split lengthwise, seeded
  and thinly sliced
1/2 small sweet onion, such as Vidalia,
  thinly sliced
1/2 teaspoon salt
1 1/2 cups diced napa cabbage or
  green cabbage

2 tablespoons cider vinegar
1 tablespoon seasoned rice vinegar
1 1/2 teaspoons granulated sugar
1 small hot pepper, sliced paper-thin
1 small piece fresh ginger (about
  1/2-inch cube), minced
1 tablespoon minced fresh chives

Combine the cucumber and onion in a colander. Toss with salt and place colander over a bowl. Place in freezer for 15 minutes. Rinse well and transfer to a mixing bowl. Add remaining ingredients; mix well and serve cold.

The weapons of your warfare are mighty as long as you camp beside your Commander.

Carrot and Celery Salad, Congealed - Layered
(This is a pretty and delicious salad)

2 small packages orange Jell-O
1/4 teaspoon salt, divided
1 cup boiling water
3/4 cup cold water
2 teaspoons vinegar
1 (3-ounce) package cream cheese
1/3 cup mayonnaise

1/2 teaspoon celery seed
1/2 cup chopped celery, finely chopped
1 cup finely grated raw carrots
1 (8-ounce) can crushed pineapple
   in natural juice
1/2 cup raisins

Dissolve gelatin and 1/8 teaspoon of the salt in boiling water. Add cold water and vinegar. Chill until slightly thickened. Blend cream cheese, mayonnaise, and celery seed; fold in about 2/3 cup gelatin mixture and add celery. Pour into desired container and place in refrigerator to congeal. Season carrots with remaining 1/8 teaspoon salt; add crushed pineapple and raisins. Fold into the remaining slightly thickened gelatin; pour on top of first layer and chill until firm. Unmold on crisp lettuce. Garnish with mayonnaise and sour cream mixture (1/2 of each), with a sprinkle of celery seed added. Makes about 8 servings.

Carrot Salad, Congealed

2 packages orange Jell-O
1 cup boiling water
1 (6-ounce) can undiluted,
   frozen orange juice

1 (20-ounce) can crushed pineapple,
   including juice
2 cups finely shredded carrots
1/2 cup finely chopped celery
1/2 cup raisins

Dissolve orange Jell-O in boiling water. Add orange juice and pineapple. Put in refrigerator or freezer until slightly thickened. Add carrots, celery and raisins. Pour into desired dish, mold, or molds to congeal. (Slightly oil container.) Top with a dollop of sour cream/mayonnaise/celery seed dressing, half-and-half mayonnaise and sour cream, and a sprinkle of celery seed.

Carrot-Apple Salad with Sour Cream Dressing

2 cups finely grated carrots
1 large sweet apple, peeled, cored and
 chopped
1/2 cup dark raisins

1/2 cup chopped celery
1/2 teaspoon salt
Dusting of black pepper

Sour Cream Dressing:
1 cup sour cream (fat-free, if desired)
2 tablespoons lemon juice
1/4 teaspoon salt

Dash black pepper
2 tablespoons sugar

Combine all salad ingredients. Combine dressing ingredients and blend well. Add to salad and stir.

Cauliflower and Green Pea Salad

1 medium cauliflower, cut into florets
2 cups fresh or defrosted Select Baby
 Sweet Peas
1/4 cup chicken broth
2 ribs celery, finely chopped
3 green onions, finely chopped
2 tablespoons chopped parsley
1/3 cup chopped red pepper

1 tablespoon balsamic vinegar
1 tablespoon Dijon mustard
3 tablespoons light sour cream
1/4 teaspoon each salt and white pepper
1 cup chopped cooked ham, optional
Chopped chives for garnish or a few
 green onion tops

Steam cauliflower and peas until barely tender. Drain well and put into a bowl. While the vegetables are still warm, pour the chicken broth over them; set aside to cool. Combine the celery, onions, parsley, red bell pepper, vinegar and mustard. Mix in sour cream; add salt and pepper. Toss gently with cauliflower and peas, adding ham if desired. Sprinkle with chives and serve.

Cauliflower Salad Delight

1 medium head cauliflower, broken
 into tiny florets
2 stalks celery, sliced
1 large bell pepper, chopped
1 (2-ounce) jar pimiento, drained
3/4 cup sliced green olives (reserve juice)

1/2 pound cheddar cheese, cubed
 or shredded
1 (8-ounce) bottle Caesar salad dressing
1 cup dairy sour cream (fat free, if desired)
2 tablespoons olive juice (reserved from
 olives)

Toss first 5 ingredients together in large bowl. Mix together remaining ingredients and pour over salad; toss until well coated. Refrigerate several hours or overnight before serving.

Coleslaw - A favorite recipe

1 large Granny Smith apple, unpeeled,
    cored and diced
8 cups slivered cabbage
1/2 cup raisins
1 tablespoon mayonnaise
4 tablespoons plain low-fat yogurt
    or sour cream

1/2 cup apple cider vinegar
2 tablespoons olive oil
6 packets Sweet & Low
1 teaspoon celery seed
1 teaspoon salt
Freshly ground black pepper

Place apples, cabbage and raisins in salad bowl. Combine remainder of ingredients and pour over cabbage mixture; toss well. Place in air-tight container and refrigerate until ready to serve.

Coleslaw - Jalapeño

1/3 cup sour cream
1/3 cup mayonnaise
2 tablespoons red wine vinegar
2 tablespoons olive oil
1 garlic clove, minced

1/4 cup chopped pickled jalapeño
    pepper (more if desired)
1/4 teaspoon salt
1/8 teaspoon pepper
1 (16-ounce) bag coleslaw mix

Combine first 8 ingredients in large bowl; add coleslaw mix, tossing to coat. Cover and chill. Yield: 4 to 6 servings.

Coleslaw - Marinated

1/2 cup sugar (you may substitute
    2 teaspoons or 6 packets of
    Sweet & Low)
1/2 cup water
1/2 cup vinegar
1 teaspoon mustard seed

1 teaspoon celery seed
1 bell pepper, chopped
1 onion, chopped fine
1/2 head of large cabbage, shredded,
    or 1 small cabbage

Combine first 5 ingredients; heat until sugar dissolves. Combine bell pepper, onion and cabbage; add marinade mix and toss. Cover tightly and refrigerate, turning occasionally, until ready to use. Keeps well in refrigerator.

Coleslaw Soufflé Salad

2 (3-ounce) packages lemon gelatin
1 cup boiling water
1 cup cold water
1 cup mayonnaise
2 tablespoons cider vinegar
1 teaspoon salt

1/4 teaspoon pepper
1/2 carrot, finely shredded
2 cups finely shredded cabbage
1/2 cup finely diced celery
1 small onion, finely diced
1 small cucumber, finely diced

Dissolve lemon gelatin in boiling water. Add cold water. Whisk in mayonnaise, vinegar, salt and pepper. Chill until becoming congealed around the edges; beat with electric mixer on medium speed until fluffy. Fold in remaining ingredients. Pour into 1 quart mold, individual molds, or dish to congeal. Vegetable garnish: Cucumber slice, celery curls, parsley or your choice. (It has the look of a sweet salad, so a vegetable garnish is good.) Very good, old, recipe.

Corn Salad

1 can white shoepeg corn
1 can Mexicorn
1 can sliced water chestnuts
1 bell pepper, red or green

1 small onion, or 3 green onions,
    tops and bottoms
2 stalks celery, chopped
Fresh ground black pepper
Ranch Dressing (made from purchased mix)

Drain shoepeg corn, Mexicorn and water chestnuts; combine and add other ingredients. Add Ranch Dressing to taste. Refrigerate.

It is not what happens to us, but what happens in us.

Corn Salad Mold - Tangy

2 cups water
1/4 cup cider vinegar
2 tablespoons Dijon mustard
2 (3-ounce) packages lemon gelatin
1 (2-ounce) jar diced pimientos, drained

1/2 cup chopped green bell pepper
1/2 cup chopped green onion
1 (15 1/4-ounce) can whole kernel corn, drained, or you may use white shoepeg corn, if you prefer

Combine water, vinegar and mustard in a saucepan; stir well, Sprinkle gelatin over vinegar mixture and let stand 1 minute. Cook over low heat, stirring until gelatin dissolves. Pour mixture into bowl and chill until slightly thickened. Fold in the remaining ingredients. Spoon into a mold or an 8 or 9-inch square dish. Cover and chill until firm. Serve on lettuce leaf with dollop of mayonnaise/sour cream (1/2 of each), and a very light sprinkle of celery seed on top. Yield: 9 servings.

Cucumbers, Sliced in Sour Cream

2 large cucumbers, pared and sliced thin
1 1/2 teaspoons salt
1 cup sour cream
2 tablespoons lemon juice

1 small onion, sliced and chopped
1/4 teaspoon sugar
Dash pepper

Toss cucumbers with salt. Set aside.
Combine sour cream, lemon juice, onion, sugar and pepper. Drain cucumbers. Toss with sour cream mixture. Refrigerate at least 2 hours before serving. Serves 4 to 6.

English Pea Salad - Dilled

1 (10-ounce) package tiny frozen green peas or 1 (16-ounce) can small green peas
1 cup diced mild cheddar cheese (4-ounces)
2 stalks celery, chopped
1/4 cup chopped dill pickle

1/2 cup mayonnaise or salad dressing
1/2 teaspoon dried dill weed or 1 1/2 teaspoons snipped fresh dill weed
1 (2-ounce) jar sliced pimientos
1/4 teaspoon salt

If using canned peas, drain well. If using frozen ones, put in a strainer and run very hot water over them for just a few minutes. Drain well. Toss all ingredients together. Chill and serve on lettuce. Makes 8 servings.

Jellied Horseradish Salad
(Delicious served with fish!)

1 (3-ounce) package lemon Jell-O
1 cup boiling water
1/2 cup whipping cream (You may
   substitute 1 cup whipped topping,
   thawed)

1 cup mayonnaise (You may use
   1/2 mayonnaise and 1/2 fat-free
   sour cream)
4 tablespoons drained horseradish
1 (3-ounce) package pineapple Jell-O

Mix the lemon Jell-O with the boiling water. Let cool until starting to set. Beat whipping cream until stiff; add mayonnaise and horseradish. Blend thoroughly with cooled Jell-O. Pour into 9x9-inch square pan, or larger if you would like the servings thinner. Mix pineapple Jell-O as per instructions on box. Let set until just slightly jelled; pour over top of first layer. Chill thoroughly and cut into squares.

Potato Salad

6 large potatoes, boiled and diced
4 hard-boiled eggs, diced
1/2 cup chopped green pepper
1/4 cup chopped onion
1/2 cup sweet relish
1 teaspoon celery seed

Salt and pepper to taste
1 cup salad dressing
1 teaspoon mustard, or more if desired
2 tablespoons sugar
1/4 cup milk

Prepare all ingredients except dressing. Mix salad dressing, mustard, sugar and milk and mix into all other ingredients. Taste, if not enough dressing, prepare and add more.

Watch, or you will miss the tiny seeds of faith you are to cultivate each day.

Potato Salad with Sour Cream Dressing

7 medium potatoes, cooked, unpeeled
   (6 cups)
1/3 cup clear French or Italian dressing
3/4 cup sliced celery
1/3 cup sliced green onions and tops
   (Reserve some tops)
4 hard-cooked eggs

1 cup mayonnaise
1/2 cup sour cream
1 1/2 teaspoons prepared
   horseradish mustard
Salt, to taste
Celery seed, to taste
1/3 cup diced pared cucumber, optional

While potatoes are warm peel and slice; pour dressing over them and chill for 2 hours. Add celery and onion. Chop egg whites; add. Sieve yolks; reserve some for garnish. Combine remaining sieved yolks with mayonnaise, sour cream and horse-radish mustard. Fold into salad. Add salt and celery seed to taste. Chill salad for 2 hours. Add diced cucumber, if desired. Mix. To garnish, sprinkle reserved sieved yolks and sliced onion tops over top. Serves 8 to 10.

Summer Tomato Salad

1 pound tomatoes, cut into wedges
1/2 small onion, sliced
2 tablespoons olive oil
2 tablespoons red wine vinegar

1/2 teaspoon garlic salt
1/4 teaspoon black pepper
1 tablespoon fresh basil or other herbs
Feta cheese

Combine all ingredients and crumble feta cheese on top.

Sweet Potato Holiday Salad
(Very unusual and very good!)

1 (8-ounce) crushed pineapple,
   undrained
1 cup apricot nectar
1 (3-ounce) package apricot flavored
   gelatin

1 (8-ounce) package cream cheese,
   cubed and softened
1 cup shredded raw sweet potatoes
   (or finely chopped)
1 cup chopped pecans
1 cup frozen whipped topping, thawed

Combine pineapple and apricot nectar in a saucepan, bring to a boil. Add gelatin, stirring until gelatin dissolves, add cream cheese, stir until melted. Chill until slightly thickened. Fold in sweet potatoes, pecans and whipped topping. Pour into 5-cup mold or 9-inch square dish. Chill until firm. Yield 9 to 12 servings.

Tomato Aspic - Special Dressing

3 envelopes unflavored gelatin
1/2 cup cold water
3 cups boiling tomato juice
1/2 cup ketchup
1/4 cup lemon juice

2 tablespoon grated onion
1 tablespoon prepared horseradish
3/4 teaspoon salt
Special Dressing (recipe follows)

Lightly oil 4-cup mold or 8 individual molds. Sprinkle gelatin in cold water. Set aside. Bring tomato juice to boil in medium saucepan. Add softened gelatin, ketchup, lemon juice, onion, horseradish and salt. Stir well. Pour into mold or molds and chill several hours or overnight. Yield: 8 (1/2-cup) servings.

Special Dressing:
1 cup mayonnaise

1/4 cup Durkee's Salad and Sandwich Sauce

Mix mayonnaise and sauce well. Chill and and keep ready to serve on aspic.

Tomato Aspic - Asheville Style

1 can tomato soup
2 envelopes plain gelatin
1/2 cup cold water
2 (3-ounce) packages cream cheese
1 cup mayonnaise

1/2 cup green pepper, chopped
1/2 cup onions, chopped
1/4 cup sliced olives
1/4 cup celery, chopped
Salt and cayenne pepper to taste

Bring soup to boil; add gelatin which has been dissolved in cold water. Add cheese slowly, creaming thoroughly. When slightly thickened, add mayonnaise and remaining ingredients. Congeal. Unmold on lettuce. Garnish with olives.

Tomato Salad - Congealed

1 can chopped tomatoes
1 (3-ounce) box lemon gelatin
1/2 cup chopped celery
10 stuffed olives, sliced

1/4 cup chopped green pepper
1/2 teaspoon salt
1 teaspoon Worcestershire sauce
Few drops of hot sauce

Heat tomatoes; stir in gelatin, cool a few minutes. Add other ingredients. Refrigerate. Serve with dollop of half mayonnaise and half sour cream.

Toss Salad - Layered

1 head Boston lettuce (rinsed and refrigerated to crisp the day before)
1 medium red onion, cut in half, sliced, rings separated
3-4 tomatoes, cut chunky
1 (10-ounce) package frozen McKenzie Deluxe Petite green peas, thawed
Cauliflower, peppers, fresh mushrooms (or whatever your family likes)
1/2 jar Bacos chips (or to taste)
1 cup mayonnaise
1 cup sour cream (fat-free)
2 tablespoons sugar
2 cups shredded Monterey Jack or sharp cheddar cheese

Break lettuce into bite-size pieces. Layer desired vegetables, beginning with lettuce; layering peas on last. Combine mayonnaise, sour cream and sugar. Spread over vegetables as you would ice a cake, sealing in vegetables. Top with grated cheese. Cover and refrigerate.

Toss Salad for 45-50 People

4 heads lettuce, broken into bite-size pieces (rinsed and refrigerated the day before)
1 bunch celery, sliced
2 red onions, sliced
6 plum tomatoes, cut vertically through center
1 (16-ounce) bag McKenzie frozen Petite Deluxe green peas
1 jar Bacos chips
1 pound sharp cheddar cheese, grated
4 packages Ranch Dressing Mix, mixed according to directions or 4 recipes of **Special Salad Dressing** (recipe follows)

Prepare and combine all vegetables; toss with your favorite dressing just before serving or serve dressing on the side.

Special Salad Dressing:

1 cup mayonnaise
1 cup sour cream (fat-free)
1 teaspoon celery seed
2 tablespoons apple cider vinegar
4 tablespoons sugar

Combine all ingredients and refrigerate over night allowing flavors to meld.

Toss Salad, Oriental
This is so good!

Salad Greens: 6 cups chopped napa
    cabbage and bok choy combined,
    or you may use 6 cups green cabbage
4 green onions, chopped, using some
    of the green

1/2 cup diced mushrooms, optional
5 radishes, sliced, optional
Soy Vinaigrette (recipe follows)

Rinse napa cabbage and bok choy, or green cabbage; seal in plastic wrap or tightly covered container, and refrigerate well ahead of use, as you would lettuce. This allows vegetables to become thoroughly crisp. Chop cabbage, bok choy, onion, mushrooms, radishes, and combine. (Be sure to use the white part of the bok choy, it is so good!) Refrigerate, tightly covered. This can be done the day before using.

Soy Vinaigrette:
1/2 cup safflower oil or vegetable oil
1/2 cup rice or balsamic vinegar
2 tablespoons soy sauce

3/4 cup sugar (or Sweet & Low,
    12 packets or 4 teaspoons)

Combine oil, vinegar, soy sauce and sugar (or Sweet & Low) in small container that you can shake. If using sugar, cook over medium heat, stirring constantly, until sugar dissolves. Cool. Set this dressing aside. If you like more dressing, double the recipe. (You may do this ahead of time and refrigerate.)

Crunchy Mixture:
1 (3-ounce) package Ramen Noodles -
    (discard flavor packet)
4 tablespoons butter or margarine, melted

1/2 cup sunflower seed
1/2 cup slivered almonds

Crumble noodles into bite-size pieces, combine with sunflower seed and almonds. Melt butter in jelly-roll pan in 350 degree oven; add seed, nuts and noodles, and toss to coat. Bake, stirring often, until lightly toasted, being careful not to over cook, as almonds will toast quickly. Cool. Seal in plastic bag until ready to use. This, also, can be done several days ahead. Do not refrigerate. Just before serving, toss all ingredients in large salad bowl. A wonderful do-ahead salad!

Vegetable Medley Salad

1 bunch fresh broccoli
1 head cauliflower
1 (16-ounce) bag petite frozen
　English peas
1 envelope Hidden Valley Ranch
　Original Dressing Mix

1 (8-ounce) carton sour cream
　(fat free, if desired)
1 cup mayonnaise
1 cup grated cheddar cheese
1 jar Bacos chips or Bacon Bits

Wash and drain broccoli and cauliflower. Cut broccoli (florets only) and cauliflower into small pieces; add peas. Mix the dressing mix with the sour cream and mayonnaise. Add bacon bits and cheese. Toss with vegetables. Refrigerate several hours before serving. Serves: 8 to 10.

Veggie Salad - Congealed

2 (3-ounce) packages lemon Jell-O
1 cup boiling water
1/2 cup cold water
1 (16-ounce) can chopped tomatoes,
　in juice
1 cup chopped cucumber, optional
1/4 cup bell pepper, chopped
1/4 cup chopped onions, sweet or spring
　(tops and bottoms)

1 cup frozen petite English peas
3 tablespoons sugar
3 tablespoons vinegar
1/2 teaspoon black pepper
3/4 teaspoon salt
1/2 teaspoon celery seed

Dissolve Jell-O in boiling water; add cold water. Add all other ingredients and refrigerate several hours or overnight. Serve on lettuce with mayonnaise/sour cream dressing, (1/2 of each.)

Sauces

Cranberry Crunch - So Good and So Easy!

2 cups fresh cranberries
1 cup sugar
1 (12-ounce) jar orange marmalade
Grated rind of 1 orange

4 ounces crystallized ginger, cut into
    small pieces, optional
1 cup chopped pecans

Rinse and pick cranberries. Place in an oblong (7x11-inch) pyrex dish. Sprinkle with sugar. Cover and seal with aluminum foil. Bake in a 350 degree oven for 25 minutes. (The cranberries will have popped.) Cool slightly and stir to dissolve sugar. Add other ingredients and refrigerate. I do not use the ginger, but you may like it. **Note:** This is a wonderful recipe, and it keeps indefinitely in the refrigerator. It is so good with chicken, turkey, and ham, and **makes very special holiday gifts!** It is also great, and pretty, as a topping on blocks of cream cheese as an hors d' oeuvre. Serve with Triscuits, or your favorite crackers.

Fruit Glaze

1 cup fresh fruit, crushed
1/3 cup sugar

2 tablespoons cornstarch
1 tablespoon water

Bring to a boil fruit and sugar over medium heat; boil 2 minutes. Whisk together cornstarch and water; stir into fruit mixture. Return to boil, stirring constantly; boil 1 minute. Cool.

Strawberry-Banana Topping for Pound Cake and Ice Cream

2 tablespoons butter
2 tablespoons brown sugar
2 tablespoons lemon juice
1/4 cup light rum

3 medium bananas, sliced (Use firm
    bananas)
6 fresh strawberries, cut in half
Commercial pound cake or vanilla ice
    cream (or both)

Melt butter in skillet. Add sugar, lemon juice and rum; stir well. Cook until sugar dissolves (2 to 3 minutes), stirring constantly. Add bananas and strawberries; cook until bananas are just a little soft, but not mushy. Serve over pound cake and ice cream, or just over ice cream.

Barbecue Sauce

1 can condensed tomato soup
1/4 cup honey
3 tablespoons Worcestershire sauce
2 tablespoons soy sauce
1/3 cup ketchup
2 tablespoons vegetable oil
1 tablespoon lemon juice

1 tablespoon mustard
1 teaspoon chili powder
1/2 teaspoon dried minced onion
1/4 teaspoon garlic powder
Dash red pepper or bottled hot sauce
(to taste)

Combine all ingredients in medium saucepan. Bring to a boil on medium heat. Reduce heat and simmer uncovered 5 minutes. Keeps well in refrigerator.
Note: A good sauce! Nice for gifts!

Barbecue Sauce for Grilled Chicken

1/2 pound margarine
1 cup lemon juice

3 tablespoons Worcestershire sauce
Garlic powder and salt to taste

Melt margarine and add other ingredients. Simmer 2 to 3 minutes, but do not boil. Grill chicken and add sauce toward the end of grilling time.

Cocktail Sauce

1 cup ketchup
2 tablespoons Worcestershire sauce
2 tablespoons lemon juice

2 tablespoons prepared horseradish
Salt to taste
Tabasco sauce to taste

Combine. Keep in refrigerator at least 1 hour before serving.

Durkee's Sauce for Chicken

1/4 cup Durkee Famous Sauce
1/2 cup mayonnaise
2 tablespoons lemon juice
1 tablespoon honey

1 teaspoon Worcestershire sauce
1 1/2 teaspoons rosemary leaves
    or dill weed, optional

This is listed in chicken recipes in this book. It is also good as a sauce for broiled or grilled fish and steaks.

Cucumber Sauce for Salmon, Salmon Loaf or Other Seafood

1/2 cup mayonnaise
1/2 cup sour cream
1/2 cup finely chopped cucumber

2 tablespoons chopped onion
1/2 teaspoon dill weed

Combine ingredients; mix well. Yield: 6 to 8 servings. This is listed with Pacific Salmon Loaf with other seafoods. This is an old recipe and very good.

Horseradish Cream

1 cup whipping cream

4-6 tablespoons horseradish (to taste),
    well drained

Beat cream very stiff. Add horseradish. Serve with beef or pork. Cover and store in refrigerator up to 3 days. You can substitute 2 cups whipped topping (thawed) for the 1 cup whipping cream.
Note: Prepare as above, except substitute 2 tablespoons Dijon-style mustard (or more) for the horseradish. Serve with beef or pork. Add mustard to your taste. You may substitute 2 cups frozen whipped topping for whipping cream. The little taste of sweet adds to the flavor, and the fluffy texture is nice.

Lemon Sauce for Veggies

1/2 cup sour cream
1/2 cup mayonnaise

1 teaspoon prepared mustard (to taste)
2 tablespoons lemon juice

Mix all ingredients and heat over very low heat. Yield: 1 cup. Good on asparagus and broccoli!

Orange Sauce

1 cup light brown sugar, firmly packed
2 tablespoons cornstarch
1/2 teaspoon salt

4 tablespoons orange peel, grated
2 cups orange juice
1/2 cup water

Combine sugar, cornstarch and salt. Stir in orange peel, juice and water. Cook over low heat, stirring constantly; until thickened and transparent. Good served with Cornish hens, turkey, wild duck, or as you like.

Elizabeth's Favorite Sauce for Pork

1 cup ketchup
1 cup water
6 tablespoons lemon juice

4 tablespoons Worcestershire sauce
4 tablespoons soy sauce
4 tablespoons brown sugar

Combine ingredients. Will keep a very long time in refrigerator. This is good to drizzle on slices when you slice your pork roast, and to serve on side along with roast. **It is a sauce, not a gravy.** Our family loves this!

Tartar Sauce

1 cup mayonnaise (You may substitute
  1/2 cup fat free sour cream for
  1/2 cup of the mayonnaise.)
1/3 cup dill pickle, finely chopped

1/3 cup onion, finely chopped
1 1/2 teaspoons capers, chopped
1 teaspoon lemon juice
1 tablespoon diced pimiento

Mix all ingredients and refrigerate at least 1 hour before serving with seafood.

White Sauce - Medium

2 tablespoons margarine
2 tablespoons all-purpose flour
1/4 teaspoon salt

Dash pepper
1 cup milk

In a small saucepan melt margarine . Stir in flour, salt, and pepper. Add milk all at once. Cook and stir over medium heat until thickened and bubbly. Cook and stir 1 minute more. Makes 1 cup.

Cheese Sauce: Same as above except leave out salt and add cheese.

Thick Sauce: (Makes 1 cup)
3 tablespoons margarine
4 tablespoons all-purpose flour
1/4 teaspoon salt

Dash pepper
1 cup milk

Thin Sauce: (Makes 1 1/2 cups)
1 tablespoon margarine
1 tablespoon all-purpose flour
1/4 teaspoon salt

Dash pepper
1 1/2 cups milk

Worry causes a divided mind, and we lose our sense of direction.

Chili, Chowders, Soups & Stews

Chili

Makes 8 quarts - (Half recipe, if desired)
(Use heat diffuser to prevent scorching!)

5 pounds lean ground beef
5 large onions, chopped
5 cans chopped tomatoes
3 cans Ro-tel tomatoes, diced
4 cans red kidney beans or pinto
    beans, drained (or you may use
    1 1/2 pounds dry beans, soaked
    overnight and cooked)
2 tablespoons vinegar

2 teaspoons garlic
2 teaspoons oregano
3 tablespoons chili powder
2 teaspoons cumin
1/4 cup sugar
1 quart water (adjust amount to
    thickness desired)
Salt and pepper to taste
Tabasco sauce, if desired

In large stock pot, sauté ground beef until it has changed color, stirring occasionally. Drain well. Add onions and allow them to cook, stirring, for a few minutes. Add all other ingredients and simmer, uncovered, 1 hour, stirring occasionally. Makes about 8 quarts. Adjust ingredients for the number of people you are serving.

Chicken or Turkey Chowder

4 chicken breast halves, skinned
    and fat discarded (or equal amount
    of turkey or other chicken pieces)
4 cups water
1/2 teaspoon salt
3 small onions, diced
2 medium carrots. sliced
2 medium potatoes, peeled and cubed

1 (17-ounce) can cream corn
1 (15-ounce) can diced tomatoes
2 cups milk, more or less for desired
    thickness
1/4 teaspoon curry powder
Instant chicken bouillon to taste
Tabasco sauce, if desired

Combine first 3 ingredients; cook until chicken is very tender. Remove chicken from broth; debone and chop, reserving chicken. Add onions, carrots and potatoes to broth and cook slowly, about 10 to 12 minutes. Add all other ingredients, including chopped chicken. Simmer about 15 minutes, until vegetables are very tender, stirring occasionally. Adjust seasoning with instant chicken bouillon and Tabasco, if desired. Serves 8, generously.
Note: For chicken and pasta chowder, add (3/4 cup) uncooked rotini (spiral pasta). Adjust milk and instant chicken bouillon, if necessary.

Corn Chowder

2 tablespoons margarine
1 large onion, chopped
1/2 cup chopped celery
1/3 cup bell pepper (optional)
2 tablespoons all-purpose flour
4 cups skim milk
2 (16 1/2-ounce) cans cream-style corn

1 (11-ounce) can yellow or white
   shoepeg corn
1/4 teaspoon thyme
1/8 teaspoon paprika
1 teaspoon black pepper, or to taste
1 teaspoon salt
Tabasco sauce to taste

Melt margarine, add onion, celery and pepper; sauté for 2 to 3 minutes. Add flour and milk, continuing to cook and stir until well mixed. Add all other ingredients and simmer for about 30 to 45 minutes, stirring occasionally. Use a heat diffuser on stove burner to keep from scorching. Yield: about 2 quarts. A favorite!
Variation: For Corn-Clam Chowder, add 1 cup frozen mixed vegetables (or 1 cup vegetables of your choice), and 1 (6 1/2-ounce) can minced clams.

Creamy Broccoli-Ham Chowder

1/4 cup butter or margarine
1 medium onion, chopped
1/4 cup all-purpose flour
1 1/2 teaspoons salt (or less)
1/2 teaspoon celery salt
1/8 teaspoon white pepper

3 cups milk
1 (6 3/4-ounce) can chopped ham
1 (10-ounce) package frozen, chopped
   broccoli
2 tablespoons chopped chives
1 cup sour cream

Microwave butter and onion in 2 to 4-quart glass casserole or soup tureen 4 to 5 minutes until tender, stirring once. Blend in flour, salt, celery salt and pepper. Stir in milk. Microwave 7 to 8 minutes or until mixture boils and thickens, stirring 3 to 4 times. Add ham, broccoli and chives. Microwave, covered, 11 to 12 minutes or until broccoli is just about tender, stirring twice. Stir in sour cream.
Microwave, covered, 2 to 3 minutes or until hot.

Shrimp Chowder

8 slices bacon, optional
1 medium onion, chopped
2 stalks celery, chopped or
   1 can cream of celery soup
2 large potatoes, chopped and cooked
   in 3 cups of water, or
   2 (10 3/4-ounce) cans cream of
   potato soup

2 (4-ounce) packages frozen salad
   shrimp or 2 (4 1/4-ounce) cans
   small shrimp, drained and rinsed
4 cups milk
1/4 teaspoon pepper
1 cup instant mashed potatoes
   (optional- use only if you want
   chowder thicker)

Cook bacon until crisp; remove bacon, reserving very small amount of drippings. Crumble bacon and set aside. In reserved drippings, (use 2 tablespoons olive oil, if not using bacon) sauté onion and celery until tender. Add potatoes (with water in which they were cooked), and remaining ingredients, stirring well. Cook over medium heat until thoroughly heated. Sprinkle each serving with bacon, if using bacon. Yield: 2 1/2 quarts.

Broccoli-Cheese Soup

1 small onion, chopped
2 tablespoons margarine, melted
2 (10-ounce) packages frozen,
   chopped broccoli (thawed)

2 cans cream of potato soup
2 cups chicken broth, or more for
   desired thickness
1 small box Velveeta cheese, cubed

In saucepan, sauté chopped onion in melted margarine. Add broccoli, potato soup, chicken broth and cubed cheese. Stir over medium heat, stirring, until cheese is melted and soup is hot. (You can make your chicken broth by adding 1 1/2 teaspoons instant chicken bouillon to each cup of water, if you prefer.)

Chicken Noodle Soup
(Suzanna's Favorite)

1 cup chopped celery
1 cup chopped onion
1/4 cup margarine
12 cups water
1 cup diced carrots
3 tablespoons chicken bouillon

1/2 teaspoon marjoram leaves (ground)
1/2 teaspoon pepper
1 bay leaf
4 cups diced cooked chicken
1 (5-ounce) package wide egg noodles
1 tablespoon chopped parsley

In a large Dutch oven, cook celery and onion in margarine until tender. Add remaining ingredients except chicken, noodles, and parsley. Bring to a boil, reduce heat and simmer 25 minutes. Remove bay leaf. Add wide egg noodles, chicken, and parsley. Return to a boil and cook 10 to 15 minutes or until noodles are tender, stirring occasionally. Makes 4 quarts.

Cabbage and White Bean Soup

1 tablespoon olive oil
3 cups thinly sliced green cabbage
1 large carrot, sliced
1 tablespoon chopped garlic
1/2 teaspoon salt
1/8 teaspoon ground pepper
2 (14 1/2-ounce) cans chicken broth
   (or make your own)

1 (14 1/2 or 16-ounce) cans diced
   tomatoes in juice
1 cup water (or water to desired
   consistency, adding chicken bouillon,
   if desired)
2 (16-ounce) can white beans
   (cannellini, or great Northern
   white beans) drained and rinsed

Heat oil in large saucepan. Add cabbage, carrot, garlic, salt and pepper; cover and cook 2 minutes until cabbage starts to wilt. Increase heat to high; add broth, tomatoes and their juice, and water. Cover, bring to a boil and cook 7 to 9 minutes until vegetables are tender. Meanwhile, remove 1 1/4 cups beans to a plate; puree remaining beans in food processor or blender. (Do this only if you would like soup thickened.) Add reserved beans and bean puree to saucepan and cook 2 minutes, until soup is hot. Makes 4 servings.

Cream of Anything Soup

1/4 cup butter
1/4 cup flour
2 cups vegetable stock (liquid in
    which your vegetable has been
    cooked)

Vegetable of your choice, precooked
Salt and pepper to taste
1/2 cup milk or cream to thin,
    (more or less, to desired thickness)

In a large pot over medium heat, cook butter and flour to make roux. Add vegetable stock. Cook until it thickens. Add vegetable, salt and pepper. Thin with milk or cream. Serve hot. Be careful not to boil. Serves 6, and works well with broccoli, asparagus or cauliflower.

Beef and Vegetable Soup
(10 to 12 quarts - You can easily make less)

2 pounds ground round, browned
    and drained
1 (16-ounce) frozen petite baby limas
2 (14 3/4-ounce) cans cream
    style corn
2 (11-ounce) cans white shoepeg corn
4 (14 1/2-ounce) cans diced tomatoes
5 ribs celery, chopped and cooked
2 large potatoes, cubed and cooked
4 large onions, chopped and cooked
4 carrots, sliced and cooked

1 (46-ounce) can V-8 100% vegetable
    juice - (use some water if you
    want less tomato taste)
Salt, pepper and instant beef bouillon
    to taste
Tabasco sauce, if desired
5 cups chopped cabbage
1 (16-ounce) package frozen, sliced,
    unbreaded okra
1 (16-ounce) package frozen petite
    green peas

Combine all ingredients except cabbage, okra and English peas. Bring to a boil and reduce heat to low or simmer. Maintain that heat for about 40 minutes; add cabbage, okra and English peas, and cook on low heat for about 30 minutes or until all vegetables are done. Adjust seasoning, if necessary. This makes about 10 to 12 quarts. I use this large amount when I want to put some in the freezer. It is so nice to have ready to take out, heat and serve.

Potato Soup - Easy and Good

4 cups diced potatoes
1 large onion, chopped
1 can cream of celery soup (or chicken)
2 cups skim milk
1/4 pound Velveeta cheese, cubed

3 tablespoons Bacos Chips or
    Real Bacon Bits, optional
1/2 teaspoons garlic salt
Tabasco sauce to taste
Salt and pepper to taste

Combine potatoes and onions in saucepan; cover with water and cook until tender. Leave water on them. Add all other ingredients and cook on medium heat until cheese is melted. We love this soup, and it is a wonderful gift for someone not feeling well.

Quick Veggie Soup

1 (16-ounce) package frozen mixed
    vegetables
1 (1-ounce) envelope dry onion
    soup mix

1 (46-ounce) can V-8 100% vegetable
    juice
1 pound lean ground beef, browned
    and drained well

Combine all ingredients; bring to a boil. Reduce heat and simmer 20 minutes. Yield: 2 quarts.

Refrigerator Soup

2 smoked turkey legs, skinned
    and chopped
1 cup dried lima beans, soaked
    overnight
1 large onion
2 cloves garlic, minced
Pinch dried thyme

1 bay leaf
Salt and pepper to taste
2 carrots, peeled and sliced crosswise
1 turnip, peeled and cubed
8 ounces potatoes, cubed
8 ounces cabbage, shredded

Place turkey legs, lima beans, onion, garlic, thyme and bay leaf in a stockpot with 5 cups cold water. Bring to a boil, reduce heat and simmer, covered, for about 50 minutes. Discard bay leaf. Season with salt and pepper. Add carrots, potatoes, turnip and cabbage. Add more water, if needed. Cook another 45 minutes. Remove turkey legs; take meat from bones and chop. Return meat to pot. Serve soup with crusty bread. Serves 4.

Smoked Chicken (or Turkey) and White Beans (Cannellini) or Great Northern Beans

Nonstick cooking spray
1 teaspoon olive oil
2 cloves garlic, minced
1 large yellow onion, chopped
2 (16-ounce) cans stewed tomatoes, with liquid
1 can Ro-tel diced tomatoes with green chiles
1/2 teaspoon dried oregano, crushed or to taste

1 teaspoon dried basil, crushed or to taste
1/2 teaspoon salt
1/4 teaspoon freshly ground black pepper
3 (16-ounce) cans white beans, rinsed and drained
1 pound smoked chicken, or turkey, skinned and chopped
1 quart of water or more (to desired consistency)
Salt and pepper to taste

Heat a large nonstick skillet and add the oil. Sauté the garlic and onion until softened, about 5 minutes, stirring occasionally. Pour into stock pot or Dutch oven; stir in the tomatoes, oregano, basil, salt and pepper. Bring to a boil, then reduce heat and simmer, uncovered, for 15 minutes. Add the rinsed beans, chopped chicken and water; mix well. Adjust liquid and seasonings, if necessary. Cover and simmer 20 minutes or until flavors have melded. Serve. Yield: About 3 quarts.

Note: This is so good! We like smoked turkey for Thanksgiving and Christmas, and we use some of the left-over turkey for this soup. It is a great change from the rich foods of the holidays, and very healthy.

Worry in Greek means "double-minded."

Beef-Taco Soup

2 (6-inch) corn tortillas, optional
Vegetable cooking spray
1 pound ground round beef
1 cup chopped onion
1 packet of taco seasoning
1 (15-ounce) can diced tomatoes
1 (16-ounce) can dark red kidney beans,
   drained and rinsed
1 (8-ounce) can tomato sauce
1 (4-ounce) can chopped green chiles,
   undrained

1 (14-ounce) can beef broth
   (or make your own: 1 1/2 teaspoons
   beef bouillon to 1 cup water)
1 1/2 tablespoons seeded and minced
   jalapeño peppers, optional
1/2 cup shredded lettuce
1/2 cup chopped tomato
1/2 cup shredded, reduced-fat sharp
   cheddar cheese

Cut tortillas into 1/2-inch wide strips; cut strips in half crosswise. Place tortilla strips on a baking sheet sprayed with cooking spray. Bake at 350 degrees for 12 to 15 minutes or until crisp. Set aside. Coat a Dutch oven with cooking spray, place over medium heat until hot. Add ground round and onion. Cook until beef is browned; drain. Add taco seasoning packet to beef and onion. Stir in canned tomatoes, beans, tomato sauce, green chiles, beef broth, and jalapeño peppers. Bring to a boil; cover, reduce heat, and simmer 30 minutes, stirring occasionally. Ladle soup into individual bowls; top evenly with lettuce, tomato, cheese, and tortilla strips. You may also garnish with 1/2 teaspoon of fat-free sour cream. Serves 8 (1-cup) servings.

Brunswick Stew - Easy!

1 (24-ounce) can Castleberry's
    Brunswick Stew
1 small can Castleberry's pork
1 small can Swanson's white chicken
1 can cream corn

1 can white shoepeg corn, or
    yellow whole kernels
1/4 cup Kraft Hickory Smoke
    Barbecue Sauce
Juice of 2 lemons
1 tablespoon Worcestershire sauce

Combine all ingredients in large saucepan or Dutch oven. Heat until bubbling. Stir occasionally to keep from sticking. Serve. (Use heat diffuser to prevent scorching.)

Southern-Style Brunswick Stew
(This is great for the freezer, or anytime!)

(All these measurements are approximate.
Vary them according to your family's preference.)

Cook your meats first; discard fat. Refrigerate broth and remove fat from top. Use needed broth in stew. You may want to freeze remainder for other uses. Prepare meats the day before you plan to make the stew, and the job will not seem so big.

12 cups chopped chicken
6 cups chopped pork (Boston butt,
    or the cut you prefer)
4 large chopped onions
    (cook in microwave)
6 (14.5-ounce) cans diced tomatoes
3 (10-ounce) cans Ro-tel tomatoes
    and green chiles
3 (14 3/4-ounce) cans cream
    style corn

3 (11-ounce) cans white shoepeg
    corn, or whole yellow kernels
1 (16-ounce) package frozen
    petite green peas (English)
2 cups ketchup
1 (10-ounce) bottle Worcestershire
    sauce
4 tablespoons lemon juice or vinegar
4 tablespoons sugar
4-6 cups broth (to desired thickness)
Tabasco sauce to taste (if desired)

Use heat diffuser to help prevent scorching! Combine all ingredients and cook, stirring, until it gets hot. Reduce heat and simmer about 1 hour. Serve, or place in pint or quart freezer cartons; allow to cool a little and freeze. Wonderful to have ready to heat and serve. This is a family favorite!

Vegetable casseroles & Vegetables

Casseroles that are named from one specific vegetable, are in alphabetical order with the vegetable in this book.

Buffet Vegetable Bake with French Beans

2 (10-ounce) packages frozen French
    beans, drained
1 can bean sprouts, drained
1 can cream of chicken soup
1 can water chestnuts, sliced

1/4 cup Parmesan cheese, grated
1/4 cup Swiss cheese, grated
1 tablespoon Worcestershire sauce
1/2 cup toasted, slivered almonds

Combine all ingredients except nuts in 1 1/2-quart casserole. Bake at 350 degrees 25 minutes or until hot. Stir; top with almonds and bake 5 minutes more or until lightly browned. Yield: 6 to 8 servings.

Life should be fun, filled with great expectations and a constant sense of true values - things that really count and make a difference in our lives and in the lives of others.

Garlic-Roasted Vegetables

1 large whole bulb garlic, optional
3 medium all-purpose potatoes,
    cut into fourths
4 small onions, each cut lengthwise
    in fourths
3 medium yellow crook-neck squash,
    cut into 3/4-inch slices

2 medium zucchini, cut into 3/4-inch
    thick slices
6 medium plum tomatoes, each cut
    lengthwise into fourths
1/4 cup grated Parmesan cheese

Seasoning:
2 tablespoons olive oil or more to
    coat all vegetables

1 teaspoon dried Italian seasoning, or
    Morton's Nature's Seasons Seasoning
    Blend
1/2 teaspoon cracked black pepper, if desired

Preheat oven to 425 degrees. Cut 3/4-inch off top of unpeeled garlic bulb, cutting through tip of each clove. Discard top portion. Wrap garlic securely with foil. Set aside. In large bowl, combine seasoning ingredients. (Our family prefers the Morton's Blend, but either is good.) Add vegetables except tomatoes; toss to coat. Reserve tomatoes in bowl to add later. Arrange all other vegetables and foil-wrapped garlic on 15x10-inch jelly-roll pan. (Line jelly-roll pan with foil for easy clean up.) Roast in 425 degree oven 30 minutes or just before crisp-tender stage, checking often. Toss tomatoes in seasoned oil and add to vegetables in pan. Continue to roast for just a few minutes until vegetable are desired doneness. Remove to large bowl or tray, or serve on foil-lined pan. Unwrap garlic; squeeze softened cloves of garlic over vegetables. Very gently toss. Sprinkle with cheese and adjust seasonings, if needed.
Note: This is a beautiful and healthy dish that has been a very popular recipe; I have shared it with many people. It also is a family favorite! To me, the secret to success with this is, to not over cook. An advantage is that you can adjust the ingredients for any number of people, and substitute vegetables to please your family!
Suggestion: Leave off the potatoes and serve over pasta with Mock Pasta Alfredo Sauce. (Recipe for sauce in Pastas.)

When circumstances of life bump into you, what spills out is what you are filled with.

Veg-All Casserole

1 can Veg-All, drained
1 cup celery, chopped
1 cup grated sharp cheddar cheese
1 medium onion, chopped
1 can cream of celery soup

1/2 cup sour cream, optional
1/2 cup mayonnaise
1 can sliced water chestnuts, drained
1 sleeve Ritz crackers, crumbled
1 stick margarine

Mix all ingredients, except cracker crumbs and margarine. Pour into casserole. Cover mixture with cracker crumbs. Melt margarine and drizzle over casserole. Bake in 350 degree oven until bubbly and light brown.

Vegetable Casserole

1 (15-ounce) can white shoepeg corn, drained
1 (16-ounce) can French-style green beans with almonds, drained
1/2 cup chopped celery
1/2 cup chopped onions

1/2 (8-ounce) can water chestnuts, sliced
1 (8-ounce) carton sour cream
1 (10 3/4-ounce) can cream of celery soup
1 sleeve Ritz crackers, crumbled
1 stick margarine

Mix all ingredients together, except crackers and margarine. Pour into casserole. Top with Ritz cracker crumbs. Melt margarine and pour over cracker crumbs. Bake at 350 degrees 30 to 40 minutes. Makes 8 to 10 servings.

In the tapestry of your life, if you are a strong, beautiful thread of faith, you will be a blessing to others.

Chinese Vegetable Stir-Fry

(This recipe is from a special Chinese friend who entertained us royally on our trip to her country, Taiwan.)

1 tablespoon vegetable oil, or olive oil
4-5 cups mixed vegetables (see suggestion)
1/3-1/2 cup **Asian Sauce** (recipe follows)
  combined with 1 tablespoon cornstarch
  and 1/3 cup water

Chicken, beef or pork strips, cooked
  (may be added, if desired)

Heat the oil in a pan or wok over high heat. Add the vegetables and stir-fry. If the vegetables begin to brown, add 1/4 cup water and cover to steam them. (Be careful not to over cook.) When the vegetables are done (and precooked meat, if using meat), remove from wok and set aside. In the empty wok, add sauce and cornstarch mixture, stirring constantly, until it comes to a boil. Return the vegetables to the wok just long enough to heat through. Serve immediately.

Suggestion: 1 medium onion, sliced lengthwise; 1 large red bell pepper, cored, seeded and cut into strips; and 4 cups broccoli florets. Any combination of vegetables you prefer will work fine.

Classic All-Purpose Asian Sauce:

1/2 cup soy sauce
1/4 cup water
1/4 cup sesame oil
1/4 cup brown sugar, granulated
  sugar or honey

1 teaspoon black or white pepper,
  or to taste
2 cloves garlic, crushed, or to taste
1 1/2 tablespoons (about 3/4-inch piece)
  crushed or pureed fresh ginger
  (can use juice as well)

In small container with cover, combine the soy sauce, water, sesame oil, sugar or honey, pepper, garlic and ginger. Heat to meld flavors. Cool and store tightly covered in refrigerator. You may like to keep this in fridge for quick meals.

Asparagus - Right Out of the Can

This is a menu for a busy day when you don't want to dress to go out to eat, and you certainly do not want to cook! It will get you by until time for the next meal with ease and good health!

1 (10 1/2-ounce) can of asparagus
   cuts and tips
Ranch dressing, as desired
1 (15-ounce) can sliced beets
1 tablespoon mayonnaise, or to taste

Pepper and salt to taste
1 (14 3/4-ounce) can salmon
Fat-free saltine crackers
Fruit of your choice

Drain asparagus and place on a small, attractive, dish. Drizzle with small amount of Ranch dressing. Drain beets and place in small bowl. Add small amount of mayonnaise, pepper, and salt to taste. Toss and put in serving dish. Drain salmon; remove skin and bones, if you can't bear to eat them, but try to leave bones in because we need the calcium! Place on serving dish and drizzle with Real lemon. Serve with fat-free Premium saltines. Have fruit for dessert. Enjoy!

Asparagus Casserole

4 tablespoons butter or margarine
4 tablespoons flour
2 cups milk
1/4 teaspoon salt
1/4 teaspoon pepper
1 (2-ounce) jar pimiento, chopped

2 (10 1/2 ounce) cans asparagus tips
1 can sliced water chestnuts
1 hard-boiled egg, finely chopped
2 cups grated Velveeta cheese
1 sleeve buttery cracker crumbs
1/2 stick margarine, melted

Melt butter or margarine in saucepan; add flour, stirring well. Gradually add milk and cook over low heat until it thickens; add salt, pepper and pimiento.
Layer in casserole dish asparagus, water chestnuts, chopped egg, grated cheese and pimiento sauce, making 2 layers. Top with cracker crumbs; drizzle melted margarine over top. Bake in 350 degree oven for about 25 minutes, or until bubbly and lightly browned.

Asparagus with Cream Sauce

2 pounds fresh asparagus or 3 cans
   or 3 (10-ounce) frozen packages
1 tablespoon butter or margarine
1 1/2 tablespoons all-purpose flour
1/2 cup chicken broth or 1/2 cup water
   with 3/4 teaspoon chicken bouillon

1/2 cup half-and-half or evaporated milk
2 tablespoons Dijon mustard or to taste
1 teaspoon lemon juice
1/4 teaspoon freshly ground pepper

If using fresh asparagus, snap off tough ends; remove scales from stalks with a knife or vegetable peeler. Cook, covered in small amount of boiling water 6 to 8 minutes or until crisp-tender; drain. Arrange asparagus spears in a row on platter and garnish with pimiento rose and fresh parsley. Melt butter in saucepan over low heat. Add flour, stirring until smooth. Cook 1 minute; stirring constantly. Gradually add chicken broth and half-and-half; cook over medium heat until thickened. Stir in mustard, lemon juice and pepper. Let stand 3 minutes; spoon over middle of row of asparagus. Makes 8 servings.

Asparagus with Curry Sauce: Just leave out the mustard and add 1 teaspoon curry powder, or to taste.

Lemon-Sesame Asparagus - Easy

1 (10-ounce) package frozen asparagus
   spears or use canned
1 tablespoon butter

2 teaspoons sesame seeds
2 teaspoons lemon juice

If using frozen asparagus, cook until just crisp-tender. Drain. Combine butter and sesame seeds in a small skillet; cook over medium heat 2 or 3 minutes or until sesame seeds are lightly browned. Stir in lemon juice; pour over asparagus. Yield: 3 servings.

Baked Beans

2 (1-pound) can pork and beans
1/2-3/4 cup brown sugar
1/2 cup ketchup
1 teaspoon dry mustard

1 large onion, chopped
or to your taste
6 slices bacon, cooked, drained
and crumbled

Combine all ingredients except bacon. Bake uncovered at 325 degrees for about
2 hours or until the serving consistency you like. We like onions added for last
30 minutes of cooking time so that they are a little crunchy. Sprinkle with crumbled
crisp bacon. These may be cooked in microwave or on top of stove, if you are run-
ning short on time. If cooking on top of the stove, it is good to use a large
non-stick frying pan. This is a very old recipe that we have enjoyed many times,
given to us by a friend.

Lawana's Green Bean Casserole

1 sleeve Ritz crackers
1/2 stick margarine
2 cans French green beans
1 (8-ounce) carton sour cream

1 can cream of mushroom soup
2-3 cups shredded cheddar cheese
Garlic powder, optional

Melt margarine and add to Ritz cracker crumbs and set aside. Mix remaining ingredients and pour in baking dish. Add the buttered Ritz crackers on top and bake in
350 degree oven until bubbly and lightly browned.

*Perhaps one of the best qualities in an individ-
ual is being willing to change. Pray to change
each day into a better person.*

Green Bean Sauté

Seasoning of your choice
(ham bouillon is good)
1 1/2 pounds fresh green beans
1 can sliced water chestnuts
1/2 cup diced yellow or red bell pepper,
optional

1 tablespoon butter or margarine
2 teaspoons olive oil
1 cup sliced onions, separated into rings
(or more, if your family loves them
like we do)

In 10-inch skillet, combine 1 cup water and bouillon. Bring to a boil. Reduce heat to low; add beans, water chestnuts and pepper. Cover and cook 3 minutes, stirring occasionally. Uncover; cook until liquid is reduced to 1/4 cup and green beans are tender-crisp (about 3 minutes). Transfer to serving platter. Keep warm. In same skillet, combine butter and oil. Heat until butter is melted. Add onions and cook over medium high heat, stirring frequently, until onions are browned (2 to 3 minutes). Spoon over green bean mixture. Pretty and good!

Green Bean and Shoepeg Corn Casserole

1 (16-ounce) can French-style
green beans
1 (15-ounce) can shoepeg white corn
1 (6-ounce) can sliced water chestnuts
1 (2-ounce) jar pimientos, optional, but
pretty
1/2 cup chopped onions

1/2 cup finely chopped celery
1 (8-ounce) carton sour cream
1 (10 1/2-ounce) can cream of celery
soup
1 sleeve Ritz crackers, crushed
1 stick margarine, melted
1/2 cup sliced almonds

Drain beans, corn, water chestnuts, and chopped pimientos. Mix well all ingredients except crackers, margarine and almonds. Place in 9x13-inch greased casserole dish. Sprinkle cracker crumbs over top and drizzle with melted margarine. Bake 30 minutes at 350 degrees. Sprinkle with sliced almonds and bake 10 more minutes, or until very lightly browned.

Swiss Green Beans

1 tablespoon butter
1 tablespoon flour
1 teaspoon salt
1/4 teaspoon pepper
1 teaspoon sugar
1 tablespoon grated onion

1 cup sour cream
4 ounces Swiss cheese, grated
2 (16-ounce) cans French green beans, drained
2 cups crushed corn flakes
1/2 stick margarine, melted

Melt butter in saucepan; blend in flour, salt, pepper, sugar and onion. Gradually add sour cream and cook, stirring constantly until thickened. Add cheese and stir until melted. Add beans. Pour into 1 1/2-quart casserole; top with cornflakes and melted margarine. Bake at 350 degrees until bubbly. Serves 8.

Broccoli - Steamed

Frozen broccoli or fresh,
(the amount you need)

Bouillon - Ham Base
(Goya, or the brand you like)

Steam until crisp-tender; sprinkle with bouillon while hot and toss. Serve. Healthy, so easy, and tasty!

The ultimate blessing of God is His Presence. The ultimate motivation for faithfulness to God is that same Presence.

Broccoli Casserole

2 (10-ounce) boxes chopped broccoli
1 (5-ounce) can sliced water chestnuts,
   optional
1 (8-ounce) carton sour cream

1 can cream of chicken soup
1 cup grated cheese
1 sleeve Ritz crackers, (or less), crushed
1/2 stick margarine, melted

Heat broccoli and drain well. Place in 9x13-inch casserole and sprinkle with water chestnuts. Mix sour cream, soup and grated cheese. Pour over broccoli. Add crushed Ritz crackers and melted margarine. Bake at 350 degrees until bubbly. **Suggestion:** If you prefer, you may omit sour cream and chicken soup and use a white sauce instead.

White Sauce with Cheese:
4 tablespoons margarine
4 tablespoons all-purpose flour
1/2 teaspoon salt

Dash pepper
3 cups milk

Melt margarine in non-stick skillet; blend in flour, salt and pepper. Slowly blend in a little of the milk and gradually add remainder, cooking slowly. Add cheese and cook until thickened; pour over broccoli and water chestnuts. Top with crushed Ritz crackers and drizzle with melted margarine. (You may like to use fat-free milk and a low-fat margarine.) Sometimes I vary the kinds of cheese with whatever I happen to have: sharp cheddar, Monterey Jack, and Velveeta are very good mixed. This is a favorite recipe! You may like to make two (8x8-inch) and freeze one for later use. (Add topping after removing from freezer.)

Broccoli-Corn Casserole

1 (10-ounce) package chopped broccoli
1 (11- to 16-ounce) can white
   shoepeg corn
1 (15-ounce) can cream corn
1 egg, beaten

1 small onion, chopped
1 stick margarine, melted
1 1/2 cups cracker crumbs (A buttery
   type is best)

Combine melted margarine and crackers. Mix all other ingredients together and add 1/2 of cracker/margarine mixture. Pour into buttered casserole. Top with remainder of cracker/margarine mixture. Bake in 350 degree oven for about 30 minutes or until lightly browned.

Broccoli Sauté with Bacon

2 pounds fresh broccoli or
  3 (10-ounce) packages frozen
8 slices bacon, crisply cooked

1/2 cup chopped green onions
3/4 cup nuts (pecans or walnuts)

Cook broccoli until tender-crisp; drain. Cook bacon in non-stick skillet; remove, drain and crumble. Drain drippings, leaving small amount in skillet. Add green onions and nuts and sauté until onions are tender; add broccoli and cook 1 minute, tossing gently. Place on serving dish; sprinkle with bacon. Yield: 8 servings.

With cold weather comes the sweetest and best priced cabbage. To stop cabbage from turning smelly, keep the cooking time short. They keep a brighter green color by cooking with the lid off.

Cabbage Au Gratin

4 tablespoons butter
6 tablespoons flour
2 cups milk
1 teaspoon salt

1 cup grated cheese
4 cups shredded cabbage
1 cup Ritz cracker crumbs

Melt butter; stir in flour. Add milk gradually; cook and stir until thickened. Add salt. Melt cheese in cream sauce. Cook cabbage in boiling water until tender-crisp, 3 to 5 minutes; drain. Pour sauce over cabbage in 7x11-inch dish. Cover with cracker crumbs. Bake in 350 degree oven until crumbs are brown, or you may brown under broiler if dish is already hot.

Cabbage and Kielbasa

1/2 medium head cabbage,
  (about 1 pound)
1 pound Kielbasa sausage, cut into
  1-inch diagonal slices

1 teaspoon caraway seeds
3/4 teaspoon seasoned salt
1/4 cup commercial Italian
  salad dressing

Cut cabbage into thin strips. Combine cabbage and remaining ingredients in a 4-quart casserole; toss gently. Cover with heavy-duty plastic wrap; fold back a small corner of wrap to allow steam to escape. Microwave at HIGH 8 to 10 minutes or until cabbage is tender-crisp, stirring at 4-minute intervals. Drain. Yield: 4 servings.

Cabbage with Onion and Carrot

1 fresh green cabbage, chop the amount you need. (Save remaining cabbage, if any, for another use.)

1 medium sweet onion, sliced vertically
1 carrot, peeled and sliced
Ham base bouillon

Cook vegetables in boiling water just until tender-crisp; drain. Add bouillon and place in large bowl to toss; serve. This dish is pretty and delicious! Be sure that you don't overcook! This is a favorite of ours. (I sometimes add Kielbasa sausage to this recipe and serve it as a main dish.)

Carrots are a healthy, pretty, and easy to prepare vegetable. I believe they are often neglected in our menus. I hope you will enjoy some of these recipes, and will have them more often.

Carrot Soufflé

1 pound carrots, sliced
Salt to taste
1 stick margarine
1/2 cup sugar

1 teaspoon baking powder
3 tablespoons flour
3 eggs
1 teaspoon vanilla extract

In a saucepan, cover carrots with water, add salt and cook until tender; drain. Combine with butter in blender or food processor. Process until smooth. Combine sugar, baking powder, flour, eggs and vanilla in bowl; mix. Add carrot mixture and mix well. Spoon into greased baking dish and bake at 350 degrees 45 to 60 minutes, or until nicely browned.

Focus on helping children to develop Christian self-esteem. We are created in His image.

Company Carrots

2 1/2 pound bag fresh carrots,
  or 2 pound bag prepared baby or
  large carrots
1/2 cup mayonnaise
1 tablespoon onion, chopped

Salt and pepper to taste
1 tablespoon horseradish
1/4 cup saltine crackers, crushed
2 tablespoons butter
Parsley and paprika, optional

Clean and cut carrots into sticks or slices. Cook in small amount of water until barely tender-crisp. Save 1/2 cup cooking water; add to mayonnaise, onion, salt, pepper, and horseradish. Mix and pour over carrots in 2-quart greased casserole. Sprinkle with crumbs. Dot with butter, parsley and paprika. Cook 30 minutes in 350 degree oven.

Apricot Glazed Carrots

4 cups sliced carrots
3 tablespoons margarine, melted
1/3 cup apricot preserves (You might
  like to use Smucker's Light.)

1/4 teaspoon salt
1/4 teaspoon grated orange rind
1/4 teaspoon ground nutmeg, optional
2 teaspoons lemon juice

Cook carrots to desired doneness in salted water; drain. Combine other ingredients and stir until blended. Spoon over hot carrots, and toss well. Serve at once for a pretty and good vegetable. Yield: 6 to 8 servings.

Caroline's Honey Glazed Carrots

3 cups sliced carrots
Ham-based bouillon
1/4 cup honey (or less)

2 tablespoons fresh parsley or
  a little dried, optional

Heat 2 inches water in medium saucepan to a boil; add carrots. Reduce heat; cover and cook about 8 minutes or until carrots are tender-crisp. (Be careful not to over cook.) Drain carrots; return to saucepan. While hot, sprinkle with instant ham-based bouillon; drizzle with honey and sprinkle with parsley, if desired. Toss gently and cover until ready to serve. This is a favorite in our family!
Orange Glazed Carrots: Leave out honey and bouillon. Cook 1/4 cup margarine, 3 tablespoons orange juice, 1 teaspoon grated orange rind, 1 1/2 tablespoons sugar and 6 whole cloves until sugar is melted and mixture is well-blended - about 3 to 5 minutes. Pour over drained carrots and toss.

Cauliflower Casserole

1 large bag or 2 boxes frozen
  cauliflower florets
1 can cheddar cheese soup
1/2 can milk
1/2 cup mayonnaise

1 egg, slightly beaten
1 tablespoon minced onion
Salt and pepper to taste
1 sleeve Ritz crackers
1/2 stick margarine

Steam cauliflower until almost done. Drain and place in 9x13-inch baking dish. Mix all other ingredients, except **Ritz** crackers and margarine, and pour over cauliflower. Top with crushed Ritz and drizzle with melted margarine. Bake in 350 degree oven for 30 minutes or until lightly browned. Serves 6 to 8.

Corn Pudding

(This is a good dish from your pantry.)

1 (15-ounce) can cream style corn
1 cup milk, heated (tepid)
3 tablespoons butter
3 tablespoons flour

1 teaspoon salt, if desired
1/8 teaspoon black pepper
2 eggs, beaten

Mix flour with corn. Add all other ingredients. Pour into buttered casserole. Bake at 350 degrees until puffed in middle and light brown. This is a very good, old recipe from the can!

Freezer-Fresh Creamed Corn

3 (16-ounce) packages frozen white
  shoepeg corn, partially thawed
  and divided
1/2 cup butter or margarine

1 3/4-2 cups milk
1 1/2-2 teaspoons salt
1/2 teaspoon pepper

Position knife blade in food processor bowl; add 1 package corn. Process until smooth, stopping once to scrape down sides. (I use my blender.) Melt butter in a large heavy skillet over medium heat; stir in pureed corn, remaining 2 packages of corn, milk, salt and pepper. Bring to a boil, stirring constantly; reduce heat and simmer, stirring often, 20 to 25 minutes or until desired thickness. Yield: 10 to 12 servings.
These are the amounts of ingredients for only 2 packages of corn:
2 (16-ounce) packages corn, divided; 1 1/2 cups milk, 3/4 stick margarine, 1 1/4 teaspoons salt, 1/4 teaspoon pepper. (Puree 1/2 package.)

Lemony Corn on the Cob

4 ears fresh corn	1/2-1 teaspoon lemon pepper
1/4 cup butter or margarine	

Spread mixture of margarine and lemon pepper on the 4 ears of corn. Wrap each ear in foil. Grill corn (or cook in 350 degree oven) over medium heat for about 20 to 30 minutes, turning after 10 minutes.

Suggested Menu: Grilled Chicken, Lemony Corn on Cobb, Grilled Zucchini Fans, Sliced Tomatoes, French Bread, Pound Cake with Strawberry-Banana Topping. Zucchini Fans and Pound Cake topping are found in this book.

Shaker Yellow Velvet

An old-time Shaker recipe, this sublime combination of crookneck squash and corn makes an ideal partner for simple grilled fish or roast chicken or pork.

3 ears corn, shucked, or frozen kernels	3 yellow crookneck squash, each about 6 inches long
1/2 cup chicken stock (make it with 1/2 cup water and 3/4 teaspoon chicken bouillon, if you like)	1 cup whipping cream or evaporated milk
	1 tablespoon snipped fresh chives or green onion tops
	Salt, freshly ground white pepper

Bring water to boil in steamer pan. Place corn on steamer rack. Cover and steam until very tender, 5 to 10 minutes. Let cool. Using sharp knife, cut off kernels from cobs. Place corn in skillet with chicken stock and set aside. Trim ends of squash. Cut into quarters lengthwise, then cut crosswise into 1/2-inch thick slices. Add to skillet. Cover and cook over medium heat until squash are tender, about 5 to 10 minutes. Uncover and cook over medium-high heat until all liquid evaporates, 5 minutes longer. Stir in cream and cook, stirring occasionally, until cream thickens, 5 minutes more. Stir in chives or onion tops and season to taste with salt and pepper. Serve immediately. Makes 4 servings.

Corn/Vidalia Onion Casserole

1 box Jiffy cornbread mix
2 large Vidalia onions, thinly sliced
1 (15-ounce) can cream corn
1 (8-ounce) carton sour cream

1/2 cup mayonnaise
1/2 teaspoon salt
Black pepper to taste

Prepare cornbread mix as directed. Spread in large baking dish which has been oiled. Spread onions on top of cornbread mix. Mix remaining ingredients. Spread over onions and bake at 350 degrees 45 to 50 minutes. Best if served immediately.

White Creamed Corn
(Southern Farms - Silver Queen Style) Frozen

2 (20-ounce) packages frozen corn   Margarine to taste - I use 1/2 stick

Place corn in casserole dish (frozen is fine); slice margarine on top, cover. Put in microwave and cook 5 minutes at the time, cutting up and stirring the corn as it thaws, until done. Serves 8. Adults and children around our house like this, and it could not be more simple!

Cucumber Pickles

4 quarts sliced cucumbers
2 large green peppers

6 medium onions

Wash small to medium size cucumbers and slice thin. Place in clean sink. Sprinkle with 1/3 cup salt and cover with ice. Leave drain open so water can drain off. Let stand for 3 hours. Remove from ice and place in boiling mixture of the following:

3 cups white vinegar
1 1/2 teaspoons celery seed
6 cups sugar

Cook over medium high heat, stirring from the bottom until they come to a boil. They will change color, and you need to keep stirring and watch for the change. As soon as they have changed, remove them from heat. Do not over cook as this will cause them to be limp. Place in sterilized jars and seal. Store in a convenient place and refrigerate well before serving.

Eggplant Casserole - with Clams

*(Eggplant has a little flavor of seafood, and this recipe
is very good with clam in it.)*

2 medium eggplants
1 cup chopped onion
1/2 cup chopped celery
1/2 stick margarine
1/4 cup flour
1 cup milk

1 (6- or 7-ounce) can minced clams,
  undrained (We like 2 cans)
1 egg, beaten
1 cup bread or saltine crackers crumbs
2 tablespoons margarine, melted
2 tablespoons Parmesan cheese

Peel and cube eggplants and boil in salted water until just tender. Drain and place in a 1 1/2 or 2 quart casserole dish. Sauté onions and celery in 1/2 stick margarine. Blend in flour, milk, and minced clams; cook until thickened. Remove from heat and stir in egg; adding just a little of hot mixture into egg mixture, stirring, and then combine the two. Pour this mixture over eggplants. Combine bread or cracker crumbs with remaining margarine and Parmesan cheese. Sprinkle over casserole. Bake in a 375 degree oven for 25 minutes or until bubbly and brown. Yield: 6 to 8 servings.

Eggplant Fritters or Fried Eggplant

1 eggplant
1 cup all-purpose flour
1 teaspoon baking powder
1/2 teaspoon salt

1/2 cup milk
2 eggs, beaten
Vegetable oil

Peel eggplant and cut into finger-sized strips. Combine flour, baking powder, and salt. Mix well. Add milk, eggs, 1 teaspoon vegetable oil, stirring until smooth. Dip eggplant strips into batter. Fry in hot oil until brown. Drain well on paper towels.

French Fried Okra

1 pound fresh small okra pods
1 egg, beaten
1 tablespoon water
1 cup self-rising cornmeal mix
2 tablespoons all-purpose flour

Salt and pepper to taste
2 cups canola or other oil for frying
2 tablespoons Parmesan or Romano
    cheese, optional

Wash okra; cut ends from pods and leave whole. (You may prefer to cut it into bite-size pieces.) In a shallow dish, combine the egg and water. Marinate okra pods in egg wash for 20 to 30 minutes. In a shallow pan, combine the cornmeal mix, flour, salt and pepper. Coat okra generously with this mixture. In a 12-inch skillet, heat oil to 360 degrees. Drop okra into oil and fry until golden brown on all sides, 4 to 5 minutes. Drain on paper towels. Sprinkle with grated cheese. Serve at once.

Okra and Fresh Corn Casserole

1/2 pound okra
3 ears corn, or about 2 cups
    frozen kernels
1/4 cup green onions
2 tablespoons butter
1 tablespoon flour

1/2 cup milk
1/4 cup shredded sharp cheddar cheese
2 tablespoons chopped parsley
3/4 cup soft bread crumbs
1 tablespoon melted butter

Slice okra into 1/2-inch pieces; slice kernels off ears of corn (if using fresh corn). In medium saucepan, cook onions in butter until soft. Blend in flour. Add milk and cook, stirring until thickened. Remove from heat; blend in cheese, stirring until melted. Fold in parsley, okra and corn. Turn into a 1-quart casserole. Combine bread crumbs with melted butter; sprinkle around edge of casserole. Bake in 350 degree oven 30 to 45 minutes or until lightly browned. Serves 6.

Steamed Okra

1 (16-ounce) package frozen baby okra   Ham-based bouillon

Place frozen okra in 8-inch fry pan. Sprinkle well with ham-base bouillon to season; toss. Cook on low temperature, covered, until tender. There is usually enough water to come out of frozen okra, but if you need to, add very small amount. This is a good Southern dish, usually boiled, but I think steaming in this manner is even better, very easy and quick. Serve as a side along with other vegetables.

Caramelized Onions

1 can whole small onions or
    equal amount of fresh, sweet onions
2 tablespoons margarine
1 tablespoon sugar

1/4 cup liquid from canned onions or
    1/4 cup water
2 teaspoons balsamic vinegar
1/2 teaspoon salt or to taste

Drain onions, reserving 1/4 cup liquid. Combine margarine, sugar, onion liquid, vinegar and salt. Cook and stir until blended. Add onions and cook until mixture browns lightly, stirring frequently, and onions are tender and crisp.

Cheese-Onion Bake

6 cups thinly sliced Vidalia onions
1/4 cup butter
1/4 cup flour
2 cups milk

1/2 teaspoon salt
1/8 teaspoon pepper
2 cups shredded sharp cheese, divided

Place onion rings in 1 1/2-quart casserole. In saucepan, melt butter; blend in flour and milk, stirring often. Cool, stir in salt, pepper and 1 cup of the cheese. Pour over onions. Top with the other cup of cheese and bake uncovered in 325 degree oven about 35 minutes. Serves 4 to 6.

Creamed Onions and Peas with Mint

10 ounces pearl onions
1 (16-ounce) package frozen
    petite green peas
1 teaspoon granulated sugar

1 cup whipping cream, half-and-half,
    or evaporated milk
1/2 teaspoon salt
2 tablespoons finely cut mint leaves,
    plus a few leaves for garnish,optional

Bring a large saucepan of water to a boil; drop in onions and boil for 3 minutes, then transfer with a slotted spoon to a colander. Reserve the water. Rinse onions well under cold water, slice off the base of each onion and pop it out of its skin. Set aside. Cook peas and sugar in 1 cup of the reserved water until just tender, about 2 minutes; drain in colander. Put the cream, salt and mint, (if using mint), in the empty saucepan with the peeled onions. Bring to a gentle boil and cook for 1 minute. Add the peas to heat through. Serve immediately.

French Onion Casserole

Butter or margarine for bread
8 (3/4-inch) slices French bread
3 large onions, thinly sliced and separated
2 tablespoon butter or margarine
2 cups shredded Swiss cheese (8 ounces)

1 (10 3/4-ounce) can cream of chicken soup
1 (5-ounce) can (2/3 cup) evaporated milk
1/4 teaspoon pepper

Spread 1 teaspoon butter on one side of each slice of French bread. Set aside. In large skillet cook sliced onions in 2 tablespoons butter until tender, but not brown. Stir often. Transfer to 7x11x2-inch baking dish. Sprinkle Swiss cheese in a layer over onions. In small bowl, combine chicken soup, evaporated milk and pepper, stirring until well mixed. Pour soup mixture into baking dish, spreading evenly over cheese layer. Layer bread slices, buttered side up, over soup mixture. Bake in 350 degree oven about 30 minutes or until onion mixture is heated through and bread slices are golden brown.

Glazed Onions

1 tablespoon olive oil
1 large onion, cut into 1/2-inch wedges

1 tablespoon steak sauce
Salt and freshly ground pepper, to taste

Heat oil in a large skillet over high heat. Add onion and cook, stirring often, until it begins to soften, 3 minutes. Reduce heat to medium and cook until onion begins to change color, 4 to 5 more minutes. Stir in the steak sauce, salt and pepper and remove from heat.

Marinated Onions

4-6 onions
1 cup sugar

1/2 cup vinegar
2 cups water

Slice onions thin and soak in water with all above ingredients overnight or at least 4 hours. Drain well and mix this with 1/2 cup mayonnaise, 1 tablespoon celery salt and 1 tablespoon celery seeds. This will keep in the refrigerator several weeks.

Vidalia Mums

4 large Vidalia onions
1 stick margarine, melted
1 (10 3/4) can cream of chicken soup

2 cups grated sharp cheddar cheese
  (8 ounces)
2 tablespoons chopped pimiento

Preheat oven to 350 degrees. Grease a 2-quart casserole dish. Cut each onion into 6 wedges, without cutting all the way through the bottom of onion (forming mum). Place onions in casserole dish. Pour margarine over onions and then spread onions with soup. Sprinkle cheese and pimiento over top. Bake 40 to 45 minutes until bubbly.

Vidalia Onion Casserole

1/2 stick margarine
7-8 large Vidalia onions, cut into
  large chunks, or 7 to 8 cups
1/2 cup uncooked rice

1 3/4 cups water
1 cup grated Swiss cheese
1 cup half-and-half or evaporated milk
1 teaspoon salt

Melt margarine in a large skillet over medium heat. Add onions and sauté until transparent. Cook rice in salted water 5 minutes and drain well. Blend into onions along with cheese, half-and-half, and salt. Pour into a buttered 7x11x1 1/2-inch casserole dish. Bake in a 325 degree oven for 1 hour. Yield: 8 servings. Nice with all meats.

Black-Eyed Peas with Lemon and Garlic

1 (16-ounce) bag frozen black-eyed peas
4 cups water
4 garlic cloves, peeled and thinly sliced
Ham-base bouillon to taste,
  about 2 teaspoons

1 cup tightly packed minced fresh parsley
4-6 tablespoons lemon juice
Salt to taste
1 lemon, cut in sections

Put the peas, water, garlic and bouillon seasoning in a heavy 3-quart saucepan. Bring to a boil, reduce heat to a simmer, cover and cook until the peas are tender, about 10 minutes. (Do not overcook.) While the peas are hot, stir in the parsley, lemon juice and salt, if needed. Pass lemon slices at the table.
Note: Bite-size pieces of lean ham can be added to this dish for the mainstay of a meal. Add coleslaw, cornbread, and enjoy!

Company Green Peas

1 (10-ounce) package frozen English
   peas, (petite)
1 (4-ounce) can sliced mushrooms,
   drained

1 teaspoon ham base bouillon
   (more if needed)
1/2 teaspoon dried onion flakes
1/4 teaspoon salt, if needed
1/4 teaspoon pepper

Cook peas according to directions on package, drain. Do not over cook. Add
remaining ingredients; cover and let stand 5 minutes. Yield: 3 to 4 servings.

Creamed Celery and Peas

1/3 cup water
2 cups sliced celery
1 (10-ounce) package frozen peas
   (English-petite)
1/2 cup sour cream
1/2 teaspoon dried rosemary, crushed,
   optional

1/4 teaspoon salt
Dash garlic salt
1 tablespoon chopped pimientos,
   drained
1/4 cup slivered almonds, toasted

Over medium heat, bring water to boil. Add celery; cover and cook 8 minutes. Add
peas; return to a boil. Cover and cook for 2 to 3 minutes; drain. Combine sour
cream, rosemary, salt and garlic salt; mix well. Toss vegetables with pimientos;
place in serving bowl. Top with sour cream mixture. Sprinkle with toasted
almonds. Yield: 6 servings.

English Pea Casserole

1/3 cup chopped celery
1/3 cup onion, chopped
1/3 cup bell pepper, chopped, optional
1 stick margarine, divided
1 can cream of celery soup
1/4 cup milk

1 small can pimientos
1 can sliced water chestnuts
1 hard-boiled egg, chopped
1 (15-ounce) can LeSueur Petite Peas,
   drained
Crushed Ritz crackers

Cook celery, onion and bell pepper in 1/2 stick margarine. Dilute soup with 1/4 cup
milk and combine all ingredients except crackers and remaining margarine. Salt and
pepper to taste. Cover top with crushed Ritz crackers; drizzle with melted margarine.
Heat in 350 degree oven until bubbly and lightly browned.

Peas - Fresh

Shell and wash; drain. Place in saucepan; sprinkle with ham base bouillon to season. Add salt, if necessary. Cover with water and cook until tender. Adjust seasoning, if necessary. Many people use meat to season, but we think bouillon is wonderful, and it is much better for you.

Scalloped Green Peas and Onions

1/4 cup butter
1/4 cup flour
1/2 teaspoon salt
1/2 teaspoon seasoned salt
1/4 teaspoon black pepper
2 cups milk

1 (16-ounce) package frozen green peas (English, petite)
1 pound small white onions, peeled and sliced thin
2 medium baking potatoes, peeled and sliced thin
1 cup shredded Swiss cheese

Melt butter in saucepan over low heat; blend in flour, salts and pepper. Add milk, stirring constantly. Cook and stir until sauce is smooth and thick. Arrange half of the peas, onions and potatoes in a buttered 1 1/2-quart shallow casserole dish. Spoon half of the sauce over vegetables; sprinkle half of the cheese over sauce. Repeat. Cover dish and bake at 375 degrees until vegetables are tender, about 1 hour. Yields 6 servings.

Cheese, seafood or any veggie will spruce up your plain spuds. For a zesty Mexican-style meal, top your baked potato with spicy black bean soup or tuna mixed with salsa.

Barbecued Potatoes

1 tablespoon olive oil
1 tablespoon honey
2 teaspoons chili powder
1/8-1/4 teaspoon garlic powder

1/8 teaspoon black pepper
3 medium-size baking potatoes, cut into 1/2-inch slices

Combine first 5 ingredients; add potatoes, tossing to coat. Spread potatoes evenly on a foil-lined, lightly greased, 15x10x1-inch jelly-roll pan. Bake at 425 degrees for 20 minutes or until potatoes are tender. Yield: 4 servings.

Campfire Potatoes

5 medium potatoes, peeled and
thinly sliced
1 medium onion, sliced
6 tablespoons butter or margarine
1/2 cup shredded cheddar cheese
2 tablespoons minced fresh parsley,
optional

1 tablespoon Worcestershire sauce
Salt and pepper to taste
1/3 cup chicken broth (1/3 cup boiling
water plus 1/2 teaspoon instant
chicken bouillon)

Place the potatoes and onion on a large piece of heavy-duty foil, about 20x20-inches.
Dot with butter. Combine cheese, parsley, Worcestershire sauce, salt and pepper;
sprinkle over potatoes. Fold foil around potatoes and add broth. Seal the edges of
foil well. Grill, covered, over medium coals for 35 to 40 minutes or until potatoes
are tender, (or cook in the oven). Yield: 4 to 6 servings.

Cream Potato Casserole

8-10 potatoes, peeled, boiled and mashed
1 (8-ounce) package cream cheese,
cubed and softened
1 (8-ounce) carton sour cream
Milk (enough to make right consistency)
2 eggs, well-beaten
1 medium onion, chopped

2 tablespoons flour
2 tablespoons margarine, melted
Salt and garlic salt to taste
Pepper to taste
1 (3-ounce) can French fried onion rings
or grated cheese on top

In a large bowl, combine the hot potatoes and cream cheese; beat, allowing cream
cheese to melt. Add all other ingredients, except onion rings. Beat 2 to 3 minutes
at medium speed of electric mixer. Pour into greased 2 1/2 quart casserole. Spread
crushed onions evenly over top. Bake uncovered at 300 degrees for 30 to 35
minutes.

Dilled New Potatoes and Sugar Snap Peas

1 pound white new potatoes	1 tablespoon olive oil
1/2 pound sugar snap peas	Salt and freshly ground black pepper
2 tablespoons chopped fresh dill	
or dried, to taste	

Wash potatoes and cut into 1 to 1 1/4-inch quarters. Place in vegetable steaming basket over 1/2 inch water. Cover steamer and place on high heat for 12 minutes. Trim sugar snap peas. Add to potatoes and steam both together for 3 minutes. Mix dill and olive oil together in a serving bowl. Add potatoes and sugar snap peas and toss well. Add salt and pepper to taste. Makes 2 servings.

Hidden Valley Ranch Mashed Potatoes

1 package Hidden Valley Ranch	Potatoes
Salad Dressing Mix	Milk
(Original Recipe)	Margarine

Prepare mashed potatoes; stir in dry salad dressing mix. Add milk and margarine to achieve desired consistency.

Try Any of These Additions to Your Favorite Mashed Potato:
Horseradish and Chives
Caramelized Sweet Onion and Sour Cream
Jalapeño and Roast Pepper
1/4 cup Olives and Roasted Garlic
Durkee's Famous Sauce and 1 tablespoon parsley for about 2 pounds potatoes,
    (about 4 large), and pepper to taste

New Potatoes with Sauce
So easy and good!

Use canned, small, potatoes - the amount you need. If preparing for a large crowd, purchase a gallon; drain liquid off and cover with white sauce, or sour cream, or a combination of the two. Add margarine and a little black pepper. Place in covered casserole and heat. Sprinkle tops of potatoes with paprika, if desired. A friend fixed these for a large crowd and they were delicious!

Potato Casserole

1 (2-pound) bag frozen hash browns, thawed
2 cups chopped onion
1 (16-ounce) carton sour cream
1 (10 3/4-ounce) can cream of chicken soup
1 stick margarine, melted
2 cups grated sharp cheddar cheese
2 1/2 cups crushed corn flakes
1/2 stick margarine

Mix hash browns, onion, sour cream and soup; add melted margarine and grated cheese. Gently toss and place in large oiled casserole dish. Top with crushed corn flakes and drizzle with melted margarine. Bake for 1 hour at 350 degrees.

Scalloped Potatoes

3 tablespoons margarine
2 tablespoons all-purpose flour
1 teaspoon salt or to taste
1/8 teaspoon pepper
2 cups milk
6 medium potatoes, or 6 cups thinly sliced
1 medium onion, chopped
Paprika

Melt margarine in 2-quart sauce pan over low heat. Blend in flour, salt and pepper. Add milk all at once. Cook until mixture thickens slightly and bubbles. Remove from heat. Place 1/2 potatoes in greased 3-quart casserole, cover with half of the onions and half of the milk mixture. Repeat layers; sprinkle with paprika. Cover and bake at 350 degrees about 1 hour. Uncover and bake 30 minutes. Serves 6 to 8.

Candied Sweet Potatoes

1 1/2 pounds fresh sweet potatoes, peeled and cut as for French fries
1 1/2 cups sugar
1/2 cup pecans, broken vertically into quarters

Place potatoes in casserole large enough to have fairly thin layer of potatoes. Sprinkle with the sugar. Bake in 400 degree oven until tender and juice is thickened a little. Lightly toast 1/2 cup pecans in just a little margarine and a sprinkle of salt. Sprinkle on potatoes just before they are done and return to oven for about 5 minutes. This recipe is from a friend who is a wonderful cook!

Crunchy Sweet Potato Soufflé

2 (14 1/2-ounce) cans cooked,
   mashed sweet potatoes
1/2 cup sugar
2 large eggs, beaten

1/2 cup milk
3 tablespoons margarine
1/2 teaspoon salt
1 tablespoon vanilla extract

Topping:
1 cup brown sugar
1 stick margarine
1 cup coconut

1 cup nuts, chopped
4 cups corn flakes, crushed

Combine the first seven ingredients. Pour into 9x13x2-inch casserole. Mix topping ingredients; spread over casserole and bake in 350 degree oven for 25 minutes. **Note:** Spices are optional. You may add 1/2 teaspoon cinnamon and 1/2 teaspoon nutmeg to soufflé, if you like, (or your favorite spices).

Sweet Potato Soufflé

3-4 pounds sweet potatoes, baked and
   mashed (Hopefully, they are red
   and juicy.)
1/2 cup sugar (or less)
3 tablespoons margarine, melted

2 eggs, beaten
1/2 cup raisins (or more, if you like)
2 teaspoons vanilla extract
Marshmallows

Combine all ingredients except marshmallows in order given. Bake in 350 degree oven about 30 minutes. Remove from oven and place marshmallows on top. Return to oven and lightly brown marshmallows. (One of my friends makes delicious potato soufflé, and this is her recipe.)

🌿 *Trust God for the results of your efforts.*
Have faith for the fruit of your teachings.

Orange Candied Sweet Potatoes

6-8 sweet potatoes, cut vertically
   into quarters or eights, depending
   on size of potato
1/2 cup sugar
1 cup water

1 cup orange juice
3 tablespoons white corn syrup
1 teaspoon grated orange rind
1/4 cup margarine

Arrange peeled uncooked potatoes in a buttered casserole. Combine all remaining ingredients and pour over potatoes. Bake in a covered dish in a 350 degree oven until tender, and juice has begun to thicken; about 1 to 1 1/2 hours. Baste occasionally. Remove lid last 10 minutes to brown.

Sweet Potato Pudding

3 cups coarsely grated sweet potatoes
1 1/2 cups sugar
3/4 cup buttermilk
1/2 cup sweet milk
1/2 teaspoon cinnamon

1/2 teaspoon cloves
1/2 teaspoon salt
1 stick margarine, melted
2 eggs, beaten
1 cup chopped nuts

Combine all ingredients; pour into oiled casserole. Bake in 350 degree oven for 1 hour. This was a favorite of my Mother-in-law, and she was a wonderful cook, and a wonderful person. I just wish I had learned more from her.

Baked Sweet Potatoes

Peel and slice into 3/8-inch rounds as many potatoes as you need. Place not more than two layers in shallow glass baking dish; sprinkle very lightly with salt and dot with margarine. Sprinkle generously with Brown Sugar Twin. Bake in 350 degree oven until done when pierced with fork. You may add cinnamon to Brown Sugar Twin, if desired. (You may wish to use regular sugar.) These really are a family favorite and so easy!

Rutabaga
(A turnip, with a very large yellowish root.)

1 rutabaga (Usually they are large, but if young and small, you may wish to purchase more than one.)

Cut into small portions and then peel. This is much easier than trying to peel the large root. Cut into small pieces or cubes. Put into large saucepan and cover with water. Allow to boil until very tender. We prefer them seasoned with ham base bouillon, but add the type of seasoning you prefer and add or adjust salt, if necessary. This is a wonderful, sweet vegetable and also very good for us. Do not neglect to use these!

Jalapeño Spinach

2 eggs, hard-boiled
1 (10-ounce) package frozen
  chopped spinach
3 green onions with tops, chopped
1 tablespoon butter
1 tablespoon flour

Salt and pepper to taste
A sprinkle of cayenne pepper
1/4 cup milk
2 ounces Monterey Jack cheese with
  jalapeño peppers, shredded
4 bacon slices, cooked and crumbled

Peel eggs, chop up whites, reserve yolks and set aside. Cook spinach with 2 tablespoons water in microwave on HIGH 2 1/2 minutes. Stir and turn dish. Cook another 2 minutes. Drain spinach, reserving 1/4 cup liquid. Sauté green onions in butter about 45 seconds on HIGH. Stir in flour, salt and pepper. Stir in milk and reserved spinach liquid. Microwave on MEDIUM-HIGH about 2 minutes, stirring after 1 minute, until sauce thickens. Fold in shredded cheese and chopped egg whites. Put in 1 1/2-quart casserole and top with crumbled bacon. Microwave on HIGH 2 minutes until heated thoroughly. Press egg yolks through a sieve, or just crumble; sprinkle around edges of casserole. Yield: 4 servings.

Spinach Casserole

4 (10-ounce) packages frozen,
   chopped spinach
1/2 cup margarine
3 tablespoons flour
1 cup milk
1 medium onion, chopped, or
   1 bunch spring onions, chopped
1 1/2 teaspoons celery salt, or to taste
1 teaspoon garlic salt, or to taste

1 (8-ounce) package mozzarella cheese
1 (8-ounce) package cream cheese
2 (4-ounce) cans mushrooms
2 eggs, well beaten
2 (14-ounce) cans artichoke hearts,
   drained
1 sleeve Ritz cracker crumbs
4 tablespoons margarine, melted

Cook spinach according to directions on package; drain well. Melt margarine in saucepan. Add flour, stirring until smooth. Add milk slowly, stirring to avoid lumps. Cook until thick and smooth; add onion and seasonings to sauce mixture. Cube cheeses and add to sauce, stirring until cheese melts; add mushrooms. Add well beaten eggs to spinach; combine sauce with spinach. Spread chopped artichoke hearts in bottom of a 3-quart casserole. Pour spinach mixture over artichokes and top with cracker crumbs; drizzle with margarine. Bake in 350 degree oven until bubbly. Yield: 12 to 16 servings.

Spinach-Stuffed Squash

4 large yellow squash
2 (10-ounce) packages frozen
   chopped spinach
1/3 cup margarine
1/2 cup onion, chopped
1 (3-ounce) package cream
   cheese, cubed

1 teaspoon garlic salt
1/2 teaspoon ground black pepper
1/8 teaspoon ground red pepper
1/4 cup grated Parmesan cheese
2 tablespoons fine, dry bread crumbs

Cook whole squash in boiling water to cover for 10 minutes or until tender-crisp; drain and cool. Cut squash in half lengthwise; remove and discard seeds. Place shells in lightly greased 9x13-inch pan. Cook spinach according to package directions; drain well, pressing between layers of paper towels. Melt butter in a large skillet; add onion and sauté until tender. Add spinach, cream cheese and next 3 ingredients, stirring until cheese melts; spoon evenly into squash shells. Sprinkle with Parmesan cheese and bread crumbs. Bake at 400 degrees for 20 minutes or until thoroughly heated. Yield: 8 servings.

Acorn Squash

2 acorn squash (about 6 ounces each),
  peeled
1/4 cup honey
2 tablespoons butter or margarine,
  melted

2 tablespoons chopped nuts
2 tablespoons raisins
2 teaspoons Worcestershire sauce

Cut squash in halves; do not remove seeds. Place cut side up in baking pan. Bake at 400 degrees 30 to 45 minutes, or until soft. Remove seeds and fibers. Combine honey, margarine, raisins and Worcestershire sauce; spoon into squash. Bake 5 to 10 minutes or more until lightly glazed. Serves 4.

Butternut Squash

2 cups squash, boiled and mashed
1 cup sugar
1 cup milk
3 eggs

3/4 stick margarine
1 1/2 teaspoons each, vanilla extract and
  almond extract

Topping, optional
1/2 cup light brown sugar
1 cup chopped pecans
1 teaspoon ground cinnamon

1 cup Bran flakes (crushed)
2 tablespoons margarine, softened

Squash must be peeled, cut up, boiled until tender, and mashed. Mix all ingredients together, pour into oiled casserole or pour into 2 pie shells (your choice). Bake until just firm in middle.
Topping: Combine all topping ingredients; top casserole or pies when about 1/2 done. Allow to brown lightly.

God will use anyone who is willing to be obedient to His will in his or her life.

Crunchy Squash Casserole

2 (10-ounce) packages frozen, sliced
   yellow squash (or equal amount of
   fresh squash)
1 cup chopped onion
6 tablespoons margarine, melted, divided
1 (8-ounce) carton sour cream

1 (10-ounce) can cream of chicken soup,
   undiluted
1 (8-ounce) can sliced water chestnuts,
   drained
1 (6-ounce) package chicken-flavored
   stuffing mix (divided)

Cook squash according to package directions, drain well. Sauté onion in 1 table-spoon margarine until just tender-crisp. Combine squash, onion, sour cream, soup and water chestnuts. Combine stuffing mix and remaining melted margarine, stir well. Add 3/4 of stuffing mixture to squash mixture. Spoon into a lightly oiled 2-quart casserole. Sprinkle remaining stuffing mix over casserole. Bake at 350 degrees for 20 minutes or until bubbly.

Roasted Squash Fans

6 yellow squash (medium size)
6 plum tomatoes (not too ripe)
2 tablespoons chopped basil (fresh)
1 teaspoon salt

1 teaspoon freshly ground pepper
1/2 cup olive oil
3 garlic cloves, pressed
Garnish: Fresh basil sprigs

Cut each squash lengthwise into 1/4-inch slices, cutting to within 1 inch of stem end. Cut tomatoes into 1/4-inch slices. Combine chopped basil and next 4 ingredients in large bowl, stirring until blended. Add squash and tomato, tossing gently to coat; let stand 1 hour. Remove vegetables from marinade, reserving marinade; insert tomato slices between squash slices and secure with wooden skewers or tooth picks. Place in foil lined, jelly-roll pan and roast in 425 degree oven just until tender-crisp, (or to desired doneness), being careful not to over cook. Garnish with fresh basil.
Note: If you would like, you may omit above seasonings and season with Morton's Natures Seasons Seasoning Blend. This is delicious!

Special Squash Casserole

2 pounds yellow squash
1 cup chopped onions
2 eggs, slightly beaten
1/2 cup mayonnaise
1/2 cup sour cream
3/4 cup milk

12 saltine crackers, crumbled
1 (1-ounce) package Hidden Valley Ranch
   Original Dressing Mix
1 cup mild cheddar cheese, shredded
1-2 cups bread crumbs, buttered

Boil squash and onions in salted water until desired tenderness. Drain. Mix other ingredients (except bread crumbs) and fold into squash and onion mixture. Pour into a 2-quart casserole dish and top with bread crumbs. Bake in a 350 degree oven 45 to 55 minutes until heated through and browned on top. Serves 6 to 8.

Squash Casserole in White Sauce
(This recipe can easily be made low calorie.)

2 pounds squash, sliced
1 cup chopped onions
1 (8-ounce) can water chestnuts
1/2 cup margarine, divided
4 tablespoons flour
1/2 teaspoon salt

Dash pepper
3 cups milk
2 cups cheddar cheese
   (or mixed cheeses are good), grated
Crushed crackers for topping

Cook squash and onions about 10 minutes in microwave, stirring after 5 minutes. Pour into 9x13-inch casserole and set aside. Top with chopped water chestnuts. In large skillet or saucepan, melt 4 tablespoons of the margarine. Stir in flour, salt, pepper and milk. Cook and stir over medium heat until thick and bubbly; stir in cheese. Pour sauce over squash and onions; top with cracker crumbs. Drizzle with the other 4 tablespoons of melted margarine. Bake in 350 degree oven until bubbly and lightly browned. You may like to make this into two 8x8-inch casseroles; serve one and freeze the other for later use. Freeze before baking. (Add topping after removing from freezer.)
Note: If you would like to make this low calorie, just leave out the margarine, use fat-free milk, and low-fat cheese.

Squash Dressing

2 cups cooked yellow squash
1 cup chopped onion
2 cups cornbread crumbs
 (like Pepperidge Farm)

2 eggs, slightly beaten (or egg substitute)
1 stick margarine, melted
1 (10 1/2-ounce) can cream of celery soup
Salt and pepper to taste

Mix all ingredients together and bake at 350 degrees for about 30 minutes, or until puffed up in center and browned. This is a favorite!

Squash Hush Puppies

Oil for frying
2 cups cooked yellow squash
 (about 1 pound), drained and mashed
1/2 cup plus 2 tablespoons cornmeal

1/2 cup saltine cracker crumbs
1 medium onion, chopped
2 eggs
Salt and pepper, to taste

In saucepan, heat oil over medium heat to 350 degrees on a frying thermometer, or until just hot enough to fry. In a medium bowl, combine squash, cornmeal, cracker crumbs, onion, eggs, salt and pepper. Mix well. Drop by rounded teaspoons into oil and cook for 1 to 2 minutes, or until each is golden brown and cooked through (fry in several batches). Drain on paper towels and serve hot. Makes 40 bite-size hush puppies, 8 servings.

Your ultimate freedom in life is how you decide to let things affect you.

Squash Soufflé

(This can be a good pantry recipe if you use the canned squash.)

2 pounds yellow squash, sliced;
  or 2 cans squash
1 medium onion, sliced
1/2 teaspoon salt
1 teaspoon sugar
2 eggs, well beaten
3 tablespoons butter or
  margarine, melted

3 tablespoons flour
1 cup milk
1/2 pound sharp Cracker Barrel
  cheese, grated
Seasoned salt to taste
Buttered bread crumbs

Combine fresh squash, onion, salt and sugar. Simmer with small amount of water for 20 minutes. Drain well. Mash with potato masher. Add eggs, melted margarine, flour, milk, and cheese. Add seasoning salt to taste. Bake in a buttered 1 1/2-quart casserole for 30 minutes. Top with crumbs and bake 10 minutes more. This can be stored in the refrigerator for 2 to 3 days, unbaked, and it freezes well.

Stir-Fried Squash

1 tablespoon olive oil, more if
  necessary
3 cups sliced yellow squash
  (about 1 pound)
1 small zucchini squash, sliced
  about 1/4-inch thick
1 sweet onion, sliced

1 small red bell pepper, sliced, optional
3 garlic cloves, minced
Morton's Nature's Seasons Seasoning
  Blend, to taste
Black pepper, if desired

Pour olive oil around top of non-stick wok or large skillet, coating sides; place over medium-high heat for 1 minute. Combine both kinds of squash, onion, pepper and garlic; add seasoning blend and toss. Pour into wok or skillet and stir fry 10 to 12 minutes or just until tender-crisp. Add black pepper to taste. Serve immediately. Yield: 4 to 6 servings.

Fresh Tomato Tart

1/2 (15-ounce) package refrigerated
   pie crusts
2 cups (8-ounces) shredded mozzarella
   cheese
3 tablespoons chopped fresh basil,
   divided

3 medium-size ripe tomatoes, peeled
   and cut into 1/2-inch slices
1 1/2 tablespoons olive oil
1/4 teaspoon salt
1/4 teaspoon pepper

Fit pie crust into a 10-inch tart pan, according to package directions; trim any excess pastry along edges. Generously prick bottom and sides of pastry with fork. Bake at 400 degrees 5 minutes. Sprinkle cheese evenly into pastry shell and top with 2 tablespoons basil. Arrange tomato slices on top; brush with olive oil and sprinkle with salt and pepper. Place tart on a baking sheet; place baking sheet on lower rack of oven. Bake at 400 degrees for 35 to 40 minutes. Remove from oven, sprinkle with remaining basil. Let stand 5 minutes before serving. Yield 8 to 10 servings. This is delicious!

Fried Green Tomatoes

4-5 green tomatoes
Salt to taste

Self-rising flour
Oil for frying

Slice tomatoes rather thin, about 1/4 inch thick. Drop into pan of salty water, 1 tablespoon salt to a quart of water. Let set 30 minutes or longer, drain and dip in self-rising flour. Fry in vegetable oil until brown. Drain well on paper towels. Have enough grease in the skillet to come up around the slices; have it frying hot, and do not crowd the slices in the fry pan. Salt to taste.

Spiritual things are not discerned by a carnal person. Spiritual things are discerned by the spiritual person.

Turnips

Turnips are a very special dish in the South that all older people know how to cook very well. They are especially good with corn bread. I think most adults in the South like most of the green vegetables. It seems most children are not so fond of them, but when they grow up, they usually learn to like them. They are very good for us and we should have them often. The nice thing is that now we have frozen ones that are very easy to prepare, and they are hard to tell from the fresh ones. In fact, sometimes people think they are fresh ones! I have never tried to fool people about that, but some have been shocked to find out they were from the frozen food section! (And, even seasoned with ham base bouillon!) Of course, in most places in the South, you can grow turnips, and some people do. If they don't have a vegetable garden, they sometimes grow them in their flower garden.

Note: Kale and collards are also green, leafy, vegetables that can be cooked the same as turnips. They, also, are very good for us.

Fresh Turnips
(This recipe is for young people.)

1 bunch fresh turnips (from grocery, or from your garden)

Remove roots from leaves and peel them, (if they have roots.) If they are very young, they may not have grown roots yet; however, I love the roots cooked with them, when available. Break each nice leaf away from bunch and with your hand strip the nice green part away from the large part of the stem; the smaller part of the stem is fine as it will cook tender. Discard large stems. When you have stripped all the nice parts of the leaves, wash several times until you do not feel any grit in the bottom of your container or sink. Expect your turnips to shrink a lot when cooked. Place them in a large pot; add about 2 inches of water in the pot, (add more as needed), and add the kind of seasoning that you like. Cook until tender. Serve with corn bread and pepper sauce. The potlicker (soup) is also very good with corn bread. Most people like turnips cooked with fresh pork of some kind, and I agree, they are good that way. (Be sure to cook pork done.) However, they are very good cooked with ham base bouillon. If you do not use bouillon, add salt to taste.

Turnips from the Frozen Food Section

1 (10-ounce) box or 1 (1-pound)
  bag frozen turnips, without roots
3 medium fresh turnip roots, sliced,
  more if you like a lot of roots (I think
  the fresh roots are the secret to
  making turnips taste like fresh ones.)

Ham base bouillon for seasoning,
  or your choice of seasoning
Salt as needed

Place turnip roots in large pot; add about 2 inches of water. Add desired seasoning. Let them come to a boil; add turnips; let them return to a boil and then reduce heat. Cook for at least an hour, or longer - until tender, on low heat, stirring occasionally and adding water as necessary. (If you should use fresh pork for seasoning, be sure and cook your meat first until almost done, and finish cooking it with the turnips.) Always serve with hot corn bread!

Zucchini Casserole with Mozzarella

4 thinly sliced zucchini
  (3 to 4 medium-size)
1 cup chopped onion
1/2 stick butter or margarine
2 tablespoons parsley flakes
1/2 teaspoon salt
1/2 teaspoon pepper

1/4 teaspoon sweet basil leaves
1/4 teaspoon garlic powder
1/4 teaspoon oregano
2 eggs, well beaten
8 ounces mozzarella cheese, shredded
1 (8-ounce) can crescent rolls
2 teaspoons Dijon mustard

Cook zucchini and onion in 1/2 stick butter until tender. Stir in parsley and other seasonings. In large bowl, blend eggs with cheese. Stir in zucchini. Line quiche pan with crescent dough (ungreased). Spread with mustard. Pour mixture into crust. Put extra cheese on top. Bake in 375 degree oven 18 to 20 minutes.

Zucchini Pie

3 cups grated zucchini with skin
4 eggs, slightly beaten
1 handful of grated Parmesan cheese

Garlic salt and pepper to taste
1 cup Bisquick baking mix

Preheat oven to 350 degrees. Spray an 8x8-inch Pyrex plate or pan with non-stick cooking spray. Mix all ingredients together in bowl and pour in pan. Bake 35 minutes. Cut into squares and serve warm.

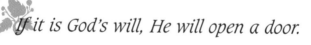

If it is God's will, He will open a door.

A

B

Delightfully Southern

Lucy M. Clark
722 East 22nd Avenue
Cordele, Georgia 31015

Please send ____copies $18.95 each
    Postage & handling first copy $3.00
    Postage & handling additional copies $.50 each

Name_____

Address_____

City_____State_____Zip_____

Phone (_____)_____

Delightfully Southern

Lucy M. Clark
722 East 22nd Avenue
Cordele, Georgia 31015

Please send ____copies $18.95 each
    Postage & handling first copy $3.00
    Postage & handling additional copies $.50 each

Name_____

Address_____

City_____State_____Zip_____

Phone (_____)_____

Delightfully Southern

Lucy M. Clark
722 East 22nd Avenue
Cordele, Georgia 31015

Please send ____copies $18.95 each
    Postage & handling first copy $3.00
    Postage & handling additional copies $.50 each

Name_____

Address_____

City_____State_____Zip_____

Phone (_____)_____